POLITICAL ARITHMETIC

Also Published in

REPRINTS OF ECONOMIC CLASSICS

By ARTHUR YOUNG

THE AUTOBIOGRAPHY OF ARTHUR YOUNG [1898]
A SIX MONTHS TOUR THROUGH THE NORTH OF ENGLAND,
4 VOLS. [1771]

POLITICAL ARITHMETIC

CONTAINING

OBSERVATIONS

ON THE PRESENT STATE OF

GREAT BRITAIN

AND THE

PRINCIPLES OF HER POLICY

IN THE

ENCOURAGEMENT OF AGRICULTURE

BY

ARTHUR YOUNG

TO WHICH IS ADDED

A MEMOIR ON THE CORN TRADE
By THOMAS POWNALL

[1774]

REPRINTS OF ECONOMIC CLASSICS

AUGUSTUS M. KELLEY · PUBLISHERS
NEW YORK · 1967

First Edition 1774

(London: W. Nicoll, *at No. 51, in St. Paul's
Church - Yard,* 1774)

Reprinted 1967 by
AUGUSTUS M. KELLEY · PUBLISHERS

LIBRARY OF CONGRESS CATALOGUE CARD NUMBER

67 - 29462

PRINTED IN THE UNITED STATES OF AMERICA
by SENTRY PRESS, NEW YORK, N. Y. 10019

POLITICAL ARITHMETIC.

CONTAINING

OBSERVATIONS

ON THE PRESENT STATE OF

GREAT BRITAIN;

AND THE

PRINCIPLES OF HER POLICY

IN THE

ENCOURAGEMENT OF AGRICULTURE.

Addreſſed to the

ŒCONOMICAL SOCIETIES eſtabliſhed in EUROPE.

TO WHICH IS ADDED,

A MEMOIR on the CORN TRADE:

Drawn up and laid before the COMMISSIONERS
of the TREASURY.

By GOVERNOR POWNALL.

By ARTHUR YOUNG, Eſq. F. R. S.
AUTHOR of the TOURS through ENGLAND—
Honorary Member of the Societies of DUBLIN, YORK,
and MANCHESTER, and of the Œconomical Society
of BERNE in SWITZERLAND.

LONDON:

Printed for W. NICOLL, at No. 51, in St. Paul's
Church-Yard. MDCCLXXIV.

TO THE SOCIETIES

ESTABLISHED IN

DIFFERENT PARTS OF EUROPE

FOR THE

ENCOURAGEMENT OF AGRICULTURE,

THIS TREATISE

ON THE PRINCIPLES OF

BRITISH POLICY

RELATIVE TO

THAT IMPORTANT DESIGN,

IS INSCRIBED,

BY THEIR

MOST OBEDIENT,

AND DEVOTED SERVANT,

ARTHUR YOUNG.

*North Mims, near
Hatfield, Hertford-
shire, April 15, 1774.*

PREFACE.

THE great encouragement which agriculture at prefent meets with in *Europe* has been either the caufe or effect (probably both) of many publications upon that part of political œconomy which concerns the culture of the earth. In feveral of thefe writings I have remarked, in fome important inftances, fuch a turn of thought, and fuch recommendations to fovereigns as appeared to me to be founded upon principles extremely falfe : At the fame time, I met with many paffages in the works of foreign writers, wherein they

quoted

quoted the example of *England*, but under great mifreprefentations. Thefe circumftances induced me to attempt a plain explanation of the fyftem of *Great Britain* in the encouragement of agriculture, in order for an opportunity to point out as well as I was able the principles of that policy which has wrought thofe effects in this country, and which give foreign authors an idea of our profperity; *Britifh* ones, a conviction of our declenfion and ruin.

If fuch a plan is executed with ability, it can hardly fail of being beneficial; for a train of conduct falfe in the very foundations of its policy, being recommended by writers of confiderable reputation, may be fuppofed to be liftened

to

to by statesmen and legislators:
—to point out such errors is incumbent on a lover of agriculture, who thinks he sees them—the world must be his judge if mistaken. At the same time to find others recommending ideas because they are realized in *England*— which in truth have no such foundation, instigates one farther to shew in what principles consists this branch of *British* policy. All this will be allowed to be an important subject; I wish it had been in more able hands; but others not having undertaken the task, is the reason that the reader finds me engaged in it.

In executing this design, it was necessary to give some account of our present state, in respect of agriculture, arts, manufactures, commerce,

merce, luxury, population, wealth, and the prices of commodities. I have dwelt upon thefe no farther than was neceffary to fhew that the principles explained had been attended with fuch and fuch effects. I had already done fomething of this fort in the obfervations annexed to the regifters of my Tours through *England*, and therefore avoided repetitions; this part of the work would have been very fhort, had not the affertions and opinions of fome writers among ourfelves (gentlemen for whofe abilities I have an high refpect) been fo very contrary to the pofitions I was laying down, that it would have been affectation gravely to explain principles as if undeniable, without removing the objections of men of repute, who denied their exiftence.

The

The obfervations I made in my journies through the kingdom, fixed my opinions concerning population —the inclofure and divifion of landed property—the prices of the earth's products, &c. I found the language of plain facts fo clear, that I could not but liften and be convinced, and I laid the facts before the world on which I founded my opinions: In oppofition to thefe facts, thofe writers have offered reafon upon reafon, argument upon argument, and have given elaborate difquifitions on fubjects which demanded facts alone. This has occafioned my fhewing in the prefent treatife how the facts I before gave are confiftent with, and even naturally arifing from firft principles. This I efteemed a neceffary

part

part of my undertaking—for if I could not fucceed here, it would be in vain to offer circumftances in our national conduct to the imitation of foreigners, which were not clearly deferving their attention.

The fubjects here treated are the moft important that can demand the attention of our legiflature—and it is of the higheft confequence that gentlemen fhould have right ideas of them; fince giving into vulgar errors, and miftaken notions on population, prices of provifions, luxury, fize of farms, inclofures, &c. muft have ill effects. If the parliaments of this kingdom once adopt the errors I here endeavour to refute, it will be a fignal of national decay; fince thofe principles

ciples of our policy which have made us the envy of the world, will then, inftead of being revered, become active againft us.

I am very fenfible that throughout thefe calculations I have taken the unpopular fide of the queftion. A work (unlefs conducted with uncommon abilities) rarely fucceeds, whofe principal aim is to perfuade a nation to be eafy and fatisfied under prefent circumftances ; and to convince them that they have almoft every reafon to be pleafed : fuch a tafk has nothing in it that flatters the multitude — you run counter to public prejudice, and all the reward you can hope for, is the approbation of a few fenfible individuals.

Gover-

*　　*　　*　　*

Governor *Pownall* was fo obliging
as to permit me to take copies of
fome important papers relative to
the corn trade. His memoir on
the uncertainty of the ftatutes, and
the means of afcertaining the prices
of corn for the purpofes of exportation, proves, in the cleareft manner, his uncommon attention to
that fubject, and his ability in dif-
cuffing it. He likewife favoured
me with the table of the expence of
fhipping corn to and from *Holland*
at page 28 ; that of the prices at
which flour from *New-York* and
Penfylvania can be landed in *England*, page 280, 281, and 282.
Alfo that of the prices of flour in
thofe colonies, page 340.

CONTENTS.

CHAPTER I.

CONTENTS.

CHAP. II.

CONTENTS.

C O N T E N T S.

POLITICAL

POLITICAL ARITHMETICK.

INTRODUCTION.

IF ever the encouragement of agriculture was a principal object of attention in the feveral governments of *Europe*, it is at prefent, when we every day fee eftablifhments, inftitutions, or laws framed with this great and laudable view. It is a fpirit which does much honour to the prefent age, and will certainly be attended with excellent effects. Having in many foreign publications feen various accounts of thefe exertions in moft of the neighbouring countries; read feveral differtations on what the French call the *Oeconomical Science*; and reflected on the propofitions which have been beft received in thofe countries, I am induced to offer a few obfervations to the public—fpeaking to other nations as well as to my countrymen. There are inftances in which appear much

more

more merit in the general defign of encouraging agriculture, than in the particular
means taken to effect it; arifing, I fhould
fuppofe, from a want of information : This
muft give concern to one who wifhes fo
well to the caufe. Defirous of being as
good a citizen of the world as my ftation
in life will allow; and feeing that the
foreign writers frequently quote the cafe
of *England*—and are eager to copy her,
let me endeavour to explain, as far as I
am able, the principles which have advanced the hufbandry of this country to its
prefent height.—Let me obferve wherein
foreigners fhould imitate us—and wherein
their imitation can be of no fervice to them.
We cannot well underftand this without.
improving the knowledge of our own interefts. I fhall do it with the greater
readinefs, as I believe the ingenious writers, who have publifhed fo much upon
thefe fubjects in *France*, *Italy*, and *Germany*, have, in feveral cafes, formed miftaken ideas of the policy and practice of
England; both have been the objects of
my particular attention, and though I may
fail in minutely tracing many effects to
their true caufes, yet a flight examination
relative to foreigners adopting what they
call our fyftem, may, I think, have its ufe
to ourfelves.

In

In the progrefs of explaining what I take to be our national advantages, and our national obftacles, I fhall naturally be led to examine fome popular opinions ftarted lately among ourfelves by other writers, as fome of them are fuch as appear to me utterly deftructive of the ends I propofe in this enquiry.

CHAP.

CHAP. I.

ENCOURAGEMENT OF AGRI-CULTURE IN GREAT-BRITAIN.

THE circumftances to which our farmers owe moft, are,

1. Liberty.
2. Taxation.
3. Leafes.
4. Tythe not generally gathered.
5. A freedom from perfonal fervice.
6. Corn Laws.
7. General wealth of the kingdom.
8. Inclofures.
9. Confumption of meat.

SECT. I.

LIBERTY.

THE advance which the agriculture of this country has made, is owing primarily to the excellency of our conftitution—to that general liberty which is dif-fufed among all ranks of the people, and which enfures the legal poffeffions of every

man

man from the hand of violence and power :
This is the original and animating foul
that enlivens the hufbandry of *Britain.*
But it is not owing to this alone that we
have attained to an high degree of excellence ; other caufes alfo have operated, and
very powerful ones, for freedom alone will
not do, as we fee by *Scotland,* where the
conftitution is the fame, but agriculture
abundantly different.   This we fee alfo in
Ireland.—Our farmers, and all the people
employed by them, enjoy that general
freedom and fecurity which is the birth-
right, I will not fay of *Britons,* but of all
mankind.   The operations of a correct and
fpirited agriculture require confiderable expence ; the returns of which are fome years
before they come in ; fuch a bufinefs,
above moft others, requires every favour
that legiflation can fhew : A great degree
of fecurity of poffeffion is neceffary in fuch
a cafe, not only from the effects of arbi-
trary power, but alfo from all oppreffions
that the nobility, gentry, and wealthy
landlords can throw upon their tenants.
An *Englifh* farmer, with a leafe, is as independent of his landlord, as the landlord
is of the farmer ; and if he has no leafe,
we may be fure he is favoured in the rent
proportionably to fuch circumftance.   This
general liberty, which our farmers enjoy

in

in common with the reft of their fellow-
fubjects, it muft be evident, to all attentive
obfervers, cannot fail of being of the
higheft confequence to the promotion of
good hufbandry. It is impoffible to enter
into a full explanation of all the advantages they receive under this general head;
which, in fact, is of all others the greateft
encouragement, not only to agriculture,
but equally fo to arts, manufactures, commerce, and, in a word, every fpecies of
induftry in the ftate *.

S E C T. II.

T A X A T I O N.

THE public revenue of *Britain* is raifed
by fuch a mode of taxation, that little of the weight falls on hufbandry. The
great

---

* Le travail eft le pere de l'opulence. La terre
inépuifable dans fes dons, récompenfe toujours la
fueur de l'homme laborieux qui la follicite, en le com-
blant de richeffes à proportion de fes foins & de fes
peines. Mais l'appas feul des jouiffances encourage
le travail. L'affurance qu'on à d'échanger à fon gré le
fuperflu, eft ce qui rée le fuperflu. C'eft cette caufe
active qui fertilife les champs, fait fouiller les mines,
enfante les inventions, les découvertes et tout ce qui
rend une nation florifante et redoutable. *Theorie du
Luxe*, 1771, tom. i. p. 170.

great divifion of our taxes is into: 1. Land;
2. Parifh; 3. Windows; 4. Excifes; 5.
Cuftoms. As to the fmaller objects of
ftamps, licences, poft-office, &c. none of
them bear the leaft upon one fet of men
more than another, nor are they burthenfome to any.

The land-tax is raifed abfolutely and
totally upon the landlord, though paid by
the tenant. In all cafes it is the fame thing
to the farmer, whether he pays his rent
immediately to his landlord, or to the King
in taxes ; the latter are firft carried to account, and the ballance to his landlord is
always proportioned to what he has already
paid for land-tax. Whether it is one fhilling or four in the pound, it is juft the fame
to the farmer—the landlord is the only one
concerned.

If he farms his own eftate, he pays it
himfelf, which makes no other difference
than the mere trouble of the payment.

An immenfe advantage is the amount of
the tax being fixed : If I buy or inherit an
eftate confifting of wafte, or poorly cultivated tracts, which let only for an hundred pounds a year, and pay a tax of five
pounds to the ftate ; and if after, by fpirited
exertions, I advance the annual value of
my eftate to a thoufand pounds a year, the
tax remains juft as it was before—no increafe.

creafe. This is an advantage, and an en-couragement to improvements which no fyftem can exceed *.

Several *Englifh* writers have pleaded for a new and more equal land-tax; which might be perhaps a good meafure if there was an abfolute certainty of its then remain-ing unchangeable for at leaft a century; but as we cannot have fuch certainty, I muft efteem it a moft dangerous idea; for if the tax was by a general new affeffment made an equal and fair one, then there would not be the fame reafon as at prefent for oppofing alterations : A tax of fo much in the pound, varying according to rent, would be at once a tythe, and the moft pernicious fyftem that could be invented, becaufe an improver would be TAXED IN PROPORTION TO HIS IMPROVEMENTS. Let therefore the tax remain upon its pre-fent footing : it is now perfectly innocent, if altered, we know not where the altera-tions would ftop.

Another

---

* In one refpect this is not fo fully the cafe; the fums which parifhes are affeffed always remain the fame ; but the officers may vary the affeffment on individuals ; but then they muft know at what rent a farm is let before they can raife any perfon's tax, and the perfon fo raifed may appeal, if every other perfon in the parifh is not equally taxed, which makes fuch alterations in the affeffment rare.

Another circumſtance which renders our land-tax ſo little burthenſome to the agriculture of the kingdom, is its being laid abſolutely upon *rent:* The aſſeſſors cannot tax the landlord for any ſuppoſed or viſible value: if a farm is ever ſo rich, or ſupports ever ſo many cattle, it is nothing to the aſſeſſor, he can tax the rent only: and if the landlord farms it himſelf, he can only be taxed according to the rent the laſt time the farm was let, though an hundred years ago, and would at preſent let for quadruple the ſum; if the old rent cannot be diſcovered, the old aſſeſſment is continued, without enquiring on what foundation it was formed.

From this ſlight review of the land-tax of *England,* it appears to be no burthen on agriculture:—no ſyſtem of taxing land could have been invented that would injure it ſo little.

It is not ſo with the pariſh taxes; they are laid immediately on the farmer, and prove a burthen to him in proportion to their weight: They conſiſt of the poor's rate, or the ſums raiſed for the ſupport of the chargeable poor: The church rate, for keeping in repair the pariſh church: The highway rate, raiſed by the ſurveyors for the repair of the roads. The latter is not general, as the ſtatute duty of ſix days work with their teams, is commonly more

than

than fufficient; and in no cafe, by act of parliament, more than a rate of fix-pence in the pound of rent can be laid in aid of the duty: this is the only refemblance we have in *England* of the *Corvees* of *France*, and the monftrous perfonal fervice which is fo deftructive to the agriculture of *Germany* and *Poland.* The amount in *England* cannot be called burthenfome; fince the fix days work are performed only at a lei-fure time of the year, and may be generally compounded for at a fourth part of the real value.

With the poor's rate there is ufually a few other fmall taxes thrown together, fuch as the . conftable's expences, which however are trivial, and the county rate, being a county expence for certain bridges and other general expences which concern the county at large; when divided among all the parifhes it is a very fmall amount. The poor's tax, with thefe additions, in-cluding the church rate, are ufually all thrown together, and raifed by a fingle rate, in which every occupier of lands or houfes are charged in proportion to his rent. The average of them in my Northern Tour, came only to 1 *s.* 1 *d.* in the pound; and in the Eaftern Tour to 2 *s.* 8 *d.*; aver-age of both 1 *s.* 10 ½ *d.* But in manufac-turing,

turing, and many other particular places, they rife much higher.

The reader will obferve that this tax is entirely regulated by the rent of the land, which is a circumftance that renders the burthen comparatively light: If a man hires an hundred acres of land for thirty pounds a year, during a leafe of forty years, and by improvement raifes the land to the annual value of an hundred pounds, ftill he can be rated only at thirty pounds a year, as the value or goodnefs of the land, and the largenefs of the farmer's ftock have nothing to do in the account; he is not to be taxed for them, but only in proportion to his rent.

Another obfervation I fhould make is, that in parifhes where the rates run very high, as in fome they do to 3, 4, 6, and even 10*s*. in the pound, in fuch, the tax is in fact on the landlord, for no tenant will hire land in any parifh without firft enquiring what the rates are; and when he finds them fo high, will give a rent only in proportion to fuch certain expence; if the rates were to be lowered from 10*s*. to 5*s*. in the pound, the landlord at the expiration of his leafes would be able to add 5*s*. in the pound to his rents.

Upon the whole, though the poor's-rate, &c. is a direct burthen on the farmers,

yet

yet the amount not being a matter of great confideration, and being laid only on the certain rent, it is not in any refpect to be confidered as checking the progrefs and improvement of agriculture: the difputes, litigations and lawfuits, which arife from the quarrels between farmers on fome being rated higher or lower than others, and between parifhes concerning the fettlement of their poor, are in fome inflances a greater abufe and burthen than the total of what they pay regularly in rates. This is an abufe of freedom, and rather marks the lightnefs of the burthens laid on our farmers, than their weight.

The tax upon windows bears not particularly upon agriculture ; the farmer pays fomething annually for each window in his houfe, proportioned to the total number, it is a regular tax, and too inconfiderable to be efteemed a burthen, certainly it has no ill confequences on our hufbandry. Were it however, as fome authors have advifed, to be the only tax, by its abforbing all others, it would be a deadly burthen to the whole kingdom; fince no man fhould pay to the amount of all taxes in proportion as he *poffeffes*, but in proportion as he *confumes* ; but of this more hereafter.

The two great branches of *Englifh* taxes are the excifes and the cuftoms ; their

their being burthenfome to agriculture depends entirely on what objects they are laid, and to what extent they are carried ; but in general I fhall remark, that they are much lefs detrimental than commonly imagined. Cuftoms on the exportation of corn would be ruinous to agriculture : excifes on wool and leather to fuch an amount as to leffen the confumption and fink the price in the hands of the farmer, would be evidently mifchievous : fuch excifes upon malt as would leffen the confumption of beer, and at the fame time cuftoms on the export of barley, would greatly hurt the culture of that crop : excifes laid on butchers for all the beafts they killed, to fuch a height as to leffen the confumption of meat, would have the fame effect ;—but thefe are cafes of which we have no inftances in *England :* our cuftoms and excifes are not prejudicial to our hufbandry but in very few cafes, the prohibition which is only another word for a very high cuftom on the export of wool, and raw leather, are certainly heavy burthens laid on agriculture in favour of manufactures, the proof of which, is the price of wool in *England* having fallen half fince that policy was embraced, which has been a tax of near two fhillings in the pound additional on land ; not that I would

venture

venture to plead in favour of the exportation of wool raw: I fhall only refer the
reader to the arguments of Mr. *Smith*, in
his *Memoirs of Wool*, where he will find
many extreme curious facts concerning
wool and the woollen manufacture.

That cuftoms and excifes do not injure in
the leaft the agriculture of *Britain*, we have
the cleareft proof, in their not lowering the
prices of any of the farmer's commodities,
(wool, &c. excepted, as above;) while they
leave them at the price they found or raife
them, certainly the farmer cannot be injured.
When they are carried too far they leflen
confumption, which in every circumftance
is the great wound the farmer has moft to
fear, becaufe his prices from that moment
will fall ; but in *England* the confumption
of every commodity has increafed under
every burthen that has been laid on it:
this has been uniformly the cafe with malt;
nor have we an inftance of either excifes or
cuftoms leffening the confumption, and
confequently the price of the farmer's products. The excellence of this fpecies of
taxation has been very ably explained by
feveral writers, who have fhewn that by the
tax being blended with the price, the pur-
chafer does not feel its weight, and never
pays the tax but when he is beft able to
pay it, that is at the moment he makes the
purchafe.

purchafe. If all the taxes of *England* were confolidated into this general branch *on confumption*, our fyftem would be ftill more perfect. As to their raifing prices, it is as I could eafily fhew an advantage to every clafs in the ftate.

From this review of the fyftem of taxation in *Britain*, it is clear that the agriculture of the kingdom cannot fuffer from any part of it, without the amount being carried to a much greater height; but hitherto we have feen nothing like even the profpect of mifchief to our hufbandry from any of our taxes. This muft arife in a great meafure from their not being laid on improvements—from their being permanent and not varying—from the affeffors, collectors, and receivers being armed with very moderate powers, and with none beyond the mere line of fraud againft the tax—from their being no refpectors of perfons, dealing equally with the duke and his little tenant.

S E C T. III.

L E A S E S.

THE improvements which have been wrought in *England* have been almoft totally owing to the cuftom of granting leafes :

leafes : In thofe countries where it is unufual to give them, agriculture yet continues much inferior to what we find it
where they are ufual, nor can it flourifh
till this cuftom is adopted. If the mode
and progrefs of country improvements is
well confidered, they will be found utterly
inconfiftent with an occupation without a
leafe. A farmer hires a tract of land in an
unimproved or inferior ftate ; he repairs
the fences, deepens the ditches—clears
away rubbifh—purchafes dung—forms com-
pofts—drains the wet fields—waters the
meadows—adds to the buildings—digs for
marle—gets the arable lands into good and
clean order ; thefe works take him three
or four years, during which time he facrifices his profits in hopes of being well paid.
Now how can any perfon poffibly fuppofe
that fuch a fyftem will be executed on his
farms, if he will not or does not grant long
leafes ? Is it to be expected that a tenant
will lay a thoufand pounds out upon improvements, and remain all the time at
the mercy of his landlord, to be turned
out of the farm as foon as the money is
expended ? The cafe is fo felf-evident that
the neceffity muft be undeniable ; no man
of common fenfe will put fuch truft in
another.

Nor

Nor is it fufficient that granting leafes is a common cuftom, they muft be fo guarded by the laws as to give the tenant the moft perfect fecurity ; he muft be fure of his term, and alfo fure of being fafe againft any ill defigning, malevolent, or infidious attacks of a wealthy landlord, and be as independent while he adheres to the contracts of his leafe, as the landlord is of him : all this is the cafe with the majority of *Englifh* farmers. It is true, there are many tracts of country in which landlords will not grant leafes, but then one of two circumftances muft exift ; either the land is of fuch a nature that no *improvements* are wanting—or, in confequence of no leafe being given, the farms are let much under their value.

In fome countries of *Europe* no leafes are granted, in others they are very weak guaranties of the tenants fecurity, and in others, the fale of the eftate vacates the leafe : Thefe are all radical evils which muft be cured, or hufbandry can never flourifh.

SECT.

S E C T. IV.

T Y T H E.

THIS is the greateſt burthen that yet remains on the agriculture of this kingdom; and if it was univerſally taken in kind, would be ſufficient to damp all ideas of improvement. Fortunately the ſpirit of our clergy is too liberal in general to live in ſuch a ſtate of warfare with their pariſhioners, as pretty generally is the caſe where they ſubmit to the trouble of gathering for the ſake of the additional profit.

In many pariſhes however, the tythes are gathered, and in them I will venture to pronounce no correct or ſpirited huſbandry will ever be met with :—and I may further remark, that in the extenſive journies I have made through this kingdom for the purpoſe of examining its agriculture, I have never met with conſiderable improvements where the tythe was taken in kind ; and a very little calculation would ſhew the impoſſibility of it. The reaſon our huſbandry has advanced upon the whole in ſo great a degree, is ſuch a large part of the kingdom not being tythed in kind, but a compoſition *per* acre or *per* pound being taken in lieu ; and ſuch a conſiderable

portion

portion of it being tythe free, which is
every day increasing by all the new inclosures. The great object at present of *British* agriculture, is to obtain a general exemption from tythe, by giving the clergy
some settled income in lieu of it.

ABOLITION OF TYTHE.

Last winter there were some respectable
meetings of gentlemen, for the purpose
of applying to parliament for an alteration in the tythe-laws: a committee was
chosen, and having made one in several
of their meetings, I am able to assert that
their designs are perfectly commendable;
having equally in view the benefit of
agriculture and the rights of the clergy.

The committee, in the petition they
prepared for presenting to the House of
Commons, names no equivalent to be given
in lieu of tythe, properly leaving that to
the wisdom of the house: It may not, however, be amiss to make a few observations
on such as have been thought of.

First, A Pound Rate. The annual value of the living for the last seven years to
be stated, and the average to be in future
raised by a pound rate; not by a fixed
sum, but at so much in the pound, consequently

quently the value of the living will rife
with the rife of land and fall of money.

There are two infuperable objections to
this fcheme. *Firft*, The difficulty of gaining a fair pound-rate is fully equal to that
of abolifhing tythes. Three fourths of the
kingdom have at times litigated their rates
with a view to honeft proportions, but in
vain; and accordingly the inequalities every
where found, and the enormous fallacies,
through various reafons, are fuch as render
the plan utterly impracticable. People
who have long occupied their own lands,
and are rated according to their laft leafe,
though an hundred years old, pay the
tythe either in kind or to the value; were
it to be paid by rate they would be exempted of three fourths of their juft contri-
butions, and the burthen fall on their
neighbours, who already pay as much as
they ought. For inftance, A. B. C. D. and
E. are the renters in a parifh, and F. and
G. farm their own lands: the former contribute to the rates proportionably to their
rents; but F. and G. only in proportion to
the laft rental of their lands: For want of
an explicit decifion of the value of F. and
G's lands, they are unjuftly favoured, and
the reft of the parifh burthened in proportion; is not this inequality fufficient without eafing F. and G. of a great part of their
tythe,

tythe, and throwing the weight on A. B. C. D. and E. who are already burthened more than they ought to be ? What fyftem can be more iniquitous ? *Secondly*, If this objection was got over, there is another great one. You want to be eafed of tythes becaufe of the enormous burthen of a payment proportioned to the crop ? How abfurd then would it be to exchange it for a direct fimilar burthen ? The mifchief of tythes, of the taille in *France*, and all taxes proportional to products, valuations, or rents, is the circumftance of taxing improvements : this monftrous evil you would not get rid of. If a man buys a farm at 50 *l.* a year, and by excellent management improves it highly, and lets it at 100 *l.* his tenant is at once doubled in the rates—the very evil which has fo often been complained of in various countries, that groan under taxes varying with rents or valuations. This fyftem therefore would be only changing one evil for another : Our poor rates are a tax liable to this great evil ; in the name of common fenfe, therefore, do not quadruple a tax which is open to fuch objections.

Secondly, It has been propofed to pay the rector by a corn rent ; with the double view of giving him his fhare of future improvements, and fecuring his property from
finking

finking with the value of money; but this is liable to moft of the objections of the pound-rate. Giving him his fhare of future improvements, is giving him the only thing we want to take away; and if the quantity of corn to be paid per acre is fixed, then you will throw a monftrous oppreffion on all the kingdom below your medium in favour of the part that is above it, which muft appear to every one an infurmountable objection.

Thirdly, It has been propofed that the compofition for tythes fhould be fixed at fo much in the pound rent, throughout the kingdom. This would obviate the objection from the fall of money, but it is open to that of the fecond propofition; and it is alfo open to another, which is the difficulty of fixing a rent to lands long occupied by their owners.

Fourthly, It is propofed to give a value in land—which, upon the whole, is that idea which appears to me open to the feweft objections: It provides for the clergy infinitely upon more favourable and liberal principles than any other mode whatever, infomuch that (which is an object, in the great work of changing tythes, of vaft importance) the clergy themfelves would probably agree to the fcheme upon this footing. It fecures them not only from
                                        fuffering

fuffering by a fall in the value of money, but alfo gives them a property which will rife proportionably to that fall. It is not open to a fingle objection upon the account of fair pound-rates, valuations of rent, or any fuch fources of knavery. It is the fame to the whole kingdom; you will not opprefs one part of it in favour of another. It is but one account; the moment it is fixed there is for ever an end of fquabbles with the clergy, whereas many of the other fchemes would perpetuate them as much as tythes in kind.

That there are objections to this idea is certain, and fome that are very weighty; but I think the whole affair muft depend on overcoming thefe objections; if you cannot do that the bufinefs is impracticable. However, I have yet heard none that are infuperable. An act might direct that the land-owners of every parifh fhould chufe one commiffioner of allotment, and the rector or tythe-owner another, which two to chufe a third, and thefe three commiffioners to be invefted with thofe abfolute powers common in all commiffions of inclofure; they fhould be tied down by the act to afcertain the average value of the living for the laft feven years, including all tythes great and fmall, and to affign, as near as may be, to the parfonage, a portion of land

fuffi-

fufficient to yield a rent equal to fuch average value. This would of courfe be done
in the ufual method of reducing the whole
parifh to money, and then gaining the
proportions. That there would be difficulties in fuch a work nobody can doubt, and
if acts of inclofure had never paffed, fuch
as would be called infurmountable ; but we
know that no difficulty could arife that
has not often been met with, and overcome in inclofures—no variety or com-
plexity of interefts, no difficulty of arrang-
ing lands—no more important interefts to
be fettled in one cafe than in the other ; why
not therefore proceed on a fyftem which is
put daily in execution in one part of the
kingdom or other ? I fpeak this under the
fuppofition that the lands affigned in lieu
of tythes were neceffarily to be in a fpot
around the parfonage ; if contiguity was
not infifted upon, all difficulties would
vanifh.

Another objection which has been made
to the whole of this idea, is the impropriety of adding to the lands in mortmain,
which are already too numerous and extenfive. This may be an impropriety, but are
improprieties to weigh down fuch amazing
benefits as would refult from the abolition
of tythe ? Adding to the inconvenience,
when no public advantages are to refult
from

from it, would be abſurd ; but the preſent is a very different caſe. The tenth part of your groſs products is already in mortmain, why not change ſuch a burthenſome payment for an aſſignment of land? This is not in any reſpect a ſimilar caſe with an increaſe by legacies, purchaſe, or donation. But farther ; lands in the poſſeſſion of rectors of pariſhes lying around their parſonage houſes, would be ſcarcely open to the uſual objections againſt mortmain : much the greateſt part would neceſſarily be kept in the hands of the reſident rectors, improved juſt as much and as well as the farms of the laity, when in their own hands. I appeal to the knowledge of gentlemen in the country, if the glebes of clergymen, when they lie conveniently for their own houſes, are not as well managed as other lands ; unleſs the neceſſary improvements are of a very expenſive nature, and the incumbent very old. And when ſuch lands are let, why are we to ſuppoſe that the rector will not, for his own intereſt, get as great a rent as he can, and if he does, then the greateſt objection to the land being in the hands of the church vaniſhes.

Lands in the poſſeſſion of a dean and chapter, or a biſhop, where the tenure is on lives, and the benefit a fine, or belonging to colleges or hoſpitals, are as entirely different as any two caſes can be. In

all

all thefe cafes, the public fuffers from the prefent incumbent preferring a prefent advantage of a fine to an annual one in rent; rents therefore are not raifed, and wherever that is the cafe, all the world knows the public fuffers from the bad hufbandry exercifed on fuch lands. It is the fame with truftees for hofpitals, &c. who never attend to the benefit of the eftates in the manner they do to their own. But in all thefe cafes, the rector of a parifh would be put on a par with other private gentlemen, having the fame interefts, and from the fituation of the land around his manfion, the fame inducement to improve for profit and pleafure. But this reafoning is upon the fuppofition that there were any folid objections to the fcheme, without attending to the advantages; reflect on the evil you get rid of—reflect on the mifchief of tythes to your eftates—reflect on the improvements made in land tythe free, which can only be made in them—reflect on the rife of your rents following fuch a plan—reflect on the folid improvement which would refult from it to the agriculture of the whole kingdom; and then determine if both public and private interefts do not ftrongly unite to promote the execution of this plan, the only one by which this enormous tax, MULTIPLIABLE ON ALL IMPROVEMENTS, can ever be abolifhed.

SECT. V.

FREEDOM FROM PERSONAL SERVICE.

FROM reading feveral *French* authors on rural oeconomy, I apprehend their farmers lie under a very confiderable and irregular burthen in the fervices performed for their landlords, feigneurs of towns, &c. and thefe appear to be of an extenfive nature—at all feafons of the year—and no equivalent or pay returned for them. Of this we have no other traces in *England*, except fuch articles as are fometimes inferted in leafes, fuch as carriage of firing, timber, and other materials of building; but thefe are always fpecified, voluntarily engaged in, and a limitation that they fhall not exceed a certain number of days work. It can in no cafe be efteemed a burthen; the exemption from fuch evils as the *French* writers defcribe, muft be efteemed as a very valuable circumftance.

SECT. VI.

CORN LAWS.

THE liberty enjoyed by every rank of our people; the eafe and impartiality

of

of our taxation—the length of our leafes—
our freedom from perfonal fervice — all
thefe would in vain fhed their happy influence, if, for want of good corn laws, foreigners were allowed, in the markets of
Britain, to rival our own farmers, or if by
prohibitory laws our products were kept at
a low price; every other advantage under
heaven would not make amends for fuch
deficiencies. It is in vain that an hundred encouragements urge the farmer to
gain great crops, if when he has gained
them he cannot find a ready market and a
fufficient price. I have, in feveral other
publications, explained myfelf fo fully
upon this head, that at prefent I have only
to make a few obfervations, which are
effential to a clear idea of the dependance
which our agriculture has upon the police
of corn *.

The

---

* One argument againft the bounty, ufed by feveral writers, is the imagination that the *Dutch* buy our
corn by means of that premium, and fell it to us again
with profit :—Which is much fuch an objection as
was made to Governor *Pownal's* bill, that the bounty
would be paid to pretended exporters, who would
carry their corn to *Holland* and then fhip it back
again. But the following table of the expences will
fhew how well 5 s. a quarter would pay for this
operation.

Corn-

The firſt great ſtep was to cut off the importation from foreign countries, unleſs when the price at home was very high; this important object preceded another of equal conſequence, the granting a bounty on the exportation when not exceeding certain prices. This was one of the moſt remarkable ſtrokes of policy, and the moſt contrary to the general ideas of all *Europe,* of any that ever were carried into execution.

The deſign was to give a premium to the landed intereſt of the kingdom, in return for the great exertion they had made to place the crown on the head of King *William.* The act declares the price of corn to be too low, and the evident deſign of

the

	s.	d.
Cornfactor's charge of ſhipping, per quarter,	1	6
Commiſſion and inſurance, ſuppoſing wheat at 43 s. - - -	1	6
Freight and primage, - -	1	8
	4	8
The charges from *Holland* are to be eſtimated at 1 s. more, - -	5	8
	10	4

The charges are the ſame to *Ireland,* but the freight higher to and from, 1 s. per quarter, 12 4

From which account it is very evident that the 5 s. a quarter bounty can have no ſuch effect.

the meafure was to raife it. It has, however, been attended with the direct contrary
effect, it has funk it confiderably; a point
not fufficiently underftood by many perfons,
who do not take into their account the fall
in the value of money, and confequent rife
in the price of all commodities, corn excepted; if this is calculated, the fall in the
price of wheat will be found very confiderable *. This fall has not been owing to
improvements in agriculture, fince they
would have operated equally in lowering
the price of meat and other products of the
farmers, which has been far enough from
the cafe. Here, therefore, remains the
paradox, how a meafure, which has funk
the price of corn, can have encouraged
agriculture?

It has certainly given a greater ftability
to prices, which is an object of confequence: It is not the farmer's intereft to
have corn three pounds a quarter one year,
and five and twenty fhillings the next.
Years in which the price is very low, are
the farmers great enemies; in the fixteen
years, from 1741 to 1756, the crops of
corn, in this ifland, were fo uncommonly
plentiful, that the price would have funk
fo

---

* In the *Expediency of a Free Exportation of Corn*,
1770, p. 11, I have fhewn this at large.

fo low as to have utterly difcouraged cultivation, had not a remarkably brifk exportation carried off immenfe quantities, and
kept the farmers from throwing their
wheat to their hogs.—Now had not the
bounty effeĉted this, the farmers would
not have fown wheat, and then fucceffive
years would have rifen fo high in price, as
to have raifed the general average of the period much higher than before the bounty
took place.

In examining the prices before the prohibition of the import of foreign corn, as
given in our only record, the *Windfor*
Table, we do not fee the *real* prices, tho'
we do fince that time : They are the prices
of corn in that market, which is neceffarily
affeĉted by all the markets around, and by
that of *London* in particular, with which
it communicates by water.—Now if the
French or *Dutch* poured in great quantities
of corn, it neceffarily funk the price of our
own, and probably gave our farmers a low
rate when they ought to have had an high
one : This operation neceffarily gave a
degree of equality to the prices before that
period, which was totally artificial, and not
owing to encouragement of our own culture, but the direĉt contrary. Yet with all
this mifchief to our hufbandry, the fyftem
very poorly anfwered the intent, for the
fluc-

fluctuation of prices was, notwithstanding, much greater than it has been since. And when the writers against the bounty speak of the cheapness of corn at former periods, they forget that they are speaking of the cheapness of *French* corn as much as of *English*, since the cheapness they falsely state was effected by importation. This was particularly the case through the reign of *James* I.

The prices since that period are real ones of our own corn, unaffected by foreign imports, and consequently shew the true degree of cheapness.

The cheapness brought on by this measure has indeed in one period been so great, that I do not think our agriculture could have supported it, and continued flourishing, unless the crops had, at the same time, been very abundant. From the year 1730 to 1756, corn was so amazingly cheap in *England*, that this nation ought not to wish ever to see such another period : During the whole of it complaints were incessant, through every part of the kingdom, of the decay and ruin of manufactures : I have a list of above one hundred and forty publications at *London*, in that period, pointing out or complaining of the decline of the woollen and other fabrics : If those complaints had any foundation (which I admit

admit is by no means clear) it certainly was
owing to this prodigious cheapnefs of provifions, which in all countries is fuch an
encourager of idlenefs, that no manufactures can flourifh under it. From 1741 to
1756, the average price of wheat at the
Windfor market was 3 *s.* 8 *d.* a bufhel, or
1 *l.* 9 *s.* 4 *d.* per quarter, which is 2 *s.* 7 *d.*
per bufhel, or 1 *l.* o *s.* 6 *d.* per quarter
Winchefter meafure, and average quality.
It was impoffible the farmers fhould be fo
wealthy as they ought, or even in tolerable
circumftances, with wheat at fuch a price ;
—and from the beft information I have
been able to gain, I have reafon to believe
that our hufbandry, in the cheap period
from 1730 to 1756, made fcarcely any
advance : I know this was not the cafe in
Norfolk, but the improvements there were
forced by the landlords, who built, inclofed, and marled at their own expence,
and then let the land at a fourth of the
rent it carries at prefent : Since 1756, that
is with a comparative high price of corn,
the tenants have done the whole, and
made more money in fixteen years than
they did before in fix and forty.

That the fyftem of exporting with a
bounty has been of infinite national importance, cannot be doubted : Between
1730 and 1756, the quantity of corn we
ex-

exported brought in many millions of money to this kingdom, and employed a great
quantity of fhipping, yet the price was
very low at home through the whole
period; to what purpofe fhould we have
kept that corn, and loft that wealth, unlefs
to fink the price, in certain years, fo low
as to ftop the plough, and confequently
occafion fucceffive fcarcities. The uniform
experience of all nations proves that where
the exportation of corn is prohibited, there
the price in abundant years falls fo low that
the plough yields no profit to the farmer—
it is abandoned, and the lands lie uncultivated—fcarcity, and even famine, are then
never far off. It is not a fatisfaction to the
farmer to tell him, that the immenfe rates
of certain years render the general average
as high or higher than in other countries :
this is no confolation to a man who has
been abfolutely ruined by the low prices of
three or four fucceffive years. His money,
ftock, and farm are gone, nor can he enter
into bufinefs again when the high prices
come. To have embraced a fyftem
directly oppofite to fuch a pernicious one,
muft be efteemed a fingular felicity in this
kingdom.

LATE SYSTEM.

It is here neceſſary to offer a few remarks on the fyſtem which our legiſlature
has purſued ſince the year 1756, becauſe,
ſince that period, an almoſt new one has
been adopted. In 1757 and 1758, the
price aroſe conſiderably, and exportation
was prohibited. In the ſix ſucceſſive years
the export continued. But from the year
1765, to the preſent time, we have had
a perpetual ſhifting policy, in which nothing has been permanent : no regular
law ; no new arrangement of prices at
which export ſhould be allowed or prohibited ; every year has produced a temporary act fuſpending the operation of thoſe
laws which had proved of ſuch excellent
utility. The legiſlature had almoſt con-
ſtantly been driven into ſuch a pernicious
fyſtem by the riots and complaints of the
manufacturing poor, and the *London* mob
—and by the fooliſh petitions of ignorant
boroughs.

Upon reviewing this period of ſixteen
years, from 1757 to 1772, both incluſive,
it is remarkable to find that the average of
the beſt wheat at *Windſor* has been only 5 *s.*
6 *d.* a buſhel, or 2 *l.* 4 *s.* a quarter ; which,
for the average quality and *Wincheſter* meaſure,

fure, is only 4 s. 4 d. a bufhel, or 1 l. 14 s.
8 d. a quarter. Now that this has not,
upon the whole, been an high price, cannot for a moment be doubted. From
1697 to 1714, throwing out two years in
which the export was prohibited, the remainder being alfo a period of fixteen years,
through the whole of which exportation
with the bounty went on, the average price,
in the fame *Windfor* market, was 2 l. 5 s.;
confequently the laft period of fixteen
years, ending 1772, was *cheaper* by 10 d.
a quarter than the other, during which the
bounty was paid! But fo far from the
bounty being paid through this, that it has
been fufpended during ten of the fixteen
years, and export itfelf prohibited during
more than half the period. This is fuch
an amazing change of policy, that no
fagacity can difcover any other reafons for
it than the tranfitory impulfe of riots and
complaints.

But let me farther remark, that the late
period, which is to be called *dear*, only on
comparifon with the fixteen preceding years,
opened with the war, which, during nine
years, added fuch an amazing mafs of bullion and paper to our circulation, and
which has, to the prefent time, been every
day increafing rather than diminifhing, by
acquifitions in the *Indies*, and by a moft
                                    enlarged

enlarged and flourifhing commerce—that it would have been a moft aftonifhing phenomenon in politics, had not the price of all forts of commodities rifen. An increafe of national debt of feventy millions, with the regular circulation of the intereft—the expenditure, during the war, from twelve to twenty millions a year—and the money brought into the nation the laft years of the war by a commerce which never was equalled;—a great increafe of taxes—and a ftill greater of paper currency of all forts, could not fail of having that effect.

But let any perfon reflect on the rife of all prices during the laft fixteen years; let them name one article, in the common courfe of purchafe and fale, which has not been confiderably advanced. All the parts of drefs, as cloth, linen, filk, lace, leather, ornaments, &c. The whole of furniture; your pictures, glaffes, hangings, carpets, fopha's, chairs, tables. Your equipage, from the gilded chariot at St. *James's*, to the one horfe chaife at *Whitechapel*. All thofe articles of food which are beyond the purfes of the poor, the whole train of delicacies. Your pleafures, your diverfions, your education, and your ftudy. Throughout all this lift, and that it might be much lengthened every one will agree, can you name a fingle article

the

the price whereof is not greatly raifed?
We fee, therefore, by this general rife,
that the caufes, I juft mentioned, have
taken their natural effect, by raifing every
thing ; and it remains to be fhewn, that
wheat ought to rife with other things.
Two words will difpatch this argument ;
if the producer of one commodity is pro-
fcribed from fo general an advantage, while,
in every branch of his confumption, he
pays amply to every one elfe—while his
rent, his labour, his rates, his tythe compofition, his wear and tear, and manufactures, all rife in price upon him, how is
he to carry on his culture? He muft be
inevitably ruined.   On the contrary, he
ought to receive equal encouragement with
any other clafs, for exactly in proportion to
his encouragement will be the fpirit and
extent of his culture and improvements.
Yet, in direct oppofition to fuch ideas, do
we every day hear complaints of the high
prices of provifions, with inflammatory
publications, defigned to fhew the too great
profits of our farmers, and attributing fuch
prices to falfe caufes—thefe are vulgar
complaints, common in all ages and all
places.   The capital of the kingdom even
petitioned parliament, laft feffions, to give
a bounty on the importation of wheat, and
actually gave one itfelf.   Let us fuppofe
the

the Houfe of Commons had adopted the
idea, and offered a bounty fufficient to have
brought in confiderable quantities of foreign
corn—the price before was a juft one, proportioned to the quantity of money in the
nation and the quantity of the preceding
crops—confequently the price was juft
what it ought to be. The import, we may
fuppofe, lowers it confiderably ; this is the
object defired—but how are the farmers to
fare ? if proportion demands 7 *s.* a bufhel,
what is he to do with only 4 *s.* ? What
fpirit will there be in his culture ? What
encouragement to raife corn ? Thus you
lay a very heavy tax (for nothing elfe
would do in a time of fuch general fcarcity) which in the expenditure is to be
ruinous to the farmers, in order that corn
may be cheap ! What a heap of abfurdity
and contradiction is fuch a fyftem ! Might
you not as well cut the manufacturers looms
in pieces, and fet fire to their warehoufes in
order to lower the price of cloth ? Would
not any perfon fuppofe that fuch ideas
were found in fome filly pamphlet, inftead
of a petition from a great city to a *Britifh*
Houfe of Commons ? From all this we
may determine, that our former fyftem of
corn law was a great encouragement 'to
our agriculture, and fince thofe laws were
reverfed, the general rife of prices has
operated a fucceeding good effect.

PERMANENT CORN LAW.

The act which paffed laft feffions, and which was brought in by Governor *Pownal,* has remedied fome of the evils which flowed from the variable fhifting policy that had for fome years been our difgrace ; yet was that bill founded on radical miftakes, fince the principles of it fuppofed that lower export prices ought to be fixed at prefent than in 1689, inftead of which they ought to be *higher:* And the only principle upon which an alteration of the prices could be juftly effected, was proving that corn, in the prefent period, ought to be confiderably cheaper than it was in the latter part of the preceding century—which affertion, to be rendered confiftent, muft be followed by another, that the farmers of this kingdom pay much lower rents than they did; have their labour, implements, furniture, and manufactures at lower prices, and pay much fmaller fums in poor rates, at prefent, than an hundred years ago. What confiftency there can be in adopting the *principle* that prices ought to fall, and making it the corner ftone of a permanent law, I cannot underftand. I do not think that a beneficial fyftem, which had ftood the teft of many years experience, fhould,

fhould, in its *principles*, be overturned. The act of 1689, declares corn, at that period, to be *too cheap*, and therefore gave a bounty at certain prices: Corn is now much cheaper, and you declare that it is *too dear*, by lowering the bounty rates : In a word, the ideas, which were our guide in 1689, were effentially different from thofe which influence our conduct at pre-fent.

In anfwer to this, I have not heard any fatisfactory motives ; it is all thrown on the difcontents of the mob, and the complaints of rioters, who infift on wheat being *cheap*, that they may afford *dear* fugar, tea, brandy, and ftrong beer ; and be able to confume four times as much of thofe commodities, as their more frugal anceftors did.

As I have declared my opinion of the new act thus far, I fhall, on the other hand, readily admit, that if the comparifon is not to be drawn with the old policy— but with the abominable fyftem that has difgraced us fince 1765, Mr. *Pownal*'s act has great merit. *Firft*, It is a permanent law, which fingle circumftance remedies abundance of evils that have perplexed us. *Second*, It preferves the bounty when corn is very cheap, the very idea of which we were in danger of lofing. *Third*, It gives the bounty whenever exportation goes on, **which**

which is a plan equally well adapted to a conftant encouragement both of hufbandry and navigation, and the only means of regaining our loft corn trade. *Fourth,* The provifions relative to importation are well imagined, to keep up a *trade* in corn when not wanted for *confumption,* and obviate the old objeftion to our laws, that fhipping in foreign countries could not be fafely done, when it was an uncertainty whether the price in *England* would allow importation.

Upon the whole, the aft has great merit, and will do more good than any other *new* meafure could have done : and I muft fay, that the father of it merits the thanks of every one, as a member who facrifices his time and attention to objefts of public import-ance. I have the pleafure of knowing, from his converfation, that his ideas are perfeftly judicious on this point, and that he neceffarily framed the bill, from a prac-tical knowledge of what would fucceed *.

VARIATION OF PRODUCTS.

It is amufing to refleft to what a variety of caufes the rife of prices has been at-tributed—monopoly of farms—inclofures —jobbers—the bounty—horfes—dogs, and all forts of abfurdities : others have had
judg-

---

* See Appendix.

judgment enough to reject thefe idle caufes, and acknowledge that there has been a *real* fcarcity owing to bad feafons. A late very ingenious author * fays, that there has been a failure of crops in general for five years paft; and Meff. *Smyth* and *Farrer* at the bar of the houfe of commons, talked the fame language. I cannot, from the moft attentive reflection, allow thefe remarks to be juft: the average *Windfor* price of fix years ending 1772 inclufive, was 2*l.* 3*s.* 6*d.* a quarter, which is, average quality and *Winchefter* meafure, only 1*l.* 14*s.* 5*d.* Does fuch a price mark any real fcarcity? Compare this price with preceding periods —reflect that it is at a time when all forts of prices are rifing, owing to the cheapnefs of money, and then tell me if it is poffible that wheat fhould have flood at fuch a rate, had there been five fucceffive bad, or even indifferent crops! A fmall deficiency in the markets has always been obferved to raife the price beyond the proportion of fuch deficiency; under which circumftance, a bad crop at a time when every thing is rifing in price from the plenty of money, muft appear to have a prodigious effect:—What therefore muft be the effect
of

* *Enquiry into fize of farms and price of provifions,* p. 51.

of five or fix bad crops, cauling a fcarcity,
while the cheapnefs of money, increafe of
confumption, wafte, luxury, &c. all con-
fpire to raife the price even of good ones?
Surely an enormous rate muft be the confequence; fo that thofe who attribute the
ideal fcarcity to bad years, but deceive the
people, as there probably will never be
better years. It is idle to flatter them in
this manner; in my own opinion, the
crops for five years paft have been not bad,
at leaft; confequently there is no reafon to
expect corn lower; — an hundred arguments might be brought to prove that it
is not high: To raife wheat to 1 *l.* 14 *s.*
5 *d.* muft fo many chimerical reafons be
brought! Surely parliament was not very
attentive, when fhe appointed committees
to enquire into the caufes of wheat getting
to fo *high* a price!

As to good and bad crops in general,
very little dependence is to be placed in the
accounts received or given by millers, meal-
men, factors, and fuch people, who depend
fo much on private intelligence, that they
are ever apt to fuppofe the language of their
interefted information, that of the kingdom,
which is generally a very great error. But
five bad crops in fucceflion, when agriculture is highly encouraged! Very fufpicious
fuch ideas—I do not believe fuch a thing
happens

happens in two centuries. Nor do I think it eafy to declare what feafon, wet or dry, beft fuits the production of corn in *England*; the foil is fo various, fuch tracts of fand, fandy loams, gravels, chalks, and other foils, to which a wet year is as fuitable as a dry one to clays. So many tracts of clay and wet loams, to which a dry year is as fuitable as a wet one to fand.—Upon the whole, I am clear that attributing the late prices of wheat *(low* I might fay with more propriety than *high)* to bad feafons, is more rational than to talk of jobbers and poft horfes, but is very far from throwing the matter into its proper light.

I have ventured this remark as an antidote to melancholy accounts of *another bad feafon*—and then we fhall hear of *another*—and another—and another—and the hand of God fuppofed to be chaftifing us for our luxury *, at the very time that he

is

---

* Our political moralifts are ever inveighing againft luxury, I think with very little reafon. And I entirely agree with a writer, who gives his opinion in the following paffage : " A clean fhirt and a laced hat are not inconfiftent with piety and virtue, nor ortolans and burgundy with temperance, nor a feather bed with fortitude, nor a pinch of fnuff with fobriety, nor a handfome woman with chaftity. A man may enjoy them all, and yet act up to the dignity of his nature, and conformably to the precepts of religion

and

is fhowering down all the bléffings of
plenty *.

S E C T. VII.

GENERAL WEALTH.

IN proportion to that wealth in a country
which is the refult not of mines, but of
induftry, will be the profperity of agriculture, arts, manufactures, and commerce :
Arguments indeed have been ufed, to
fhew

---

and morality. Neither, on the other hand, does a
man's confining himfelf to the ufe of fat bacon, *Lace-*
demonian broth, muddy beer, coarfe woollens, a leather doublet, a canvas fhirt, and a thatched hovel
upon a common, render him the more pious, tem-
perate, fober, chafte, religious and virtuous ; for he
may confine himfelf to the ufe of all thefe, and yet
be a moft flovenly finner and beaftly profligate. And
it feems that the refined debauchee is the moft eligible
character of the two." *A Vindication of Commerce and*
the Arts, 1758, p. 51.

* Let it not be imagined that I fuppofe bad crops
cannot happen : In 1698 and 1699, the crops are
fuppofed to have been very bad, and the fame in
1709 and 1710, in which two years wheat at *Wind-*
for was 3 *l.* 18 *s.* a quarter : reckoning the fall of
money, this is not far from being equal to 6 *l.* 10 *s.*
or perhaps more. And if we had what really deferved
to be called a general bad crop, it is not to be
doubted but the price would rife much higher than
any thing we have experienced of late years, the
prices of which, even 1757 itfelf, fpeak not any thing
like a great fcarcity.

shew that the two laft *may* fuffer from great
wealth, though not, I think, conclufive
ones ; but I am clear that agriculture muft
always flourifh in proportion to the general
wealth of a country ; and I attribute the
flourifhing ftate of the hufbandry of this
kingdom greatly to the quantity of our
riches. But as there is a fyftem of reafoning which may be ufed againft this idea, it
will be proper to fhew upon what grounds
the opinion is founded.

Many writers have remarked that agriculture is much encouraged by fimplicity
of manners—that luxury is an enemy to
it ; that it flourifhed more among the old
Romans, with their minute divifion of the
foil, when a whole family had but a few
acres, than in the more brilliant and wealthy
period, the age of *Auguftus*. But the idea
is very falfe : for let us grant the fact, that
when a family has juft land enough for its
fubfiftence, that portion will be well cultivated; what ufeful deductions are to be
drawn from it relative to modern policy ?
Of what ufe in a modern kingdom would
be a whole province thus divided, however well cultivated, except for the mere
purpofe of breeding men, which, fingly
taken, is a moft ufelefs purpofe : A province of fuch farmers would live only to
themfelves—they would confume nothing
but

but the produce of their lands—they would not be able to buy manufactures—and they could pay no taxes without an oppreffion which would reduce them to indigence and mifery : Such a population is of no ufe in a modern ftate. In the early times of the *Roman* republic they were of great ufe, for the more men the greater the tax paid, *viz.* the perfonal fervice in arms. This diftinction is fo ftrong, that the fame divifion of land, which, in one cafe, was a political excellence, is, in the other, a political evil. It is of no confequence to fay, that the little portion of land is perfectly cultivated, if its perfection is of no benefit to the ftate. Hence arifes the neceffity of diftinguifhing between the practice of agriculture as a mere means of fubfiftence—and practifing it as a trade. The former is of no benefit to a modern ftate, the latter of infinite importance.

Now fimplicity of manners, and a freedom from the effects of luxury, are beft exhibited in a country portioned into fuch little properties as are merely fufficient for fubfiftence : Luxury recedes, and fimplicity advances, as you withdraw from mankind. But that caufe, which deftroys a fimplicity that operates in preventing agriculture being exercifed as a trade, is highly beneficial to a modern ftate ; this is public wealth :

wealth: As money flows in, such little portions of land muſt diſappear *, by becoming united in large parcels, wherein agriculture is exerciſed as a trade— wherein products are raiſed in ſurplus—carried to market—ſold—taxes paid—and the circulation of money active. Upon what conſiſtent principles, therefore, can that cauſe be condemned, which works juſt the effects that are eſſentially neceſſary in a modern kingdom?

Now, to quit the period of change from one ſtate of property to another, let us ſee the effects of great national wealth, when the change is effected. Let any perſon conſider the progreſs of every thing in *Britain* during the laſt twenty years. The great improvements we have ſeen in this period, ſuperior to thoſe of any other, are not owing to the conſtitution, to moderate taxation, or to other circumſtances of equal efficacy, ever ſince the Revolution, as the exiſtence of thoſe circumſtances did not before produce equal effects.—The ſuperiority

---

* Suppoſing the country ſo divided before, as was the caſe at *Rome*. The contrary effect happened in the kingdoms portioned out in the feudal ſyſtem; great tracts were reduced; but the principle of the change was the ſame in both; *agriculture for ſubſiſtence*, was in both changed for *agriculture for trade*, and in both the improvement of the national territory was proportioned to this change.

ority has been owing to the quantity of wealth in the nation, which has, in a prodigious degree, facilitated the execution of all great works of improvement.

This idea is, in part, contrary to a common one, that the price of commodities is proportioned to the quantity of money; and confequently that a crown in one age is as effective as a guinea in another; this is very true, but the great difference lies in the fuperior eafe of getting money in the wealthy period. When the quantity of money in circulation is very great, it is furprifing to fee the facility with which all kinds of great works are undertaken and executed: the money when raifed goes not proportionably farther than a fmaller fum in a poorer age; but the greater fum in the wealthier period is gained, acquired, borrowed, raifed a thoufand times eafier than the fmaller fum in the poorer one, and this is the circumftance which gives the fuperiority; and which invigorates to fo great a degree the whole range of induftry.

In this enquiry no diftinction fhould be made between money and paper, as the effects are exactly fimilar; and the great figure made in active induftry, by this country, has been almoft totally owing to the introduction, increafe, and fupport of
paper

paper credit. Let thofe who doubt of this
fact, reflect on the progrefs which agriculture, manufactures, &c. made in a few
years in *Scotland*, from the inftitution of
land-banks, which threw into actual circulation a large part of the value of the
eftates of that kingdom. While the paper
of thofe banks circulated in full credit, no
undertaking was too great — money was
always to be had; and confequently
the improvement of lands was rapid. —
New manufactures, upon the largeft fcale,
were every day eftablifhed, and commerce
in all her ports increafed. But fince the
fhock, which almoft deftroyed that credit, no undertaking of any magnitude has
been thought of.—Many that were in
action have received fuch a blow, that they
expired, and others can fcarcely be faid to
exift.

Let us, in the next place, confider,
what a ftagnation has, in *England*, been
experienced fince the bankruptcy of Mr.
Fordyce. There is no branch of induftry,
whether agriculture, arts, manufactures,
or commerce—no public works depending
on private fubfcriptions—none carried on
by borrowed money, but what have felt
the evils of that fhock to credit. If it
is faid that credit was carried too far,
and the confequences neceffarily mifchiev-

bus,

ous, I admit it; but this proves nothing
againſt my poſition, which is, that the
flouriſhing ſtate of agriculture is principally
owing to general wealth: this leads at
once to the queſtion, whether our public
paper is to be ranked in ſtability with the
credit of Mr. *Fordyce*; an enquiry which I
ſhall leave to itſelf.

Nor do the advantages of which I ſpeak,
depend only on the *eaſe of raiſing money*;
another circumſtance of great importance,
is the increaſe of luxury, which increaſes
conſumption: firſt, from increaſing the
number of the people: ſecondly, from
feeding them better and more plentifully:
and, thirdly, from waſte.—All theſe circumſtances are but other words for an increaſe of the farmer's market. If the number of the people is increaſed ſince the
revolution, of which there can be little
doubt, the food they eat yields that increaſe
of demand. Of the better living of every
claſs, of which no doubt can be entertained,
the ſame effect is evident: This better living conſiſts in the people conſuming more
food, and of a better ſort; eating wheat
inſtead of barley, oats, and rye — and
drinking a prodigiouſly greater quantity of
beer. This is not the caſe only among
the lower claſſes, but in all the middle
ranks, and in the kitchens of every family
of

of fortune in the kingdom. Nor is the article of wafte of lefs importance : if we confider the number of dogs kept in every houfe, and the profufion in which people of fortune live, we fhall be convinced that this article includes no inconfiderable part of our confumption, and is far greater in a refined and luxurious age, than in a plain and frugal one. It is exactly proportioned to luxury — and is to be efteemed as much a market to the farmer, as the regular and frugal confumption at the poor man's board. I have here confined myfelf to wheat—but the remark is yet more ftriking if we name horfes, which raife a vaft demand for other products of the farmer, and are in numbers exactly proportioned to the general wealth of the nation *.

Thofe

---

* It is incredible that the *French* œconomifts fhould fo far miftake the very principles of encouragement to agriculture, as to declaim againft luxury, which they define, l'interverfion de l'ordre naturel, effentiel des dépenfes nationales qui augmente la maffe des dépenfes non productives au préjudice de celles qui fervent à la production et en même tems au préjudice de la production elle même. The expences which flow from luxury not productive ! What can be meant by this ? The increafed confumption and wafte of all the products of the farmer ; is not this a market to him ? The circulation and rife of all prices, which, though an attendant, and not the effect of luxury, is a cir-

cum-

Thofe who urge that the fimplicity of living in frugal times is the moft beneficial to the culture of the earth, fhould reflect on the probable circumftances of a decline in that wealth which they are fuch enemies to.   Let me fuppofe that fuch a declenfion comes — that the people decreafe — that the reft eat lefs in quantity, and poorer in quality, than before—that the greater poverty of the times ftrikes off all wafte : In fuch a fituation the farmer finds a great change in his landlord or rich neighbour— inftead of a profufion in the confumption of bread, beer, mutton, and beef, thofe articles are reduced; the number of fervants is leffened — a pointer and a fpaniel occupy the place of a pack of hounds — a chaife and pair inftead of a coach and fix— ten horfes kept inftead of thirty or forty.— All thefe reductions are fo much taken from the farmer's market; he cannot, from that day, fell fo much cattle, corn, hay, and ftraw as formerly; confequently will not raife

---

cumftance of the higheft confequence to agriculture. And what a contradiction is it to efteem all expences unproductive, that are not actually employed in cultivation.   If the luxurious way of fpending a fortune in this age, was changed for the fimple manners of three hundred years ago, would agriculture be encouraged thereby ?   Such ideas are extremely ill founded, and can never be reduced to practice without the moft mifchievous confequences.

raife fo much. But this is not the only
effect; in fuch a decline he will neceffarily
raife more than demanded, the prices will
then fall, and *all* his product will be
affected by the fall in only a part of his
markets: This is the very progrefs to ruin
—he can no longer pay the fame rent,
labour or taxes — no longer execute the
fame fpirited cultivation :—the next ftep is
his land becoming wafte. This degradation
is not an opinion—it is an evident fact—a
matter of calculation; it is the very train
into which fo many of our writers are defirous we fhould fall—fince it is but another word for a general fall of prices: a
more fatal miftake could never have been
adopted: a GENERAL RISE is the great
fignal of national vigour and health; a
GENERAL FALL the fure criterion of
decay.

If I am told that an increafe of general
wealth is more favourable to the confumption of foreign, and other luxuries, than
of the products of our foil, and that a decreafe of it would alfo be more felt by
them; I reply, that the proportion between
their fufferings is difficult to calculate; but
the obfervation has fome truth in it;
but this does not impeach my affertion;
however the venders of fuperfluities may
fuffer, yet the farmers will certainly fuffer

with

with them ; for in all the articles I recited above, the rich man muſt curtail his ex-pences, and he cannot do that without leſſening the farmer's market.

It ſhould farther be conſidered, that the manufacturers and ſailors with their de-pendants, who are employed by the con-ſumption of luxuries, form another con-ſiderable branch of market to the huſband-man ; and if the decline of national wealth decreaſes that conſumption, this is a freſh wound to that market.

L U X U R Y.

A late writer *, for whoſe abilities I have the higheſt regard, ſeems to condemn what is called luxury, for the waſte it creates—for the number of domeſtic ſervants—for horſes—and for the ſlaughter of calves and lambs, which, he thinks, makes mutton and beef dearer. I am ſorry I cannot fully agree with him ; we both ſpeak of theſe matters, not with a view to viſionary uſe-leſs ideas of the manners of the people, but relative only to the encouragement of agri-culture and increaſe of plenty. In this light, what difference is there between

waſte

---

* *Enquiry into Price of Proviſions, and Size of Farms,* p. 47. In other paſſages, however, he juſtly allows luxury its merit as a market to the farmer.

waste and *regular consumption?* Between bread eat at my lord's table, and barley confumed by his hounds, or oats by his horfes? All thefe *methods* of confumption are nothing to the farmer—the mere pur- chafe of the commodities is what encourages him, in confequence of which he fets heartily about a farther production of them. And how is the confumption of calves and lambs to leffen the quantity of beef and mutton? The farmer brings thefe things to market becaufe they are demanded. if inftead of demanding ten pounds worth of lamb, you go to market for ten pounds worth of beef, he will bring the beef for you. Here is a given demand for beef; it is fupplied: luxury adds another for veal, it is fupplied, certainly without taking from the beef—and if luxury doubles that de- mand, the farmers will anfwer it, and fupply the old one of beef befides. But it is faid, there is a given number of calves every year; if the confumption of veal was ftopped, fo many more would of courfe come to market as beef, and this additional number would furely make beef more plen- tiful, and confequently cheaper. Granted. And fo you would encourage the farmer to continue this plenty of beef by lowering the price of it!—This is that univerfal combination which runs through the fupply
of

of all forts of markets—the cafe of corn has been pretty well underftood ; but ftill the remnants of thefe prejudices hang about us in calves, pigs, lambs, and fo forth. —On the contrary, you ought to act upon the reverfe of thefe principles. Your given fact is the dearnefs of beef, and you want permanently to make it cheaper :—Your only method is to raife the price. Encourage the flaughter of calves, which is fuch an encouragement to the breeder and grazier, as the export of wheat is to the corn-grower ; his prices rife—he becomes more fpirited in his bufinefs—he brings more to market. Confider this train from the beginning—is it poffible it fhould have any other confequence ? A century ago, thefe things were fo ill underftood, that our anceftors gave a bounty on the export of corn, *in order to make it dear :* they never dreamt that they were taking the moft effectual means to make it cheap ; and yet it would doubtlefs have been thought a glaring paradox to affert, that taking great quantities of corn from our markets, was not a way to raife the price. And for what I know, the idea I have juft dropped, that *in order to make beef cheaper, you muft make it dearer*, will even in this age be thought another paradox.

I am

I am here aware of an objection which will be made to this : It may be faid, that the demand for calves lays a tax on the grazier in the progrefs of his bufinefs, by raifing the price of what may be called his raw commodity; not fimilar to the *export* of beef.—I admit this, and am fenfible that the export of beef would be a better method of effecting it; but let it be confidered that the way in which export encourages the product of a commodity, is leffening the quantity in the markets while the demand continues the fame, and confequently raifing the price;—now the objection to killing calves, is, that it raifes the price of beef : this is what I contend for. It is of little confequence what does it—if the price is raifed, the producer of the commodity is encouraged—and in confequence, will bring forth a proportioned plenty *. Who can fuppofe that preventing all the calves of *Effex*, *Surry*, and *Hertfordfhire* from coming to market in the fhape of fat oxen, will

---

* ————que la fource des dépenfes eft la dépenfe elle même ; que plus on dépenfe pour la production, plus on obtient de produits ; que *confommation* enfin, *eft mere de la production*. Cette fource eft un mèandre ; & les anciens peignoient à bon droit la nature, fous l'emblême d'un ferpent qui mord fa queue. Mais ne confondons pas la tête & la queue. *Elèments de la Philofophie Rurale*.

will not be an encouragement to the graziers of *Norfolk* and *Northampton* ?—Thefe
are my reafons for thinking that luxury does
NOT raife the price of provifions, though it
will raife the price of whatever 'can be produced in the markets only in limited quantities, as early ftrawberries, afparagus, green
peafe—the works of the fine arts, &c.—
Thofe who doubt this, may confult the
prices of common food and *luxuries* at *Rome*
in the age of *Auguftus* *.   At the fame
time, I do not here mean, that a great increafe of wealth will not raife *all* prices :   I
fhall never affert that every thing is now as
cheap in *England* as in the fifteenth century.   The argument demands it not.

If the principles here laid down are not
true, how will the gentlemen who have
written fo much on the high, exorbitant,
monftrous, marvellous price of provifions,
account for the low prices of thofe and
other commodities compared with the increafe of money.   Bread, meat, labour,
manufactures, &c. ought in direct proportion to the increafe of wealth to have been
far higher than they are at prefent :   it is
the caufe I have now explained that has
kept them down.   The increafe of wealth
and luxury has had a gradual tendency to
raife

---

* *Arbuthnot's tables of antient weights and meafures.*

raife all thefe prices, which, as I before ftated, has been a gradual encouragement to their production, and confequently created a regular increafe of quantity. The operation of this caufe of plenty in the cafe of provifions, was as I have already fhewn; and I have little doubt but the fame thing has happened with labour.

PRINCIPLES OF POPULATION.

The national wealth increafed the demand for labour, which had always the effect of raifing the price; but this rife encouraged the production of the commodity, that is, of man or labour, call it which you will, and the confequent increafe of the commodity finks the price. Increafing the demand for a manufacture does not raife the price of the labour, it increafes the number of labourers in that manufacture, as a greater quantum or regularity of employment, gives that additional value to the fupply, which creates the new hands. Why have the inhabitants of *Birmingham* increafed from 23,000 in 1750, to 30,000 in 1770? Certainly becaufe a proportional increafe of employment has taken place. Wherever there is a demand for hands, there they will abound: this demand is

but

but another word for eafe of fubfiftence, which operates in the fame manner (the healthinefs of one, and the unhealthinefs of the other allowed for) as the plenty of land in the back country of *America*. Marriages abound there, becaufe children are no burthen—they abound in *Birmingham* for the fame reafon, as every child as foon as it can ufe its hands, can maintain itfelf, and the father and mother need never to want employment, that is, income—land —fupport. Thus where employment increafes, *(Birmingham)* the people increafe: and where employment does not increafe, *(Colchefter)* the people do not increafe. And if upon an average of the whole kingdom employment has for a century increafed, moft certainly the people have increafed with it.

Go to the fhipping of the kingdom, it will be found the fame; our failors have increafed. Why? Becaufe their employment has increafed. As long as the demand for feamen increafes, that demand will be anfwered, let it rife as high as it will.

Nabobs from the *Indies*, planters from *America*, merchants from the exchange, fettle in the counties, they farm, garden, plant, improve—they want men, their demand is anfwered, and was it regular,

would

would around every great houfe found and fupport a town.

Go to the villages, the fame truth will every where be apparent: if hufbandry improves, it will demand more labour—that demand is the encouragement of the production of the commodity demanded—and it will be fupplied. Who fuppofes that a county of warrens, heaths, and farming flovens, converted to well tilled fields, does not occafion an increafed demand for hands? —And was it ever known that fuch a demand exifted without being fupplied?

But the hands, it is faid, leave certain villages and go to towns. Why? Becaufe there is not employment in one cafe, and there is in another—their going to the town, proves that they go to employment —they go to that very circumftance which is to increafe their number. They go, becaufe they are demanded; that demand it is true takes, but then it feeds them.

Let any perfon go to *Glafgow* and its neighbourhood, to *Birmingham*, to *Sheffield*, or to *Manchefter*, according to fome writers, every caufe of depopulation has acted powerfully againft fuch places: how then have they increafed their people? Why, by emigrations from the country. It would be very difficult for any perfon to

fhew

fhew me a depopulation in the country
comparable to the increafe of towns, not
to fpeak of counter tracts in the country
that have doubled and trebled their people :
But why have not thefe emigrations been
to other towns, to *York*, to *Winchefter*, to
Canterbury, &c. ?   Becaufe employment
does not abound in thofe places—and
therefore they do not increafe.   Does not
this prove that in every light you view it,
it is employment which creates population ?
A pofition impoffible to be difproved ; and
which, if allowed, throws the enquiry
concerning the depopulation of the kingdom into an examination of the decline or
increafe of employment.

But fo much land may be thrown into
grafs, and confequently fo much employment
cut off, that depopulation may enfue.   Impoffible ; this caufe can never operate beyond thofe lands, more proper by nature
for grafs than tillage, for if it did, it would
at once counteract itfelf ; corn would then
rife to a price beyond the proportion of
meat, and of courfe it would be more profitable to *plough*, than to *lay down*.   This
is a circumftance that ought to fhew the
enemies of inclofures that they are fighting
againft a chimera—they complain of meat
being dearer than corn, in the fame breath
that they fay the country is depopulated by
converting

converting arable to grafs—What a contradiction is this; meat being what they call
fo dear, is a clear proof that a greater proportion of land is not laid to grafs than is
broken up for corn, otherwife corn inftead
of being cheaper than meat would be
dearer.

I fhall carry this idea yet farther. I have
confidered an increafed demand, which
raifes the value of a commodity, to be the
means of increafing the quantity of that
commodity, by encouraging the production
of it; and I have applied it to beef, to
mutton, to wheat, and to labour. I remarked that leffening the quantity in the
market while the demand continued the
fame, operated as an encouragement, and
prefently fupplied more than the ufual
quantum : it is the fame with population.
You fight off your men by wars—you deftroy them by great cities—you leffen them
by emigrations — moft infallible method
of increafing their number— PROVIDED
THE DEMAND DOES NOT DECLINE.
This is exactly the fame thing, as rendering beef fcarcer by the flaughter of calves,
and wheat by exportation—take a quantity
from the market, certainly you add to the
value of what remains, and how can you
encourage the reproduction of it more
powerfully than by adding to its value?

What

What are the terms of complaint for depopulation in this kingdom ?—People fcarce —labour dear ;—would you give a premium for population, could you exprefs it in better terms ? The commodity wanted is fcarce, and the price raifed ; what is this but faying, that the value of MAN is raifed. *Away! my boys—get children, they are worth more than ever they were.* What is the characteriftic of a populous country ? *Many people, but labour dear.* What is the mark of a country thinly peopled ? *Few people, and labour cheap.* Labour is dearer in *Holland* than in any part of *Europe,* and therefore it is the moft populous country in *Europe.*

Dr. *Price* fays, that for the laft 80 years, there has not been one great caufe of depopulation which has not operated among us *. What is the great encouragement of population ? *Eafe of acquiring income:* It is of no confequence whether that income arifes from land, manufacture, or commerce ; it is as powerful in the pay of a

manu-

---

* " The humour of blaming the prefent, and admiring the paft, is ftrongly rooted in human nature, and has an influence even on perfons endued with the profoundeft judgment and moft extenfive learning." *Hume's Effays,* 8vo. 1764, vol. i. p. 490.

manufacturer †, as in the wilds of *America.* What is the great obstacle to population? *Difficulty of acquiring income.* Here then we have a criterion, by which to judge of the population or depopulation of any period. If you view the country and see agriculture under such circumstances that the farmer's products will not pay his usual improvements, and consequently, dismissing the hands he formerly kept. If the manufactures of the kingdom want a market, and the active industry, exerted in them, becomes languid, and decays. If

com-

---

† I do not here mean that our manufacturing towns increase as fast as the settlements in *America*— I mean only that the *principle* in one case is as powerful as in the other: the difference in point of health is one obstacle—but nothing to another, which is manufacturing employment in these towns not keeping full pace with the increase of people. In the back settlements plenty of land *(income — employment)* keeps pace with the most rapid increase; whereas, if the manufacturers of *Birmingham* had a demand for all the wares they could make, I suppose it would not be long before they could supply half a dozen worlds—their hands would increase almost as fast as in *America*; their trade would double every twenty years, and their people with it. By the way, I do not think I should be far from the truth, if I asserted, that some of our manufacturing places, particularly *Burslem*, for a certain period increased as fast as any of our colonies, which is nothing more than saying, that employment has kept pace with population.

commerce no longer fupports the feamen
fhe was wont to do.   If private and public
works, inftead of entering into competition
for hands with the manufacturer and the
farmer, ftand ftill amidft numbers who cry
in vain for work *.—If thefe effects are
feen, a WANT OF EMPLOYMENT will
ftare you in the face, and that want is
the only caufe of depopulation that can
exift.   Have thefe fpectacles been common
in the eyes of our people fince the revolution ? Are they common at prefent ? Does
not the great active caufe, EMPLOYMENT,
operate more powerfully than ever ? Away
then with thefe vifionary ideas, the difgrace
of an enlightened age—the reproach of
this great and flourifhing nation †.

Sir

---

* ——" when labourers are plenty, their wages
will be low, by low wages a family is fupported with
difficulty; this difficulty deters many from marriage."
—*Obfervations concerning the increafe of mankind*, faid
to be by Dr. *Franklin*; where more good fenfe upon
thefe fubjects will be found (mixed with a few
thoughts not equally ftriking) than in half a fcore of
complaining volumes.

† *Davenant* gives the figns of a declining nation,
which well deferve confideration.   " Where a nation
is impoverifhed by a bad government, by an ill managed trade, or by any other circumftance, the intereft of money will be dear, and the purchafe of lands
cheap : THE PRICE OF LABOUR AND PROVISIONS
WILL BE LOW ; rents will every where fall ; lands

Sir *James Stewart* has an obfervation fimilar to the idea which I am now explaining, that if *Africk*'s fons were all returned her, who can fuppofe fhe would be the more populous? But he founds this idea on the quantity of food in the country: but I mean to throw the point of food out of the queftion, taking it always for granted, if a man gains employment which gives him the value of food, that he will never go without it. Increafe your people as much as you pleafe, food will increafe with them. Notwithftanding the increafe of people which muft have taken place in this kingdom fince the revolution, added to the wafte of luxury, and alfo exportation, yet the price of corn has fallen.—Population merely for want of food, will not ftop till every acre of the territory is improved to the utmoft.

We are told that fince the revolution, this country has loft a million and a half of people: this therefore implies that the caufes of population were more powerful in the laft than

---

will be untilled, and farm houfes will go to ruin; the yearly marriages and births will leffen, and the burials increafe. The ftock of live cattle muft apparently diminifh; and laftly, the inhabitants will by degrees, and in fome meafure, withdraw themfelves from fuch a declining country." *Davenant's Works,* vol. i. p. 358.

than in the prefent century; thefe caufes, we
are told, are fmall farms, open field lands,
and fimplicity of living; which is not very
far from afferting, that the lefs employment
there is in a country, the more populous
it will be. Small farms with their univerfal
attendant, *poor farmers*, can never form fuch
a fyftem of employ as richer farmers, for
this plain reafon,—they cannot work equal
improvements—nor ever were known to
do it—and improvements in hufbandry are
but another word for increafe of labour.
Befides, we fhould reflect, that agriculture
in general, by whatever farmers carried
on, had not received that improvement in
the practice, and operofe methods of culture which have fince been introduced; and
of which a long catalogue could be given.

A county divided into little farms, with
many little eftates fupporting little landlords, has certainly the appearance of population: thefe writers fay, that if the
fmall farms are thrown into large ones,
many of the people will difappear: let us
(which we need not do) grant this fact. It
is faying, that when the country was more
populous, its inhabitants eat much more
food than at prefent, confequently could
not fpare fo much for towns. The people
employed in the country in raifing the
fruits of the earth, may be employed with
                                                    fo

fo little oeconomy as to eat up the whole produce; in which cafe, there can be no towns. Thus the population of the country depends partly on the manners of the age; if it is not the cuftom to live in towns, there will be little demand for the products of farmers, confequently they and their dependants will confume them: but if, as in this age, people gather very much into towns, they demand the products in competition with the ufelefs hands before fupported by the land, who, not being able to ftand that competition, gradually take refuge in towns, as manufacturing employment arifes. This is a change, advantageous in every refpect that can be named. You had before a population ufelefs, becaufe not induftrious; who, inftead of adding to the national wealth, only eat up the earth's produce; this population is changed for induftrious manufacturers, artizans, and feamen, who eat the fame produce, but pay you amply for it. With one population, let it be ever fo great, you muft be a poor and a weak nation: with the other, you are a wealthy and powerful one.—In this argument, I fuppofe hufbandry in the improved period, to raife no more products than in the other period, accounting only for the change of thofe who eat its products. But the contrary is

well

well known to be the cafe, confequently as
there is much more food raifed, we may
fuppofe more people who eat it. I have alfo
taken for granted, that in the latter period,
fewer hands are employed on the foil,
which would be the cafe if the agriculture
was the fame in both, but improvements
far more than ballance the number of farmers, and render the population of the
modern period far greater in the country,
than that of the remoter one.

Refpecting open field lands, the quantity of labour in them is not comparable to
that of inclofures ; for, not to fpeak of the
great numbers of men that in inclofed countries are conftantly employed in winter in
hedging and ditching, what comparifon
can there be between the open field fyftem
of one half or a third of the lands being in
fallow, receiving only three ploughings ;
and the fame portion now tilled four, five,
or fix times by Midfummer, then fown
with turnips, thofe hand-hoed twice, and
then drawn by hand, and carted to ftalls
for beafts ; or elfe hurdled out in portions
for fatting fheep ! What a fcarcity of employment in one cafe, what a variety in
the other ! And confider the vaft tracts of
land in the kingdom (no lefs than the
whole upon which turnips are cultivated)
that have undergone this change fince the

laſt century. I ſhould alſo remind the
reader of other ſyſtems of management;
beans and peaſe hand-hoed for a fallow—the
culture of potatoes—of carrots, of coleſeed,
&c.—the hoeing of white corn—with the
minuter improvements in every part of the
culture of all crops—every article of which
is an increaſe of labour. Then he ſhould
remember the vaſt tracts of country uncultivated in the laſt century, which have
been incloſed and converted into new farms,
a much greater tract in 80 years than theſe
writers dream of: all this is the effect of
incloſures, and conſequently they alſo have
yielded a great increaſe of employment.

Laſtly, with reſpect to ſimplicity of living—in what does this conſiſt? Why, it
conſiſts in all the claſſes of the people
being ſatisfied with a leſs conſumption of
all ſorts of commodities than at preſent.
Living in ſmaller houſes; with leſs and
worſe furniture; fewer carriages; leſs
change in theſe articles; wearing fewer
cloaths, hats, ſhoes, ſtockings, &c.; uſing,
in a word, fewer manufactures of every
ſort and kind, and never thinking of a
variety, now common in every family.
Contented with a worſe and more difficult
carriage; no great roads; no navigations;
and very few public works; much leſs
ſhip building, and fewer of the variety of
fabrics

fabrics which the fitting out a ſhip con-
ſumes.—In a word, a ſmaller general conſumption of all ſorts; what is this but
LESS EMPLOYMENT *, and of courſe,
fewer people? But is it neceſſary to reaſon
how theſe cauſes muſt have operated? Does
not the knowledge of all old people, and
all regiſters, prove the general increaſe of
towns? Nay, theſe writers themſelves admit it, and ſpeak of it as the cauſe of depopulation † !

But it is ſaid, that the prices of neceſ-
ſaries have riſen ſo much ſince the laſt century, that the eaſe of living has declined,
and conſequently depopulation come upon
us.

---

* It is a great income that cauſes a great expence,
and it is a great expence that augments population.
Encyclopedie, vol. ii. Art. *Grain.*

† Manuſacturers, Artizans, Fiſhermen, Seamen, Soldiers, Miners of all ſorts, Colliers, Carriers of all ſorts, and navigators of rivers, Domeſtic ſervants, Merchants, and their train, Inkeepers, and their train, Inhabitants of towns in general, The claſſes ſupported by the public taxes.

Let theſe ſeveral ſets of men be conſidered, and
the moſt inattentive obſerver will at once ſee that all
are amazingly increaſed ſince the laſt century: who
can imagine that ſuch an increaſe is not ſufficient to
anſwer the decline (ſuppoſing there is one, which I
do not believe) in the number of farmers.

us. Firſt I ſay, the fact is certainly falſe
taken in general, though, for what I know,
it may be true taken in one particular: in
manufactures, I am told that the price of
labour has riſen very little *; here therefore this obſervation is partly true; but the
pleaſant thing is, that manufactures are out
of the queſtion, becauſe there cannot be a
man ſo ſenſeleſs as to ſuppoſe as many
perſons maintained by them in the laſt age
as at preſent. Dr. *Price* expreſsly admits
this, and throws the depopulation on country pariſhes. In them the firſt fact is by
no means true, for I have it on good authority in moſt parts of the kingdom, that
huſbandry labour has riſen greatly. I have
ſhewn the riſe of it in very many places,
to be much beyond that of proviſions; the
riſe of which has been very little, conſider-
ing the importance of bread in general conſumption, as far as we can judge from regiſters that are authentic. Very many of
the labouring poor are become chargeable
to

---

* At the fame time that the nominal pay of manufacturers who work by the day, is not riſen equally
with that of huſbandry labour, yet we ſhould remember that it ought not to have riſen equally, as we have
it on various authority, that manufacturers had in
the laſt century double the pay of labourers in huſ-
þandry.

to their parifhes ; but this has nothing to
do with depopulation ; on the contrary, the
conftantly feeing fuch vaft fums diftributed
in this way, muft be an inducement to
marriage among all the idle poor—and
certainly has proved fo. The reafon the
rates have increafed fo much, is the increafe
of national wealth and the fuperior eafe of
the poor. This has enabled them to confume the greater quantity of fuperfluities,
and that confumption (as it always does in
all claffes) has grown upon them. Let our
poor give up tea, fugar, fpices, brandy,
rum, gin, and ale in immoderate quantities, and they will not feel the high price
of provifions, even in manufactures. As
to hufbandry, they indulge in all thofe expences, and yet live well *—exceptions
there will be, and doubtlefs, always were,
for the nature of man is the fame in all ages.
Admitting

* Our farms and the cottages of our labourers will
ftand the teft, which *Rouffeau* would bring a kingdom
to.——C'eft en lui que confifte la véritable profpérité
d'un pays, la force, & la grandeur qu'un peuple tire
de lui-même, qui ne depend en rien des autres nations, qui ne contraint jamais d'attaquer pour fe fou-
tenir, & donne les plus fûrs moyens de fe deffendre.
Quand il eft queftion d'eftimer la puiffance publique,
le bel-efprit vifite les palais du prince, fes ports, fes
troupes, fes arfenaux, fes villes ; le vrai politique
parcourt les terres, & va dans la chaumiere du laboureur. Le premier voit ce qu'on a fait, & le fecond ce
qu'on peut faire. *Julie*, tome v. p. 33.

Admitting that the eafe of living in manufactures was greater—yet the numbers
in manufactures are vaftly increafed. In
villages, the eafe of living is not a whit
leffened, confequently there is no reafon
from thence to fuppofe a decline. Let us
reflect on the different circumftances of the
two periods in another light. In the laft
century, the farms it is faid were fmaller,
and confequently more farmers and their
families. But let me afk what a little
farmer or a labourer did with his family?
That furplus of the population of villages,
which in the prefent age finds at all times
a refuge in manufactures, commerce, arts,
or fome branch of induftry, (all which are
infinitely increafed) could not do the fame
then; for they had not fuch abundance of
employment to refort to; and if the villages
were better peopled, this muft have happened at a time when fuch a refort was much
more wanted. What muft have been the
confequence of this? Why the little farmers houfes and the cottages muft have
been crouded with people *without employment*, and confequently *without the means
of living:* this might go to a certain point,
as far as relations would fubmit to be burthened, but it would go no farther, and
muft operate as a great difcouragement to
marriage. A great family where there is
plenty

plenty of employment for all ages, is not a burthen long; but where there is no employment, of what ufe to fay that provifions were 15 or 20 *per cent.* cheaper; it muft have been a monftrous burthen. Now we have reafon to think that this was not the cafe, becaufe if it had, the poor's rates would probably have fhewn it; the inference therefore which I draw, is, that no fuch population exifted, that the villages had not more people than to be on a par with manufactures, arts, and commerce, and not near fo populous as at prefent. Let any unprejudiced reader who has the leaft conception of the oeconomy and management of a fmall farm, reflect for a minute on an occupier of from 20 to 50 acres, with a family of 8 or 10 children, moft of them unable to maintain themfelves from the fmall progrefs of arts and induftry. Lownefs of rents, and a cheapnefs of labour, the confequence of hands without work, would enable him to fupport more perhaps than at prefent: but how can any one from fuch a fyftem, deduce the caufes of population? Here arifes a frefh reafon to fuppofe the country could not be fo populous as at prefent, which was labour being dear; if there were fo many more little farmers and labourers, whofe

children

children manufactures could not take off, how should labour be dear?

Here Dr. *Price* says, " as the number of occupiers of land was greater, and all had more opportunities of working for *themselves*, it is reasonable to conclude, that the number of people willing to work *for others*, must have been smaller, and the price of day labour higher—this is now the case in our *American* colonies."—My conclusion is directly the contrary.—Is it to be supposed that *England* in the last century, was in the same situation as the colonies, every one to inclose and take land that pleased? You say the number of occupiers was greater : you admit they had families —here comes the difficulty—*what did they with those families?* Not take fresh farms, for all were full : not take refuge in towns, there was not employment for them ; not carry their cultivation by the spade and hoe to the highest perfection, their husbandry was miserable, not a tenth so operose as at present—what therefore could the surplus of this great system of population do to support itself? Nothing but regorge in the cottages—render labour too cheap— become a most miserable burthen on parents —and an effectual check on marriage— What comparison can be drawn between this situation and *America,* where every
child,

child, as foon as arrived at man's eftate, marries, and has a *new* farm immediately.

Mr. *Walace* fays, " Suppofe the great body of manufacturers in fome trading nations that have a large territory, to lay afide their manufactures, and employ themfelves in agriculture, pafturage, and fifhing; they would provide a vaft quantity of food, they would make all the neceffaries of life cheap, and eafy to be purchafed; and it would foon become vifible how great a difference there is between agriculture and manufactures in rendering a nation populous*."

I cannot agree entirely to this reafoning; Mr. *Walace* would give thefe manufacturers fmall portions of land, fufficient to yield the neceffaries of life, and no more. In the fuppofition of fuch a fmall divifion of the foil, the clafs of farmers eats up all the earth's produce. Now I fee no difference in point of numbers, between the manufacturers being fed by the farmers, or feeding themfelves: in both cafes they are fed —and they can be no more. But fuppofe them turned farmers, every man with his little farm—this fuppofes no more increafe than before. What are their families to do? Are they alfo to marry and turn farmers?

---

* *Differtation on the Numbers of Mankind,* p. 27.

mers ? If you anfwer in the affirmative,
then your obfervation may all be blotted
out, and inftead thereof, you may fimply
fay, that plenty of land to be had for nothing as in *America*, greatly increafes the
people. Who can doubt it ? But this is
not the pofition. You are fuppofing the
manufacturers in a peopled country, which
is already property, converted into farmers
—I accept your fuppofition, and I fay that
then every family, inftead of being fed by
labour in the manufactory, will be fed by
the portion of land affigned them, but there
will be no more increafe in one cafe than
in the other, becaufe the people bred in
thefe farms, and alfo in the old ones, (as
manufactures are fuppofed to be at an end)
will have no employment or means of fupport, confequently can neither marry nor
multiply beyond the fixed number of farms.
Nothing can be clearer than this. But
there is another confideration ; while the
manufacturers formed a diftinct body, the
old farmers had a market, in which their
products yielded a value in money, the fale
of thefe muft neceffarily enliven their bufinefs, and enable them to improve their
culture ; and the higher the prices, the
more they would be encouraged to work
improvements and increafe the quantum of
food, all which caufes would be at once cut

off

off in the above idea, and of courſe their effects would vaniſh. Thus the tendency of the propoſition, inſtead of being favourable to increaſe, would be prejudicial to it.

Nor can it ever be too much inculcated, that the taking people from towns and ſpreading them over the country, is attended no farther with *increaſe*, than in proportion as you have a demand for that increaſe. A man and woman in *London* do not marry. *Why not?* Becauſe a family, if they had one, would, for want of employment, be a burthen. This is ſuppoſing what is the caſe, that there are people enough in the kingdom to anſwer all demands for hands. Take the couple into the country, the caſe will be juſt the ſame; a family there, ſticking to the cottage, will be juſt as great a burthen. Such effects are not commonly ſeen in the country now, becauſe manufactures, arts, &c. take off the ſurplus of its population; but if theſe were converted into freſh cottages we ſhould ſee it every day.

As little reaſon is there for drawing the cauſes of depopulation from every refinement that is made upon the ſimple ſtages of civilization, which Dr. *Price* ſays, " favour moſt the increaſe and the happineſs of mankind: For in theſe ſtates, agriculture ſupplies plenty of the means of ſubſiſtence; the bleſſings of a natural and a ſimple life are

are enjoyed; property is equally divided;
the wants of men are few, and foon fatisfied, and families are eafily provided for:
on the contrary, in the refined ftates of
civilization, property is engroffed.—Our
American colonies are at prefent in the firft
and the happieft of the ftates I have defcribed."——Relative to the advantages of
the prefent *American* fyftem, I agree entirely with the author; but I think no ufeful conclufion can be drawn from the fact:
what country can poffibly be produced in
any period to which hiftory goes back, that
is a parallel to a new planted colony, with
the immenfity of land without any property in it but that of the crown—and
ready to be granted to whoever will take
it? The young fociety under the protection
of a formidable power, and enjoying the
freedom of the nobleft conftitution in the
univerfe? At what period of our hiftory
was this ifland in fuch a fituation? Go
back to the ages in which luxury and refinement were out of the queftion, was not
property engroffed? Did a great quarrel-
fome, fiery, tartar of a baron, give up his
eftate of 900 or 1000 manors to be fettled
by peafants in property? And had he done
it, would propagation in thofe barbarous
ages have gone on as at prefent in *America?* The fyftem of which country is fo

peculiar,

peculiar, that a parallel was never to be produced. In any age from *Alfred* to king *William*, landed property in *England* has been decided — no land for thofe who to take poffeffion of it — much greater inequality of eftates than at prefent — hence therefore depopulation cannot have come upon us from any caufes the reverfe of thofe which operate at prefent in *America*, but which did not operate in the laft century in *England*.

ENGLAND MORE POPULOUS THAN EVER.

It is for thefe reafons that I fuppofe the country at that time could not poffibly be fo populous as at prefent, becaufe the population of the villages muft depend on other caufes for taking off its furplus—it can never advance beyond that point—the moment it produces a greater furplus than can be taken off, it counteracts itfelf, and will infallibly leffen. This production of the village commodity (people) depends on the demand for that commodity occafioned by manufactures, arts, commerce, wars, &c. This is a univerfal truth in the production of all commodities. And as that demand in the laft century was not comparable to what it is in the prefent, there thence refults

the

the cleareft impoffibility of population in the country being equal to what it is at prefent.

To illuftrate the contrary idea, chalk out a line of country; fuppofe it divided into farms of 20 acres, fix an occupier in each, and force this country to fupport its own population, that is, cut off the demand of arts and manufactures; there will be a family to every 20 acres. How are the parents to maintain the children? The whole produce of the earth is eaten up, and is infufficient, the children will be the moft dreadful burthen imagination can paint— population will deftroy itfelf—the farmers if not ftarved, will be bankrupts, and nothing can prevent defolation but their either living all unmarried, or elfe the farms running into one another, and fome means taken to reduce the people *. But fuppofe manufactures, luxury, great cities, and recruiting ferjeants to operate, then the farmers may go on getting children as faft as they pleafe, for the very circumftance of the furplus becoming bur-thenfome will drive it away: And without fuppofing

---

* ———le plus grand produit total n'eft pas l'in-térèt de l'etat fi ce plus grand produit eft confommé par de plus grands frais de culture. *Eléménts de la philofophie rurale.*

suppofing in one cafe that nothing will leffen the furplus, or in the other, that the
whole fhall be demanded ; yet will the effect
of the demand be proportioned to it.

Can any thing be more fimple than this
principle? Can any thing prove clearer
that the idea of a village population beyond the demand for its furplus is chimerical? Is it not evident that demand for
hands, that is employment, muft regulate
the numbers of the people? And that if
employment in this age is greater than in
the former, the total of the people muft
be greater? Ideas of purity and fimplicity
of living in little farms, with the farmers
engaged as much in propagation as in culture—the women bringing forth with all
poffible expedition—and every movement
in the whole rural machine nothing but
increment and multiplication—all thefe notions are fine fpeculative fancies, equally
removed from reafon and experience. It
certainly is the cafe upon the *Ohio*, but for
the fame reafon that it is not fo upon the
Thames.

As I have through thefe papers laid it
down as a principle that population is proportioned to employment, it neceffarily
follows, that the population of agriculture
depends on the employment of agriculture,
and the population of manufactures on the
employ-

employment of manufacturers—and from hence I give no credit to the reafoning ufed to convince us that we are lefs populous than at the revolution, or any remoter period. This principle guides us alfo in giving credit to or rejecting opinions of any other period. I have been informed, that feveral of our manufactures have declined fince the peace of 1762*, which may indeed eafily be conceived from the amazing and unnatural height to which the commerce of this country was carried by the war—being literally erected on the ruins of that of half our neighbours,—fuch a decline in certain fabrics muft be attended with a proportionable depopulation, if others have not made a correfponding advance.—And fuch a depopulation in manufactures, muft affect our general numbers, unlefs the population of agriculture has proportionably increafed, which is a matter of opinion; it appears to me that it increafes every day.

But why will you reafon againft facts? Are not the public lifts of houfes and windows lower than they were in the laft century? This is the only apparent *fact* for fuppofing the people lefs numerous.

Thofe gentlemen who have taken the trouble to calculate the number of the people, have differed very much in their opinions.

---

* See Appendix.

opinions. Sir *W. Petty* made the number in *England* and *Wales* in 1682, amount to 7,400,000 *.—*Davenant* in 1692, made them 7,000,000 †—but in the fame tract, he makes them 8,000,000—and in 1700, he quotes and approves from Mr. *King* a computation of 5,500,000 ‡. — Sir *M. Decker* fuppofed them in 1742, (from 1,200,000 houfes, at 6 to a houfe) 7,200,000 ‖—Dr. *Mitchel* fays the number is 5,700,000 §—Mr. *Walace*, 8,000,000 ¶ —*Templeman* makes it the fame **—Another fuppofes it 6,000,000 ††—Another, 5,480,000 ‡‡ —Mr. *Smyth*, 6,000,000 §§ —Dr. *Brakenridge*, 5,340,000 ‖‖—Another, 8,000,000 *†—Dr. *Price*, 4,500,000 ††.

From

---

* *Political Arithmetic*, p. 15.

† *An Effay upon ways and means*, p. 136.

‡ *An Effay upon the probable method of making a people gainers in the ballance of trade*, p. 18.

‖ *Serious Confiderations on feveral high duties*, 8vo. 1744, p. 15.

§ *Prefent State of Great Britain and North America*, p. 113.

¶ *Differtation on the Numbers of mankind*, p. 41.

** *Survey of the Globe*. Plate 5.

†† *Poftlethwayte's Dictionary of Commerce*. Art. *People*.

‡‡ *Confiderations on the Trade and Finances*, &c. 79.

§§ *Three Tracts on Corn Trade*, p. 181.

‖‖ *Phil. Tranf.* Vol. 49, p. 877.

*† *Houghton's Hufbandry*, vol. ii. p. 465.

†† *Obfervations on reverfionary payments*, p. 184.

From the accounts we have had of former enumerations, there are reafons to think they were taken with much inaccuracy; but what is decifive in the comparifon, the laft public lifts of 1759 and 1766, are known by experiment to be falfe. Catalogues were taken in a variety of parifhes about *Wentworth Houfe* in *Yorkfhire*, by order of the marquis of *Rockingham*; and fimilar trials were made elfewhere, in all which, the number EXCEEDED the reports of the furveyors; who, in moft parts of *England*, paid little attention to houfes exempted from the tax: of which the deficiencies I have mentioned, are the moft fatisfactory proofs. When the treafury wants to know the number of cottages exempted from all payment, the receivers general of the land-tax may have orders to direct fuch a report. But how are they obeyed? Like all fuch orders in this country, where no penalty to an informer is fixed. The collectors are chofen from among low and illiterate men; fome may think fuch an order a preparatory ftep to a new tax; others are carelefs and forget it; others fet down what cottages they recollect, and do not take the trouble to ride through their parifh; an hundred fuch reafons may operate in lowering the truth at a time that not a fingle one can occafion an exaggeration.

tion. However, the circumstance that causes it is not of consequence—the fact we know is so.

In the next place, if you got the number of houses, you have not that of the people.; here the authority is as rotten as elsewhere: in some places you have gained the number of people *per family*—but what has that to do with the number *per house?* Are not many houses the habitation of several families? But farther, from the most extraordinary prejudice in the world, you collect the numbers *per* house in many places, constantly rejecting hospitals, prisons, colleges, schools, and poor houses *—you then say—there are so many houses in the kingdom—such is the result *per* house of my enquiries—consequently you have but so many people, MAKING NO ALLOWANCE FOR THE BUILDINGS YOU HAVE OMITTED. Is this a fair way of calculating?

Further, how do we know that a house at present contains on an average of the kingdom no more souls than 80 years ago? I have

---

* *London* is also forgotten, in which *Grant* asserted, that among tradesmen there are 8 to a *family*; in higher ranks 10; and in the poorest, near 5: how much more *per house* he does not tell. At present the number *per* house is probably 9 or 10, perhaps more.

have little doubt but the population *per* houfe is greater †.

Upon the whole, we may determine that the facts upon which the arguments for our depopulation are founded, are abfolutely falfe : that the conjectures annexed to them are wild and uncertain, and that the conclufions which are drawn from the whole, can abound in nothing but errors and miftakes.

SIGNS OF DEPOPULATION.

As ideas of depopulation have in all ages been fo common, and complaints of mifchiefs in the government and policy of ftate ever annexed to them, and generally without any reafon ; it may not be amifs to beftow a few reflections on thofe figns of depopulation, which, whenever they appear, may be fuppofed to fpeak truth. I have faid, that populoufnefs in *England* depends on employment, which here operates on the fame principles as plenty of land in *America*; this offers a very fimple idea of depopulation—*employment leffening.* Not leffening in the parifh A, while increafing in the town B ; or leffening in B, while

---

† See the appendix, for other obfervations on this fubject.

while increasing in A, but a general visible declension; such as would take place if the national wealth was to decline, which generally being the effect of *employment*, must mark the state of its cause. If the seamen lessen and your shipping falls away, it is a circumstance which to this nation would be of the highest consequence, and mark a variety of declension—if at the same time the great manufactures of the kingdom could no longer find a vent, and consequently their people without employment, it would be a mark not less equivocal—if the cultivated soil lessens—if tracts once valuable, become waste, and rents fall, it is an unerring sign of decay—if the prices of labour and commodities in general sink, it is no less to be depended on. These signs of national decay need not be multiplied, whenever they are seen they must mark in proportion to their extent, the declension of our prosperity.

Decrease of shipping—decline of manufactures—decline of agriculture—a general fall of prices.

It appears to me that these are circumstances which involve every other cause of national declension; they mark a loss of wealth—A DECREASE OF EMPLOYMENT, which must universally bring down population with it.

When-

Whenever therefore we hear of other caufes of depopulation, fuch as engroffing farms, inclofures, laying arable to grafs, high prices of provifions, great cities, luxury, celibacy, debauchery, wars, emigrations, &c. we may very fafely refolve them into a ftring of vulgar errors, and reft affured that they can have no ill effect, while the five great caufes mentioned above, do not fubfift.

LAW OF SETTLEMENTS.

Having ventured thus far on the activity of the caufes of the population of *England*, which I think far fuperior in power to any tendency there can be found to the contrary, I fhall very freely acknowledge there is one caufe of depopulation among us, however it is in general overcome by favourable circumftances; this is the *law of fettlements*, the moft falfe, mifchievous, and pernicious fyftem that ever barbarifm devifed. By forcing every parifh to maintain not the refident, but the fettled poor; and by difenabling the poor from fettling where they pleafe, you give a ftrong and effective motive to very many people to do every thing in their power againft population, by raifing an open war againft cottages. The landlord and
the

the farmer have almoft equal motives to reduce the number of poor in their parifhes : marriages are very frequently obftructed ; the couple muft, if they marry, ftay at home ; the overfeers of the poor will grant no certificates ; if they marry therefore, where are they to live ? No cottage is empty—they muft live with their fathers and mothers, or lodge ; the poor abhor both as much as their betters, and certainly in many cafes, run into licentious amours, merely for want of a cottage or a certificate. The whole fyftem of our poor laws is fo mifchievous, that it muft be attended with this effect. Suppofe an unmarried labourer applies to the lord of a manor for leave to build a cottage on the wafte—*No*, fays the gentleman, *the cottage when built, will be a neft of beggars, and we fhall have them all on the parifh*. Can you wonder at fuch language from a man who probably can let land worth 20 *s.* an acre, for no more than 14*s.* on account of high poor rates ? It would be amazing if he acted otherwife.

Dr. *Price* quotes with applaufe, an obfervation of Lord *Bacon*, in praife of the act of *Henry* VII. which prohibited all new cottages with lefs than 4 acres ; but what tendency had this but the evil I have now defcribed ? If a poor man buys half a rood of land to build on, he cannot do it ; he

muft

muft buy four acres!—This is the very
circumftance that now gives the power of
reftraining the erection of cottages.

Our policy is weak beyond all doubt,
becaufe it confifts of prohibiting the natural
courfe of things : all reftrictive forcible
meafures in domeftic policy are bad ; population fhould not be exprefsly encouraged,
but it is ridiculous to throw wanton reftrictions on it : It ought certainly to be left to
its own courfe; people will not multiply
beyond the demand for the furplus of their
increafe, but thus far they ought to be
allowed ; and to prohibit cottages, which
when built, would be filled with induftrious
inhabitants, is a violent and a mifchievous
fyftem. It is true, the caufes of population
in this kingdom are fo powerful, that they
overcome thefe obftacles ; but this is no
reafon againft remedying them. The firft
effectual cure is to annul the law of fettlements, and allow every man to fettle where
he pleafes : the fecond, to repeal the act
which allows no cottage with lefs than 4
acres. This would do a great deal ; but a
great caufe of the evil would ftill remain,
for as long as the poor are fupported by
the parifh, it will be the intereft of every
landlord and farmer to oppofe their increafe ; but this would be much remedied
by breaking the laws of fettlement, fince
any

any couples who wanted to marry and fettle, if refufed at home, or if no habitation could be found for them, might then go fettle where a cottage and employment were eafieft had.

POPULATION IN NORFOLK.

Since the preceding obfervations were written, the fecond edition of Dr. *Price's Appeal to the Public on the National Debt* came to hand : Annexed to it is a very fenfible and well written memoir on the decline of population in the county of *Norfolk*; in which many appearances and reafons are fet forth, to prove that the people of that county are much decreafed. If this is really the cafe, the principles which I have advanced, if not falfe, will at leaft have received a wound ; for a county which has been improved more than moft others, to have fallen off in population, would be an exception to all rules. But the gentleman who has examined this matter, carries back the period of fuperior populoufnefs to the reformation, not acknowledging any fuch effect fince the revolution, which is a declaration extremely counter to the whole argument of Dr. *Price*.

But what caufes more favourable to population could have exifted before the reformation,

mation, which have not exifted fince the revolution? This will be very difficult to fhew: I fhall attend not to churches, manor houfes, names of fields, gateways, and foot paths, but to firft principles—living effective principles. Was liberty in that age clearer and more explicitly defined? Was it practically better among the lower claffes? Were farmers and peafants more independent of the nobility, lords of manors, &c.? Was there more employment for the poor in a more correct hufbandry—more flourifhing manufactures, or more extenfive commerce? Were other demands for the furplus of the country population more powerful?——What, but an abfolute negative, is to be the anfwer to all thefe queries? And fhall we then believe numbers under thofe circumftances to have exceeded the prefent!

If none of thefe circumftances operated, pray what were thofe which did caufe fuch an effect? I know not what can be mentioned, unlefs it be the charity of the monafteries—that charity I can conceive to have maintained numbers of idle poor, but that it could poffibly equal the reverfe of the circumftances I juft now mentioned, appears to me utterly incredible. For fuppofing very confiderable revenues fpent in the fupport of the attendants on monks and

and friars, and thereby to have been a parallel to a part of modern labour, this muft then be confidered as the *employment* of thofe people, who fince have turned labourers; but what demand for the furplus of their population? What parallel to modern manufactures, arts and commerce? The clafs fupported by charity, muft have multiplied like other lower claffes, without an outlet for their furplus, which, whereever wanting, is poifon to population, and the mark of a fyftem utterly inconfiftent with it. If it is faid that charity was the parallel, not of modern labour, but manufactures, &c. then I fay, you fuppofe agriculture in that age to have been as good and operofe as at prefent—and if on that propofition you will reft your argument, nothing farther can be made of it.

The truth is, there was not in that age an employment for the people comparable to what there is at prefent, how therefore could there be as many people? Let their maintenance be pointed out. But it is amufing to fee the faculty men will have of complaining of prefent times, and lamenting the paft; we are not fatisfied with our numbers, but affert that *England* was better peopled in *Henry* VIII's time; and nothing was fo common in that age as the fame complaint, as we learn even from the ftatute

tute books.   To what period I wonder did
the croakers of that age refer ?   To that of
the defolation I fuppofe which flowed from
the quarrels of the rofes—or the tumults of
the barons of King *John*.

Compare the fuppofition before us with
every poffible caufe of it, and the refult
will be, that no fuch effect could ever take
place.   But let us examine into the foundations of the idea.

*Large churches are found where the people
are not numerous enough to fill a fingle aile ;
and fome to a fingle family.*   This gentleman
admits, that churches were often built more
for oftentation than ufe.   If in thofe bigotted
times, legacies were left for church building where none were wanted, what could
the pious executors of fuch teftaments do,
but raife ufelefs edifices ?   No fatisfactory
way of accounting for the fact—but if
oftentation was their motive to one degree
of folly, why not to another.   Befides,
moft of the *Gothic* religious buildings in
the kingdom, wherever money enough was
to be had, were confpicuous for this extravagance : what idea of utility could be the
guide in conftructing many of the cathe-
drals ?   While this fpecies of expence was
the fafhion of the times, and while we
every day fee proofs that the mere idea of
religious magnificence and little thought of
utility,

utility, was the motive of such works, why should we now think of measuring the population of that age by the edifices of sacred shew?

Proper names, distinguishing fields, inclosures, roads, trees, gateways, &c. now almost forgotten. This I think is but a very slight presumption of a superior population; we cannot know what were the original causes of such names, whether the residence of a proprietor, or the wantonness of straggling shepherds and warreners: it is possible to have been, as the writer mentions; it is very possible not to have been so.

Roads and foot paths at present altogether needless. This is an argument which proving too much, proves nothing. We have them common in this country *(Hertford-shire)* within less than 20 miles of *London*, and in great numbers; if they are a proof that *Norfolk* was better peopled above 200 years ago, they are also a proof that this county was the same, which was simply impossible. But the original reasons for marking all the roads we now see, is so difficult an enquiry that it cannot be brought to prove any thing; chance probably, and unnoticed use, were the fathers of numbers, and as some became common, others were neglected, without population having any thing to do in it.

Houses

Houfes appearing in ruins—villages on the sea coaft fcenes of defolation. This is pofitive evidence, and more deferving attention than any of the other reafons. What does it prove? It proves depopulation in the parifhes of A, B, and C. But have not D, E, and F, increafed? This we are not told, but if it is not known, what proof can be fixed in the oppofite facts? Can the writer imagine that *Lynn* 200 years ago was what it is now? *Wells* he acknowledges to be almoft a new town. *Norwich* certainly was not what it is. There are no appearances to make one fuppofe *Yarmouth* more populous two centuries ago, and the fame obfervation might be made on many others. But among the villages, probably many of them have much increafed :—at leaft, thus much we may venture, that if the contrary is not proved, no proof arifes of general depopulation from fome being in ruins.

When it is confidered that fo large a part of this county was fheep walks, which is now under an excellent corn culture, it is incredible that it fhould have declined in population : fince to have done fo, employment of the people muft have been pernicious to their increafe, and the inhabitants moft numerous when they had the feweft means of living.

While

While I am writing this, I have the pleafure of the company of fome *Norfolk* gentlemen in my houfe : I made enquiries of
them ; they confirmed part of this gentleman's account ; in fuch a place the cottages
in ruins.—*The farmers then do not cultivate
the lands?* Yes they do, better than ever.
Where do the men come from then? From
other places.—This is the general round ;
it is a circle ; depopulation here; population
there.—They named many parifhes which
they knew to be confiderably increafed.

But I think I can account in a very plain
manner for the moft important of all the
reafons affigned by this gentleman—that of
fo many villages being in ruins.—When a
whole parifh becomes one farm, under one
landlord, the power over both the poor and
their habitations will center in fuch landlord
and tenant. The tenant pays the poor-
rates, and perhaps as a part of his agree-
ment, repairs the cottages ; here therefore
are two ftrong reafons why he fhould drive
the people away, and let their houfes go to
ruin, or perhaps advife his landlord to pull
them down ; firft, he eafes himfelf of rates,
and fecondly, he gets rid of repairs. As
to his labour, he hires men from parifhes
not in the fame predicament, of whofe population, as he does not pay to it, he regards
not. This may alfo be the cafe where a
parifh

parifh confifts of two or three farms, provided the farmers agree. This is certainly
an evil, but it is owing to the abfurdity
of our poor laws, not to great farms:
however, the amount of it is by no means
of confequence, and for this reafon : The
farmer's want of hands when he has deftroyed population in his own parifh, is directly
to its amount, a premium upon the population of the neighbouring parifhes ; upon
the principle of *demand* which I have before
explained. It is then impoffible but the
people in them muft proportionably increafe. Thus the very exiftence of the evil
in one place is a demonftration that there
muft be a cure for it fomewhere elfe; for
this county is not one whofe farms are
laid to grafs ; the depopulation complained
of, is in the midft of tillage.

The great leading fact is admitted
by every one — the rural employment
has not declined; on the contrary, it has
much increafed ; for every one knows,
that inclofing, marling, dunging, ploughing, turnip-hoeing, &c. are in this refpect
very different from fheep and rabbit feeding As *the work is done*, it muft be done
by fomebody; and whether that fomebody
lives in one parifh or another, has nothing
to do in the enquiry.   Much of the harveft
is got in by *Scotch* itinerants.   There is
nothing

nothing to object to in this; where the people come from is not the enquiry; all I look to is, that from somewhere they must come. This supply of *Scotchmen*, however, is only in harvest; the works of the rest of the year are sufficient to establish the truth of my observation. *Irishmen* do most of the reaping in *Hertfordshire*; this is so little a proof of depopulation, that great tracts of our county (most of it) are almost a continued village.

Upon the whole, I cannot, upon the most attentive reflection, on the cases brought by Dr. *Price*'s very ingenious correspondent, find any reason to consider them as exceptions to the general principles I before laid down. They certainly carry the appearance of depopulation, perhaps an undeceiving appearance; but we must never form conclusions from such particular instances.

POPULATION IN FRANCE.

The most particular registers of population that I have met with, are those of *M. Messance*, in his *Recherches sur la Population*, printed at *Paris* in 1766. This gentleman gives the progress of population in several of the provinces of *France*. The following extracts will shew the increase of people in those provinces,

Auvergne, 162 parishes.

Births from 1747 to 1757,   68,934
          1690 to 1700 *,   56,814

Ditto, 38 parishes.

      1747 to 1757,   – 13,547
      1700 to 1710,   – 11,146

Ditto, 119 parishes.

      1747 to 1757,   – 20,611
      1710 to 1720,   – 17,953

Ditto, 61 parishes.

      1747 to 1757,   – 23,047
      1720 to 1730,   – 21,258

Lyon †, 133 parishes.

      1749 to 1759,   – 40,126
      1690 to 1700,   – 35,228

Ditto, 118 parishes.

      1749 to 1759,   – 32,014
      1701 to 1711,   – 25,318

Ditto, 72 parishes.

      1749 to 1759,   – 40,145
      1710 to 1720,   – 30,380

Ditto, 109 parishes.

      1749 to 1759,   – 30,968
      1720 to 1730,   – 26,532

Rouen ‡, 541 parishes.

      1752 to 1761,   – 123,037
      1690 to 1699,   – 120,691

And in general he finds the present population

---

* Page 18.   † Page 35.   ‡ Page 77.

lation of the three generalities of *Auvergne*, *Lyon*, and *Rouen*, to be to the population of 1700, as 1456 to 1350*.

Provence, *Auch*, *Pau*, *Burgundy*, &c. 1752 to 1763†,   -   426,035
1690 to 1701,   -   390,375

General View.

Comparison between the present population of *France*, and 60 years ago.

	Parishes.	BIRTHS.	
		First period.	Second period.
Auvergne, -	162	5681	6893
Lyon, - -	133	3523	4012
Rouen, - -	541	12069	12303
Lyon City, -	——	3775	4137
Rouen, - -	——	2449	2271
Paris, - -	——	16988	19221
Marseille,	——	3465	3218
Toulon, - -	——	1416	1073
Aix, - -	——	989	822
Montaban, -	——	607	602
Sezanne, - -	——	185	160
Vaison, - -	38	1023	1183
Carcassonne, -	——	495	523
Valence, - -	——	259	266
Vitry, - -	——	416	250
Burgundy, *Provence*, &c. }	1278	32531	35503
		‡ 85871	92437

* Page 128.   † Page 268.   ‡ Page 272.

From the whole of *M. Meſſance's* examinations, it appears that the people of *France* have increaſed in the laſt 60 years. I cannot but quote this faĉt for the opportunity of aſking the *Engliſh* complainants, if the cauſes of depopulation have not been *almoſt* as ſtrong in that kingdom as in *England?* If under thoſe circumſtances, *France* has increaſed her people, may we not liſten to the voice of reaſon, which tells us that *England* has done it in a much greater degree? It is true, complaints of depopulation have been as common in that kingdom as with us; and I ſuppoſe there never was a period or a country where ſuch complaints were not in the mouths of many *

---

* In the courſe of theſe papers I took occaſion to quote a paſſage from Mr. *Hume*, not omitting to pay that tribute to his political ſagacity which I ſhould ſuppoſe every one muſt acknowledge. I ſhall now tranſcribe an obſervation from another writer, whoſe admirable talents enlighten every ſubjeĉt he pleaſes to undertake. A man who deſcribes with pleaſure the proſperity of his country.

————" to make ſettlements in the moſt diſtant parts of the globe, and by a wiſe and happy conjunĉtion of our labours both there and in *Britain*, at once extended our wealth and power without the leaſt diminution of our people, contrary to the effeĉts of plantations made from other countries, which have ſuffered at home by aggrandizing themſelves abroad ;

whereas

IMPORTANCE OF WEALTH.

It is upon thefe principles that I reckon wealth but another word for confumption; and efteem it as the foul of agriculture:
had

---

whereas our domeftic power is conftantly augmented in proportion to the advantages derived from our fettlements abroad; and to this circulation of our commerce it is in reality owing that our ftrength is fo much greater, our lands fo much more valuable, and our intrinfic wealth fo much increafed, as it is fince that time; and this in fpite of long wars and other intervening accidents, not at all favourable to our interefts.

This may look like a paradox to fome, and there may be others who perhaps will regard it as a thing taken upon truft. But in reality, the facts are abfolutely certain, and it is to the wonderful growth of our plantations that we owe the ftrength and populoufnefs of this ifland, which could never otherwife have attained its prefent condition. A very little attention will make this plain. The commodities and manufactures of any country, have a certain limit, beyond which, it is impoffible they fhould extend, without an alteration of circumftances; that is to fay, when they are carried fo high, as that no new markets are to be found, domeftic induftry can proceed no farther. Now it is owing to our colonies that hitherto we have not been very fenfible of this truth; for the people fettled there from a variety of caufes, into which I have not room to enter at prefent, take off much greater quantities of our commodities and manufactures than if they had remained at home. So that one of our countrymen eftablifhed in *America*,
finds

had not very ingenious men held a direct contrary opinion, I fhould have thought my time as ill fpent in explaining it, as in demonftrating that 2 and 2 make 4. Thofe princes and ftates therefore who would wifh to have the agriculture of their dominions flourifh, fhould wifh to fee the general wealth of their fubjects increafe, and encourage every branch

---

finds full employment for feveral hands here; and AS FULL EMPLOYMENT WILL ALWAYS DRAW PEOPLE, it plainly follows from thence, that our fettlements abroad muft increafe the number of people at home. As this method of arguing fhews the reafon of the thing, fo the truth of it may be likewife demonftrated from experience. It is certain that the number of people in the city of *London* is about five times as great as at the death of Queen *Elizabeth*; and though it cannot be fuppofed that the number of people in this ifland hath increafed in the fame proportion, yet it is certain that they have very much increafed, as is apparent from the growth of other great cities, the fwelling of fmall villages into large towns, and the raifing on our coafts of many new fea ports. It may indeed be objected, that if people remove out of the country into great towns, this augments the number of their inhabitants, but not that of the nation; but then the fact muft be proved, which is a thing impoffible; for fuch as dwell in great towns confume a larger quantity of provifions and all other neceffaries than fuch as live fcattered up and down the country, they muft confequently be fupplied with thefe, and therefore *the growth of towns muft increafe the number of people in the country about them.* Thus the farther we trace this matter, the clearer and the more certain it appears, and therefore what is deduced from it cannot be rationally called in queftion." *Prefent State of Europe,* 3d edit. p. 508.

branch of induſtry that can render their people rich—they ſhould remember that when
they exhauſt a country by ill deviſed taxes,
or otherwiſe, they as effectually ruin
huſbandry as if they burnt all the ploughs
in their territories, and prohibited the future
uſe of them : deſtroying the farmer's market is, in effect, doing this.

It is alſo deſtroying it for no good purpoſe, ſince a cheapneſs of proviſions is not
attended with the leaſt advantage to any
claſs or order of a ſtate *. Nor let him in
the

---

* A writer in the laſt century has a very good obſervation on this : "It is the dearneſs of corn that
encourages the farmer, not only to pay his rent well
and give good prices, but alſo to live high, and improve all his unimproved land within his reach, which
will ſtill increaſe trade and revenue, and the neceſſity
will make the manufactors work harder, and that
will increaſe manufacture, and that will make us ſell
cheaper, till we have gotten ſo many new, or ſo improved our old cuſtomers, as that our quantities will
not ſerve. Anno 1683, I offered to make it appear,
that this kingdom will thrive more, and the manufactors live better when proviſions are dear than cheap.
There I ſhewed that plenty or cheapneſs cauſed lazi-
neſs, that dearneſs, that induſtry, and that plenty ;
and alſo, 'TWAS GOOD TO ENCOURAGE THE PEO-
PLE TO A HIGH LIVING, and the conveniences
of it : That if the manufactors cannot live as they
uſe to do, by three days in a week working, they
muſt work four, or find ſome quicker way, and that
will produce a fourth part of more manufacture, which
muſt

the right progrefs of his policy be turned afide by erroneous ideas concerning the luxury that flows from this wealth; let him equally difregard the gloomy notions of depopulation, fecure in the idea that if he gives wealth to his people, he gives employment, and of courfe they will multiply.

PRICES

---

muft caufe it to be fold cheaper. I there alfo fhewed how 'twas the king's intereft to give money for exporting corn, and our intereft to have the excife higher, and a duty not only on brewers but on all that brew." *Houghton's Collection of Hufbandry and Trade*, vol. ii. p. 266. The idea of encouraging the people to live high, is a very bold, but I believe a juft one. In another place he fays, " If corn was fold at 12 s. the bufhel, and beef 6 d. the pound, by means of an encouragement for their exportation, or double confumption, I fhould not be forry." Vol. iv. p 91. At page 382, he enlarges the idea. It is not only in *England* that provifions fhould be dear—the inconveniences of cheapnefs are the fame all the world over. It is fo in *Afia:* Dr. *Campbell* defcribing the great plenty in the *Maldives*, fays, " The natives it's true, don't grow rich, and that i take to proceed from their cheap and eafy living, which encourages them to negligence and idlenefs." *Harris's Voyages*, vol. i. p. 706. And of *Siam* he fays, " The peafants lead a miferable life, by reafon that provifions are fo cheap here, that they cannot get any thing by their labour." p. 782.

PRICES DEPEND ON QUANTITY OF MONEY.

Here it is proper to remark that the importance which I give to general wealth is founded on the fame principle with that laid down by *Montefquieu* and Mr. *Hume, that the price of commodities is proportioned to the quantity of fpecie.* But as Sir *James Steuart* has oppofed this idea, and endeavoured to eftablifh another in its room, it is neceffary to fay a word or two upon his arguments; becaufe if they are juft, my obfervations on the confequence of national wealth to agriculture, muft be erroneous, or at leaft but indifferently founded. There may be (according to Sir *James*'s idea) a great influx of wealth, and yet no rife of prices, and confequently no benefit accruing to the farmer: The paffages I mean are the following:

" I have laid it down as a principle that it is the complicated operations of demand and competition, which determines the ftandard price of every thing. If there be many labourers and little demand, work will be cheap. If the increafe of riches therefore have the effect of *raifing* demand, work will increafe in its value, becaufe *there* competition is implied; but if it has

only

only the effect of *augmenting* demand, prices
will stand as formerly."—" Let the specie
of a country therefore be augmented or
diminished in ever so great a proportion,
commodities will still rise and fall according to the principles of demand and competition, and these will constantly depend
upon the inclinations of those who have
property or any kind of *equivalent* whatso-
ever to give, but never upon the quantity
of *coin* they are possessed of *."

There is an obscurity in the distinction
between *raising* and *augmenting* demand,
which is not at first to be dissipated; but
the point principally to be attended to, is
another distinction, which I humbly apprehend may be without a difference, *viz.*
that between *specie* and *demand.* I never
understood either M. de *Montesquieu* or Mr.
Hume to assert or mean, that very great
variations would not be frequent, indepen-
dantly of the quantity of money : Nobody
could suppose they were so short-sighted as
to form such ideas : If there is much corn
brought to market this week, and few buyers, prices will certainly be higher than
in another week, when there is little corn
brought, but many buyers : Mackarel are
                                        certainly

---

* *Enquiry into the Principles of Pol. Oeconom.* vol. i.
p. 400.

certainly cheaper when many boats arrive than when but few come : If any commodity in general and regular demand, is brought to market at a particular feafon in much greater plenty than at any other feafon, who can doubt but the price will be low? All fuch variations are perfectly confiftent with the idea that the price of commodities will depend on the quantity of fpecie; becaufe this idea is not relative to certain days, weeks, months, or markets, but to general periods in which money has increafed or decreafed; one century compared with another;—one 50 years with another 50; twenty years fince a peace with twenty before it, &c. In fuch a comparifon, and neither the *French* writer nor Mr. *Hume* could have any other in view, the idea of demand and competition, is abfolutely loft in that of fpecie, becaufe they are in fact the fame thing. Sir *James* will keep clofe to the circumftance, that the quantity of money has nothing to do in the cafe, if a man will not *fpend* when he *poffeffes:* but this appears to me to be taken for granted: relative to a market day, or other point of competition, I admit of it; but I think it fhould be rejected in application to *a period.* Suppofe foreign commerce increafes from a war or other reafons, fo as to add immenfely to the

national

national wealth; an additional income is added to the fortunes of many men, thefe men will in general increafe their expences, and confequently demand. I have no idea of a great increafe of national wealth any where without an increafe of the expences of individuals following; there certainly may be fuch cafes, but they muft carry rather the appearance of exceptions, than the ground of new principles. Why did land fell in the laft century for 15 years purchafe? Becaufe there was fo little fpecie that there was no comparative demand; people who have not MONEY do not add to *demand*. Why is land at prefent fo much higher? Becaufe a greater plenty of fpecie has given a greater demand. Demand and competition appear to be *effects*; money the *caufe*.

Sir *James* fuppofes it remarked—" that articles of indifpenfable neceffity muft remain conftantly in proportion to the mafs of riches. This I cannot by any means admit to be juft. Let me take the example of grain, which is the moft familiar. Is it not plain from what we have faid above, that the proportion of wealth found in the hands of the loweft clafs of the people conftantly regulates the price of it; confequently let the rich be ever fo wealthy, the price of fubfiftence can never rife above the faculties of the poor."—In anfwer to this

it

it may be obferved, that the price has rifen far beyond what the faculties of the poor in former times could purchafe, and they would now all be ftarved, if *quantity of wealth*, that is *demand for labour*, had not rifen the price of it, as well as of wheat.—— Through whatever political mazes we are carried, we fhall find that an increafe in the national wealth will be only another word for increafe of demand ; fo as to be fcarcely poffible for one to fubfift without the other.

From various of the inftances quoted by Sir *James*, there is reafon to believe he principally draws his argument from the demand and competition at certain times, for certain commodities; at a market for corn ; at ancient *Rome* for a mullet ; prices in *January* 1759, &c. and what is remarkable, he fays nothing of the increafe of money from the difcovery of *America*, on which *Montefquieu* founds his idea ; and it is from a gradual increafe of wealth from induftry that Mr. *Hume* fupports his. And yet Sir *James* afferts, that the money in *Europe might* be increafed to ten times the prefent quantity, without the prices of commodities being affected.—Upon the whole, the matter turns principally on the proportion which holds between money and demand—throughout this effay I have fup-
poſed

pofed them the fame thing; becaufe I fee, whichever way I look, the expences of all ranks of people increafe, with an increafe of their incomes, and luxury fpreading through countries in proportion to their wealth : now luxury is wealth—is demand —is competition for the thing defired, and prices rife in proportion to expences, that is to money. If this is not true, how are we to account for the prices of a thoufand things before the difcovery of *America,* compared with the prefent prices of the fame commodities ;—or, without going fo far back—for thofe in the laft century, not only of rarities, but almoft every commodity that can be named, provifions, labour, manufactures, land, &c. Why is labour, provifions, houfe-rent, land, and commodities in general, except foreign manufactures, cheaper in *Sweden* or *Norway* than in *England* or *Holland?*—Surely it is becaufe thofe countries are not equally wealthy. You may, if you pleafe, add the confequence, that there is not an equal demand. Further, let us take Sir *James's* fuppofition; fuppofe our national wealth to be increafed to ten times the prefent amount; how would it be poffible for the prices of commodities not to rife immenfely, unlefs every man became a hoarder, which I fhall never fuppofe? Thus every man

poffeffing

poſſeſſing ten times his preſent wealth and income, immediately increaſes his expences; increaſes his ſervants, equipages, labourers, builders, artizans; his houſe-keeping expences multiply; more is eaten, drank, and waſted; all this forms a freſh demand for every article; and as the wealth of others has the ſame effect with them, here is competition; if prices in conſequence of this demand and competition ſhould not riſe, ſurely it would be miraculous? This was the idea of Meſſrs. *Monteſquieu* and *Hume*, who, from ſeeing an univerſal effect regularly following a viſible cauſe, juſtly attributed the former to the latter; they ſaw that a great increaſe of national wealth always cauſed a great riſe in prices; and that in poor countries commodities were cheaper than in rich ones; hence they deduced their reaſoning; and what we have ſince ſeen and felt in this country, would, if any proof was wanting, confirm their doctrine.

This I think is the direct and plain way of attributing the effect in queſtion to its proper cauſe. But here I readily admit a partial exception; an exception which Sir *James* ſeems to have wrought into a complete hypotheſis: I admit that to an unknown degree, an increaſe of wealth increaſing the demand for certain manufactures,

tures, will increase the quantity brought to market, and prices stand as they were : For instance, send a gradual increase of orders to the manufacturers of *Manchester*, *Norwich*, *Birmingham*, &c. and they will answer the increased demand for perhaps a long time, without an increase of prices ; because the people will increase with their industry, and a want of hands will not be felt. This is the strongest exception that can be put to the rule of Mr. *Hume*, yet is it not of importance enough to overturn his idea, since the word *commodities* includes such a variety of things besides certain manufactures, that his expression may be deemed sufficiently accurate : land, houses, labour, provisions, &c. are all clearly within his rule, not to speak of a variety even of manufactures, not wrought in great manufacturing towns.

But even in this great exception of Sir *James*'s, there are some circumstances which favour Mr. *Hume*'s hypothesis : Why are not all manufactures cheaper now than they were 300 years ago ? If the argument urged by Sir *James* is just, they ought to be cheaper, or at least not dearer ; but if the difference of the periods be considered relative to favouring manufactures of every kind, they ought now to be produced 500 *per cent.* cheaper. Yet in 1460, good. cloth,

cloth, fuch as was to ferve the beft Doctor
at *Oxford*, was fold at 3 s. 7 d. a yard; but
as there were 30 fhillings in the pound at
that time, we muft call this near 7 s. 6 d.
whereas now the proper cloth for fuch a
perfon would coft 18 s. In *William* the
Conqueror's reign the ferjeant of an infir-
mary had a coat for 4 s. I inftance thefe
only to fhew, that in periods very diftant,
the rife even of manufactures depend on
the quantity of money; and if their rates
in the laft century be examined and compared with what they are at prefent, it will
be found that fcarce an inftance is to be
produced in which there has not been a
confiderable rife; which muft be owing to
the increafe of money.

In any one period of no great extent,
the increafe of demand from the increafe
of wealth, may not be found to operate
its natural effect; but in a longer period a
change happens from a gradual and almoft
imperceptible progrefs; and then manufactures as well as all other commodities
get up to a proportion with the quantity of
money. That this muft be the cafe during
a long period cannot be doubted, when we
confider that the price of labour has much
more than doubled in a century, and that
feveral articles of raw materials in many
fabricks have rifen equally with labour;
and

and if we take a larger fcope, and go back
to the period when provifions, labour, and
every other article were not a fourth of the
prefent price, how are we to conceive that
manufactures could be as dear as we pay
for them ? And to what caufe is it poffible
to attribute the change but to the fuperior
quantity of fpecie ?

I have been led into this difquifition
from its intimate connection with my fubject, as I cannot but efteem great national
wealth as one of the moft important circumftances in the encouragement of agriculture ; and if the reafoning laid down by
Sir *James Steuart* is juft, as I underftand
it, this wealth muft be of little importance,
and my reafoning fallacious. It is with
diffidence I venture an opinion, contrary to
the ideas of a writer of fuch diftinguifhed
abilities ; and who has given fuch uncommon attention to every part of the fcience
of political œconomy : nor perhaps would
this apology be deemed fufficient, had not
Sir *James* taken the fame liberty with the
illuftrious *Montefquieu* and the fagacious
Hume.

S E C T. VIII.

I N C L O S U R E S.

THE next article I fhall mention is the circumftance of fo large a part of the kingdom being inclofed, and the policy in the legiflature of conftantly increafing inclofures.—To enter into a detail of their advantages here, would be a ufelefs undertaking—the prejudices of fome of our writers, who have even to the prefent day declaimed againft them, are to be reckoned among thofe abfurdities that never die— they are to be found in every branch of philofophy, literature, and art. I fhall here reply to one affertion thrown out by the enemies of inclofures—They fay that rich lands after inclofing, are laid down to grafs, and the kingdom thereby depopulated. Suppofing the cafe in the firft inftance, yet I have a great doubt whether the hufbandman converting his farm to that ufe for which the foil is moft adapted, which pays him beft, and confequently adds moft to the national wealth, can depopulate the country :—it may depopulate one parifh, but probably others will gain beyond the proportion by it. However, granting the pofition, which is more than there is occafion to do, yet I think

think population is but a fecondary object: The foil ought to be applied to that ufe in which it will pay moft, without any idea of population: A farmer ought not to be tied down to bad hufbandry, whatever may become of population. Population, which, inftead of adding wealth to the ftate, is a burthen to the ftate, is a pernicious population—and will be found fo in every country where the national ftrength does not depend on troops ferving without pay. As to attributing to inclofures the many evils, moft of them imaginary, which fome writers have laid to their charge, they are merely ideal.

That many abfurd opinions fhould be commonly embraced concerning *new* meafures, is natural enough, but that we fhould fee the fame errors relative to matters of which we have had long experience, is certainly remarkable. The complaints againft inclofures are of a very long date; we have had them between two and three hundred years, and they never appeared without receiving the moft folid and fatiffactory refutation. One of the moft remarkable inftances is in the reign of *Elizabeth*; the following extract from a very curious tract will fet this matter in a clear light.

A

A Compendium, or brief Examination of certayn ordinary complaints of divers of our countrymen in thefe our days. By W. S. *(fuppofed to be* WM. SHAKESPEARE) 1581.

Hufbandman.] Marry for thefe inclofures doe undoe us all : for they make us pay dearer for our lande that we occupy, and caufes that we can have no lande in manner for our money to put to tyllage, all is taken up in pafture. I have known of late a dozen ploughs within lefs compafs than fix miles about me, layd down within thefe feven years, and where threefcore perfons or upwards had their livings, now one man with his cattel has all, which is not the leaft caufe of former uprores : for by thefe inclofers many doe lack lyvings and be idle; moreover all things are fo deere that by their day wages they are not able to lyve *.

Capper.] I have well the experience thereof, for I am faine to give my journeymen two-pence in a day more than I was wont to doe, and yet they fay they cannot fufficiently lyve thereof.

Merchaunt.] Moft parte of all the towns of *England*, *London* only except, are fore decayed in their houfes, &c. whereof it is

long,

---

* One would have thought, without feeing the title, that this had been a tranfcript of the common complaints of the prefent time.

long, I cannot well tell, for there is such
a general dearth of all things, as before 20
or 30 years hath not bene the like, not
only of things growing within this realm,
but of all other merchaundize that we buy
from beyond the sea, as sylkes, wines, &c.
then all kind of vittayle are as deere or
deere agayne, and no cause of God's part
thereof as far as I can perceive; for I never
saw more plentie of corn, graffe, and cattle
of all forte than we have at this prefent,
and have had (as ye know) all these 20
yeares paffed continually.

Knight.] Since ye have plentie of all
things, of corne and cattel (as ye fay) then
it fhould not feem this dearth fhould be
long of thefe inclofers, for it is not for
fcarcenefs of corne, that ye have this dearth,
for (thanked be God) corne is good cheap,
and fo hath been thefe many years paft.
Then it cannot be the occafion of the dearth
of cattle, for inclofure is the thing that
nourifheth moft of any other * : yet I confefs
there is a wonderful dearth of all things ;
and that doe I, and all men of my forte
feel moft grief in, which have no way to
fell, nor occupation to lyve by, but only
our lands. For you all with other artificers
may fave yourfelves meetly well. Foraf-
much

---

* An admirable reply to the croakers of the prefent
age.

much as yee, as all things are dearer, do aryfe in the pryce of your wares and occupations accordingly.

Hufbandman.] Yee rayfe the pryce of your lands, and ye take farms alfo, and paftures to your hands, which was wont to be poor men's lyvings fuch as I am.

Merchaunt.] On my foul yee fay truth.

Knight.] Syr, as I know it is true that yee complayne not without caufe, fo it is as true, that I and my forte, I mean all gentlemen, have as great, yea, and far greater caufe to complayne; the pryces of things are fo rifen on all hands, we are forced either to minifh the third part of our houfehold, or rayfe the third part of our revenues; and for that we cannot fo doe of our own landes, that is already in the hands of other men, many of us are enforced to keep peeces of our own landes, when they fall in our own poffeffion, or to purchafe fome farme of other men's landes, and to ftore it with fheep, &c.

Hufbandman.] Yea, thofe fheep is the caufe of all thefe mifchieves.

Doctour.] I perceive by you all, that there is none of you but have juft caufe to complayn.

Knight.] I marvel much, maifter doctour, what fhould be the caufe of this dearth, feeing all things are fo plentiful.

Doctour.]

Doctour.] Syr, it is no doubt a thing to be mufed upon. *Qyere,* Whether if the hufbandman were forced to abate the pryces of his ftuff, this dearth would be amended; if he fhould be commanded to fell his wheat (for inftance) at 8 *d.* the bufhel, rye at 6 *d.* barley at 4 *d.* his pig and goofe at 4 *d.* his hen at 1 *d. ob.* his wool at a marke a tod, the landlord to return to his old rent, &c. would goods in that cafe from beyond feas be brought as good cheap after the fame rate ? A man would think yes. For example, if they now fell a yard of velvet for 20 *s.* or 22 *s.* and pay that for a tod of wool, were it not as good for them to fell their velvet for a marke a yard, fo they had a tod of wool for a marke * ?"

In another part he fays, " that in 20 or 30 years before 1581, commodities had in general rifen 50 *per cent.*; fome more. Cannot you neighbour remember, fays he, that within thefe 30 years I could in this town

---

* *Memoirs of Wool,* vol. i. p. 113. I tranfcribe this extract from Mr. *Smith,* not having been able to procure the original. He tells us, that the *Doctour* refolves the general dearnefs into the greater plenty of money from increafe of trade, and accounts for wool being dearer in comparifon than corn, from the former being allowed to be exported, and the latter too much reftrained in that refpect ; but that by giving an equal liberty to both, notwithftanding inclofures, the ballance would be preferved by the farmer fhifting from fheep to corn, and *vice verfa.*

town buy the beft pig or goofe I could lay my hands on, for four-pence, which now cofteth twelve-pence, a good capon for three-pence or four-pence, a chicken for a penny, a hen for two-pence." P. 35.— Yet the price of ordinary labour was then 8 *d.* a day, p. 31 *.

As a commentary on thefe extracts I fhall give the price of wheat through the 16th century, in the coin of the prefent ftandard †.

			£.	s.	d.
1500, Wheat the quarter,		-	0	6	7
1504,	——	——	0	8	9
1514,	——	——	0	5	6
1519,	——	——	0	5	6
Average of 20 years,			0	6	7
1521,	——	——	1	7	7
	——	——	1	15	10
1527,	——	——	0	19	9
Average of 7 years,		—	1	7	8
1532,	——	——	0	8	10
1550,	——	——	0	5	1¾
1551,	——	——	0	1	9

* *Mr. Hume's Hiftory of England,* vol. v. p. 484.
† This I take from *Combrune's Enquiry,* folio.

			£.	s.	d.
1552,	——	——	0	2	4
1553,	——	——	0	8	2
1554,	——	——	0	8	2
1555,	——	——	0	8	2
1556,	——	——	0	6	4
1557,	——	——	1	2	6
1558,	——	——	0	11	$2\frac{1}{2}$
1559,	——	——	0	8	2
1560,	——	——	0	8	2
1561,	——	——	0	8	3
1562,	——	——	0	8	3
Average of 31 years,	-		0	8	$3\frac{1}{2}$
1573,	——	——	2	1	$2\frac{1}{2}$
1574,	——	——	2	1	$2\frac{1}{2}$
1575,	——	——	1	4	9
Average of 3 years,	—		1	15	8
1586,	——	——	2	18	8
1587,	——	——	3	6	6
1588,	——	——	0	6	5
1592,	——	——	0	19	$6\frac{1}{2}$
1594,	——	——	3	2	10
1595,	——	——	2	3	6
1596,	——	——	1	17	4
1597,	——	——	2	14	6
1598,	——	——	2	4	2

		£.	s.	d.
1599,	—— ——	1	10	6
Average of 14 years *, -		2	2	4

It is upon record that the rife of price in 1573, was not owing to any natural fcarcity ; and it is farther known, that in 1561, a free export was allowed and continued for fome years. It has been afferted that the fucceeding high prices were owing to that freedom of exportation : The whole of this table fhews the contrary ; exportation, whenever it raifes prices, raifes them immediately ; for inftance, in a few weeks inftead of years ; yet the price in 1561 and 1562 continued low.

But it appears from the dialogue quoted above, that from 20 to 30 years preceding 1581, prices had rifen 50 *per cent.* It is plain that this had nothing to do with wheat, which continued at a tolerably fteady

---

* This table, as I mentioned before, is taken from *the Enquiry into the Prices of Wheat, Malt,* &c. folio ; but I muft remark the authority not much to be depended on. The author afferts his having reduced the prices to the prefent ftandard, but bill op *Fleetwood* gives 5 *l.* 4 *s.* the price of 1597, and 4 *l.* that of 1596: I have taken this fallible guide, becaufe I confider here merely the comparifon of the periods : I have before fhewn what little dependance is to be placed on a man who makes the profit of arable land in fallow, wheat, barley, 78 *per cent.*

fteady price till 1573, and then arofe for many years more than 50 *per cent.* The author of the dialogue writes in 1581, and in it inclofures are much arraigned for converting arable into grafs for fheep; but mark, that this complaint followed 31 years, the average price of which was 8 *s.* 3 *d.* ½, and we are told that the labouring poor could not live, whofe wages were 8 *d.* a day! Such are the prepofterous and abfurd complaints, which, like thofe of depopulation, are, as Mr. *Hume* moft juftly remarks, *a vulgar complaint in all places and all ages* *. We have Sir *W. Petty's* pofitive authority that day labour was 8 *d.* a day a century after this period; and at prefent it is 16 *d.* on an average.

But how could inclofures act againft the plenty of corn, while wheat for 31 years ftood at 8 *s.* 3 *d.* ½ prefent money? Does not this palpable contradiction fhew the folly of fuch an idea: Does it not fhew, what we have fo often remarked, that any operation which has a tendency (like throwing arable to grafs) to raife the price of any particular product—has in its very nature a tendency to the direct contrary effect. Throw fo much arable to grafs as to raife the price of corn, and you encourage the

corn

---

* *Hift. Eng.* vol. v. p. 482.

corn farmers fo much, that an increafe of
culture immediately follows. Every very
high period in the preceding table is furely
followed by a low one, until wheat came to
3 *l.* 6 *s.* 6 *d.*; the higheft price of all : what
followed ? Why 6 *s.* 5 *d.* a quarter the
very next year; fuch an encouragement to
the farmer was the former price that it at
once produced the latter. The fame remark is juft in every table of prices that
has been publifhed throughout *Europe.*
And the low price being an equal difcouragement, it muft at once produce an high one.

Is it not evident therefore that the *Knight*
in the dialogue has reafon to fay that it
could not be owing to inclofures that corn
was dear ; nor could they make cattle dear,
for inclofures caufe plenty of cattle. This
is the very mirrour of the prefent ftate of
England : Inclofures are condemned for
raifing prices : How do they raife prices ?
Why they raife wheat to 2 *l.* 3 *s.* 6 *d.* a
quarter for 7 years *, and they make beef
and mutton dear by infinitely increafing the
number of fat fheep and oxen !—When
fhall we fee an end to thefe abfurdities ?

The author of the dialogue tells us, that
in the 20 or 30 years preceding 1581,
commodities in general had rifen 50 *per
cent.*

----

* *Obfervations on Reverfionary Payments,* 3d Edit.
p. 383.

cent. and fome more : and the fhort-fighted good people of thofe days attributed this evil to fheep, inclofures, grafs, and great farms; they would not look at the right caufe with *Shakefpeare,* the increafe of money : it is the nature of the vulgar, great and fmall, in all ages, to attribute evils to fuch a caufe as may be changed; becaufe the malignity of man loves an opportunity to quarrel with government. If fheep are the caufe ; prohibit, fay they, great flocks ; if horfes, tax them ; if great farms, divide them : fuch caufes admit of remedies, which if not applied, give an opportunity of clamour : but attribute them to an increafe and confequent cheapnefs of money—to publick wealth—to national profperity— the profpect is too brilliant for a jaundiced eye, that can look with pleafure only on ideal evil and chimerical declenfion.

Among the prefent complaints of the high prices of provifions, we are told by fome writers that it is not the rates of wheat that opprefs the people, but thofe of meat. Among thefe, Dr. *Price* is pleafed to rank himfelf : he fays that it is the fuperior price of flefh that hurts the poor, as it forces them to confume bread only, confequently they could before live better when wheat was high, than they can now while it is comparatively low. I cannot fubfcribe to this

this obfervation, for the reafons I am going to produce; nor do I put much faith in the regiftered prices of meat, from their being fo uncertain and defultory; we have them not (except at the victualling-office) in the fame regular manner as the *Windfor* prices of wheat and malt. In Mr. *Combrune's* table of prices, who fupports the fame general argument as Dr. *Price,* we have the following minutes :

		£.	s.	d.		£.	s.	d.
1309,	Wheat,	1	1	11	An ox,	2	14	0
1314,	—	3	1	2	—	3	13	6
1315,	—	3	1	2	—	7	6	9
1336,	—	0	6	1½	—	1	0	4¼
1349,	—	0	5	6	—	0	18	4
1444,	—	0	9	0	—	3	4	9
1532,	—	0	8	10	—	1	16	6
1550,	—	0	5	1¾	—	0	18	0
Averages,		1	2	4	—	2	14	0

Hence it appears that a fat ox in thofe days was worth as much as 20 bufhels of wheat. If we call the prefent price of wheat 6 s. 6 d. a bufhel, it is for 20, 6 l. 10 s.; then if we confider that the improvements in hufbandry for two centuries have contributed more to improve the food and fize of cattle than any other article

ticle; we fhall have great reafon to think
that fuch an ox as in that period yielded a
price equivalent to 6 *l.* 10 *s.* would not at
prefent yield more. If the total want of
turnips, and thofe other means of winter
fatting, long fince difcovered, be confidered
—and that hay fold as well or better than at
prefent, and confequently muft be fparingly
ufed, we may conjecture to what fize their
cattle arofe; and then judge if they were
probably better than the *Scotch* black cattle
bred on mountains with little winter food,
which fell fat from 5 *l.* to 10 *l.* at prefent.

		£.	s.	d.		£.	s.	d.
1309,	Wheat,	1	1	11	Sheep,	0	9	1
1314,	—	3	1	2	—	0	3	7
1336,	—	0	6	1½	—	0	2	0¼
1310,	—	0	17	9	—	0	3	9
1448,	—	0	13	0	—	0	5	0
1531,	—	0	8	10	—	0	3	10¾
1532,	—	0	8	10	—	0	5	6½
1558,	—	0	11	2½	—	0	3	6
Averages,		1	0	0		0	4	6

The value of a fheep therefore was equal
to 1 bufhel 3 pecks and ½ of wheat: this
at prefent would be at 6 *s.* 6 *d.* a bufhel,
12 *s.* 2 *d.* for more than which I do not
apprehend one of the fheep of thofe days
would

would fell, for the fame reafons I before mentioned in refpect to oxen *.

In 1532, when wheat was 8 s. 10 d. a *fat* fheep is 5 s. 6 d. ½; this is equal to 5 bufhels, a much higher price than they yield now; and difference of breed confidered, probably double.

But Dr. *Price* gives, from a manufcript of the Duke of *Northumberland*'s, the following particular: " In 1512, the price of wheat was 6 s. 2 d. a quarter, that of a fat ox, 13 s. 4 d.; the price of wheat therefore, fays he, was about a feventh of its prefent price; that of meat, only a fifteenth." Here therefore we find the Doctor fixes the prefent price of the fat ox at 10 l.: But on what poffible authority can he fuppofe, fuch oxen as were fed in *York-fhire* 150 years ago, to be of a fize that would now yield that fum: if the confiderations I before urged are admitted, I fhould rather fuppofe the oxen of thofe days no better than *Scotch* runts at prefent. At beft therefore it is only one fuppofition in fupport of another fuppofition; an uncertainty

---

* I muft remark on both thefe articles that it is uncertain whether the oxen and fheep were fat or lean; but in all probability both; as they are fometimes called an ox *fat*; a fheep *fat*; if all were fo, it would not be fpecified fo in particular years, and not all.

tainty that muft run through all accounts of the price of cattle, which vary fo prodigioufly, that 20*l.* may be very cheap for an ox, and 5*l.* very dear. Further, a wether (not faid if fat or lean) is 1*s.* 8*d.* or equal to 2 bufhels 1 peck of wheat: That quantity of wheat at 6*s.* 6*d.* is 14*s.* 7*d.* a very good price for a wether at prefent through the North of *England*; and in fome parts of the North, an high one: the fame obfervation is applicable to the hog at 2*s.*

The Doctor next quotes from *Maitland* another proportion. Wheat, 12*s.* An ox, 1*l.* 18*s.* A wether, 3*s.* Butter, $\frac{3}{4}$ and 1*d.* a pound. Cheefe, $\frac{1}{2}$*d.* Thefe are,

The ox, —— 26 bufhels of wheat.
The wether, - 2 ditto.
Butter the pound, 2 quarts ditto.
Cheefe ditto, - 1 quart ditto.

The prices of thefe commodities at prefent would be (wheat at 6*s.* 6*d.*)

	£.	s.	d.
The ox, ——	8	9	0
—— wether, ——	0	13	0
—— butter *per* pound, -	0	0	4¾
—— cheefe, ——	0	0	2½

From thefe prices I muft draw very contrary conclufions from the Doctor: the ox and the wether are probably as cheap now as before, but what amazes me is the article of butter; which he prints in italicks, that it may be remarked. Salt butter is frequently

quently in the prefent period 6 d. a pound,
and butter in 1549, fo high as 4 d. ¾! Is
this produced to fhew the difproportion of
the products of cattle to wheat? Twenty
years ago butter in *London* was cheaper than
200 years ago. If the butter is fuppofed to
be frefh, the price is high, but why may we
not think it all falt fo foon after an age that
had no mutton in winter but what was falted?

No idea on thefe fubjects is more miftaken than the fuppofition that butter in
this age is dearer than formerly: very many
inftances might be produced of the contrary. Inftead of being dearer, it has not
advanced near fo much as moft other commodities. In *June* 1695, *Houghton* exprefly fays, frefh butter *in the country* 70
miles from *London* fold at 6 d. a pound,
and he mentions it as a common price *.
Cheefe is low, but unlefs we knew what
cheefe it was, we can found no conclufions:
In *Norfolk* and *Suffolk*, cheefe is at this
time but 3 d. ½, and fome under that. But
let us quit fuch uncertain conjectures
founded on accidental circumftances—the
prices of fingle years—of particular purchafers, which can give us no more
knowledge than we at prefent reap from
hearing that *Nokes* bought beef laft *Satur-*
day

---

* *Collection for Improving of Hufbandry and Trade,*
vol. i. p. 390.

day at 2 *d.* a pound, or *Stiles* butter for
11 *d.* What was the quality? Was the
market day high or low? Did others buy
fo? Such infulated circumftances fcraped
our of dufty libraries and records are not
worth tranfcribing for fuch general ufes as
are too often made of them. The only
regifter of the prices of meat that carries
with it the leaft degree of authenticity is
the records of the victualling-office, the
prices of which are always cheaper than
the common ones in the market, but this
is not of confequence, when one period
is compared with another, as that circumftance operates equally in all. The following table of the *London* prices of beef and
pork, will fhew us how much thefe commodities are advanced.

Years.			Beef per Cwt.			Pork per Cwt.	
			s.	*d.*		*s.*	*d.*
1683,	-	-	18	8	—	25	$1\frac{1}{2}$
1684,	-	-	20	0	—	26	0
1685,	-	-	20	0	—	26	6
1686,	-	-	17	0	—	26	0
1687,	-	-	20	$0\frac{1}{4}$	—	25	3
1688,	-	-	20	6	—	23	9
1689,	-	-	20	10	—	31	8
1690,	-	-	20	4	—	25	0
1691,	-	-	19	3	—	24	2
1692,	-	-	18	6	—	24	11

Years.	Beef per Cwt.			Pork per Cwt.	
	s.	d.		s.	d.
1693,	22	0	—	29	6
1694,	23	4	—	32	6
1695,	26	0	—	32	3
1696,	25	2	—	29	6
1697,	25	0	—	31	0
1698,	26	0	—	32	6
1699,	21	9	—	33	10
1700,	25	0	—	33	10
1701,	24	6	—	32	$4\frac{1}{2}$
1702,	27	3	—	33	$7\frac{1}{2}$
1703,	22	6	—	27	6
1704,	21	2	—	24	0
1705,	25	7	—	27	$10\frac{1}{2}$
1706,	21	5	—	27	5
1707,	19	0	—	25	$7\frac{1}{2}$
1708,	20	6	—	28	$4\frac{1}{2}$
1709,	26	0	—	30	$7\frac{1}{2}$
1710,	31	0	—	45	$7\frac{1}{2}$
1711,	39	6	—	58	6
1712,	23	10	—	31	9
1713,	23	1	—	30	9
1714,	21	10	—	29	10
1715,	23	3	—	28	0
1716,	23	9	—	31	3
1717,	22	0	—	30	9
1718,	23	0	—	29	$10\frac{1}{2}$
1719,	24	$7\frac{1}{2}$	—	27	6
1720,	29	3	—	37	9
1721,	21	9	—	43	3

Years.	Beef per Cwt.			Pork per Cwt.	
	s.	d.		s.	d.
1722,	26	9	—	31	0
1723,	18	0	—	24	0
1724,	21	6	—	31	0
1725,	20	8	—	34	6
1726,	26	$1\frac{1}{2}$	—	37	6
1727,	21	9	—	35	6
1728,	19	$7\frac{1}{2}$	—	32	0
1729,	26	0	—	40	6
1730,	18	6	—	29	3
1731,	18	3	—	24	5
1732,	16	9	—	19	0
1733,	16	1	—	25	0
1734,	16	5	—	23	$5\frac{1}{2}$
1735,	13	3	—	21	$2\frac{1}{2}$
1736,	13	7	—	23	11
1737,	13	5	—	22	6
1738,	18	7	—	30	1
1739,	18	$1\frac{1}{2}$	—	25	$9\frac{1}{2}$
1740,	23	$7\frac{3}{4}$	—	31	$0\frac{1}{2}$
1741,	24	$9\frac{1}{2}$	—	36	$3\frac{1}{4}$
1742,	24	4	—	32	9
1743,	19	$2\frac{1}{2}$	—	27	$2\frac{1}{4}$
1744,	18	$3\frac{1}{2}$	—	22	$5\frac{1}{4}$
1745,	18	$9\frac{1}{2}$	—	21	$9\frac{1}{4}$
1746,	21	$3\frac{3}{8}$	—	24	$8\frac{1}{4}$
1747,	19	$4\frac{1}{4}$	—	24	$0\frac{1}{2}$
1767,	25	$5\frac{1}{2}$	—	none bt.	
1768,	25	$3\frac{1}{2}$	—	ditto.	
1769,	22	9	—	33	0

Years.	Beef per Cwt.		Pork per Cwt.	
	s.	d.	s.	d.
1770, - -	22	$2\frac{1}{4}$	41	5
1771, - -	22	6	43	$5\frac{1}{2}$
Average of the last 5 years, -	23	7	39	3
Average of the 17 years of the last century, - -	21	5	28	1
Former dearer by - - - -	2	2	11	2
Average of the years 1709, 10, 11, 12, - - - -	30	1	41	7
Last 5 years,	23	7	39	3
Former dearer by - - - -	6	6	2	4

If the 17 years ending 1771 were known, the average would probably be lower, or at least as low as the 17 of the last century. I think this is upon the whole, a reply to the observation of Dr. *Price* [*], that the exportation, which in 1697,

---

[*] Page 383. The uncertainty which attends the antient registers of prices (except those of wheat and malt

1697, went on without clamour, though at
3 *l.* a quarter, was becaufe meat was fo reafonable as to enable the poor to live on
that: On the contrary in 1697, beef was
2 *s.*

---

malt at *Windfor*) is fo great, that I fhould never have
thought of making ufe of them had not others given
them an importance which they do not deferve.
While it is fo difficult to know thefe prices at prefent,
how can we fuppofe it fo eafy to know thofe of the
15th century? Before the late act of parliament for
publifhing the prices of corn, how did any perfon
know what was the price even of wheat? *I bought
at* 5 *s. Nay*—fays another, *I gave* 7 *s.* 6 *d.* A third
in company (from a place where the meafure is 11
gallons) 9 *s.* A fourth, who bought the worft wheat
he could find in the market, 3 *s.* 6 *d.* A fifth, who
looked for the fineft, 8 *s.* If any one of them happened to make a minute in a book which is found 300
years afterwards, the price minuted is afferted to be
that of the period. We find in thefe old regifters
wheat, *fo much*, oats, *fo much*, an ox, 1 *l.* 16 *s.* Very
pretty regifters truly! How came the gentleman who
made fuch a minute, to know what the price of an ox
was? He might buy an ox, and minute the price of
it—and fo may I now go into *Smithfield* and buy one
wortn thirty guineas, or I may buy one worth 5 *l.*
10 *s.*; but am I in either cafe to fay for the information of pofterity, *fuch is the price of an ox?* It is the
fame with calves, fheep, pigs, and geefe, any of
which may be dear or cheap, without conveying the
leaft information if all the caufes are not explained.
I have mentioned above the price of labour being 8 *d.*
a day in 1581, and the fame in 1681, on the authority of *Shakefpeare* and Sir *W. Petty:* but muft it not
ftrike every one, that neither of thefe writers could
know any thing of the matter? They fpeak of 8 *d.*
being

2 s. 6 d. *per* cwt. dearer than in 1771, and
pork only 2 s. a cwt. cheaper than in 1769.
Let me alfo remark, that for this fact I
have not only publick contracts to quote,
but alfo private prices. In 1682, the common price of beef was 3 d. *per* pound *.

And

---

being the common price of a day's labour. Where
was it the common price, at *London*, or in the mountains of *Yorkſhire?* Was it the price in hay, in har-
veſt, or in winter? Thus Mr. *Combrune* tells us that in
1351, the price of labour was 2 d. ¾ a day, but reapers
had 4 d. ½, threſhers 7 d. and mowing graſs, 1 s. 1 d. ¾
per acre or day, I know not which, but either is an ab-
ſurdity, for no ſuch proportions could poſſibly exiſt in
any age. There is an extreme difficulty in knowing
what the price of labour is at preſent in any place,
for in many, there are three or four prices *per diem* in
the year; ſome with board, others excluſive of it;
beſides which, there are many ſorts of work generally
done by the piece, inſomuch that a man whoſe nominal pay ſhall be 1 s. a day, ſhall on an average of the
year, earn 1 s. 4 d. From all which conſiderations
it is ſurprizing that writers, very acute in other matters, ſhould readily accept any information which
tends to ſhew prices in former times, while they muſt
know it to be ſo difficult to gain thoſe even of the
preſent. And this conſideration ought to make us
value the regiſters on real authority much the more,
ſuch as the *Windſor* prices—the regiſter act—and the
prices of meat laid before parliament by the victualling-office, all of which, though not infallible, are
far more deſerving of notice than the goſſiping tittle
tattle of converſation, in which every man remembers
juſt thoſe prices that ſuit his argument, and quotes
purchaſes that have about as much authority here,
as they have in the Moon.

* *Houghton's Huſbandry*, vol. iv. p. 91.

And in 1768, I fhewed, that on an average
of a great part of the kingdom it was 3 d.
and even at *London* only 3 d. ½ † How
upon the whole is it poffible for any perfon
to affert, that the export of corn—monopoly
of farms—or inclofures, have raifed the
price of beef and pork fo as to exclude thofe
poor from eating them now, who in the
laft century eat them on wages of 8 d. a
day ?

All thefe ideas are contrary to the nature
of things ; we alfo find them contrary to
the few facts that can be gained. As little
reafon is there to think that the proportion
between the prices of bread and meat has
varied in any degree fufficient to be the leaft
oppreffive :—none of thefe circumftances,
nor any others that can be named, are comparable to the rife of hufbandry labour and
poor-rates throughout the kingdom.

But the fame writer, whofe accurate in-
veftigation of other fubjects makes his opinions on this point the more to be lament-
ed, has other arguments againft inclofures,
which muft not be overlooked. He fays,
the increafe of tillage is now at an end,
and adds, " I have lately received an account of a large common field in *Leicefterfhire*, which ufed to produce annually 800
quarters

---

† *Six Months Tour*, vol. iv. p. 278.

quarters of corn, befides maintaining 200 cattle, but which now, in confequence of being inclofed and getting into few hands, produces little or no corn, and maintains no more cattle than before, though the rents are confiderably advanced *." If the Doctor had formed his tables of Obfervations on no better authority than this, they would not have been very famous. *Rents raifed—corn difappeared—cattle not increafed* †*!*—What are we to think of fuch facts? I travelled through *Leicefterfhire* and *Northamptonfhire*, and not I think without attention. I faw great tracts of country inclofed, and laid from arable to grafs; but I faw throughout the graziers fields, fuch herds of fat fheep and oxen, as delighted

---

* *Obfervations on reverfionary Payments*, p. 388.

† " We fhall only obferve, that it feems more the national intereft of *England* to employ its land to the breeding and feeding of cattle, than to the produce of corn; for, as Mr. *Fortrey* has well noted, " the profit of one acre of pafture in the flefh, hide, and tallow of an ox, or in the flefh, wool and tallow of a fheep, or in the carcafe of a horfe, is of fo much greater value abroad, than the like yield of the earth would be in corn ; that the exportation of this nation might be at leaft double to what it is, if rightly difpofed." *Davenant's Works*, vol. ii. p. 229. Sir *Thomas Moore* fays, that a fhepherd and his dog will eat up townfhips; but will not the wool and fkins produced by an acre of pafture, make greater employment than the tillage of fuch an acre can? I queftion it not." *Houghton's Hufbandry*, vol. i. p. 49.

delighted the eye—the generality of thefe
lands are ftocked at the rate of a large ox,
and 2 ½ fheep to every two acres ; and the
foil does fo well in grafs that they fat large
fheep the winter through.—Before the inclofure, thofe lands were managed in the
courfe,

1. Fallow,
2. Wheat,
3. Spring corn.

How in the name of wonder were fat oxen
and fheep kept before ? Upon the fallows ? Or upon ftraw ? That the corn
difappears is moft certain ; but that it is
amply made up in beef and mutton is as
certain.

The fyftem of inclofing arable lands
and laying them down to grafs, leffens the
quantity of corn—yet does the Doctor admit
that corn in the prefent period is cheap :
This fyftem increafes greatly (as *Shakefpeare*
well obferved) beef and mutton ; yet the
Doctor complains of thofe commodities
being dear, and *owing to inclofures*. What
is this but in other words faying, that we
leffen the quantity of beef by increafing
the number of oxen :—and render mutton
extremely dear, by making fheep more plentiful ! But thefe marvellous effects take
place at a time when, according to the
fame writer, depopulation operates like a
peftilence :

peftilence: here, therefore, is a frefh reafon why meat is dear—the mouths that eat it being daily leffened !

The fact is this; in the central counties of the kingdom, particularly *Northamp-tonfhire, Leicefterfhire,* and parts of *Warwic, Huntingdon* and *Buckinghamfhires,* there have been within 30 years large tracts of the open field arable under that vile courfe, 1 fallow, 2 wheat, 3 fpring corn, inclofed and laid down to grafs, being much more fuited to the wetnefs of the foil than corn ; and yields in beef, mutton, hides and wool, beyond comparifon a greater neat produce than when under corn. At that time, the horfes that tilled the land eat up the few grafs inclofures near the farm houfes, and a confiderable part of the fpring corn, whereas at prefent, many farms of from 500 to 1000 acres have not more than two or three nags on them for the farmers, to ride and fee their ftock. Thus the land yields a greater neat produce in food for mankind—the landlord doubles his income, which enables him to employ fo many more manufacturers and artizans —the farmer increafes his income, by means of which he alfo does the fame— the hides and wool are a creation of fo much employment for other manufacturers
—How

—How any one from fuch a fyftem can deduce the melancholy profpects of de-population, famine and diftrefs, is to me amazing.

But further; Dr. *Price* and the other writers who affure us we fhould throw down our hedges, and wafte one third of our farms in a barren fallow by way of making beef and mutton cheap, will confine them-felves to the inclofures which have converted arable to grafs. What fay they to thofe which have changed grafs to arable? They chufe to be filent. I do not comprehend the amufe-ment that is found in conftantly looking at thofe objects which are fuppofed to be gloomy—and in regularly lamenting the evils that furround us, though they flow from caufes which fhower down much fuperior bleffings. When I look around me in this country, I think I every where fee fo great and animating a profpect that the fmall fpecks which may be difcerned in the hemifphere, are loft in the brilliancy that furrounds them. I cannot fpread a curtain over the illumin'd fcene, and leave nothing to view but the mere fhades of fo fplendid a piece *.

What

---

* A *French* writer has a very good obfervation on the diftempered imaginations of our croaking politi-cians: " L'Angleterre fe trouve dans l'état d'un homme qui fe porte bien, qui jouït d'une fante brillante, qui

a la

What will thefe gentlemen fay to the inclofures in *Norfolk, Suffolk, Nottinghamfhire,
Derbyfhire, Lincolnfhire, Yorkfhire,* and all
the northern counties? What fay they to
the fands of *Norfolk, Suffolk* and *Nottinghamfhire,* which yield corn and mutton and
beef from *the force of* INCLOSURE *alone?*
What fay they to the wolds of *York* and
Lincoln, which from barren heaths, at 1*s.*
per acre, are *by* INCLOSURE *alone* rendered
profitable farms? Afk Sir *Cecil Wray* if
without INCLOSURE he could advance his
heaths by fainfoine from 1*s.* to 20*s.* an
acre.—What fay they to the vaft tracts in
the peak of *Derby,* which *by* INCLOSURE
alone are changed from black regions of
ling to fertile fields covered with cattle?
What fay they to the improvements of moors
in the northern counties, where INCLO-
SURES alone have made thofe countries
fmile with culture which before were dreary
as night?—What have thefe gentlemen to
fay to thefe inftances? Cannot they manage
to affure us the profpect is delufive? They
can.

---

a la refpiration libre, mais qui ne connoît pas affez
l'anatomie pour fentir quels font les principes de la
fanté dont il jouït; fi quelqu'un lui dit que fon em-
bonpoint pourroit bien être le principe mafque d'une
maladie, il craint, il s'allarme, il fe trouble, l'in-
quiétude le gagne." *Traité de la Circulation et du
Crédit,* 1771. p. 44.

can. Hear how they are characterized.—
" Inclofures of wafte lands and commons
" *would* be ufeful *if* divided into *fmall al-*
" *lotments,* and *given up* to be occupied at
" moderate rent, by the poor. But *if* befides
" leffening the produce of fine wool *, they
" bear

---

* How far the produce of wool is declined, may
partly be gathered from the rates at which it has been
fold in different times, being now as cheap as it was
centuries ago; while the value of money has funk fo
much, that moft other commodities have greatly rifen
in price.

Years.				*l.*	*s.*	*d.*
1198, Wool,	—	—		0	15	0
1337, —— the beft,	—	—		1	8	0
1339, Wool,	—	—		1	10	3
1353, Wool,	—	—		1	10	4
1390, —(the fale reftricted to certain places)				0	10	11
1425, Wool,	—	—		0	17	5
Average,	—	—		1	1	11
1533, —— the beft cloathing,	—			0	13	4
1581, Wool,	—	—		0	18	5
1622, Wool,	—	—		1	3	8
1641, Wool,	—	—		1	4	0
1647, Romney Marfh,		—		1	17	6
1648, Ditto,	—	—		2	0	0
1651, Ordinary,	—	—		1	8	0
Civil War,	—	—		1	19	8
1656, Wool,	—	—		2	1	3
Average, from the beginning of the civil War to the Reftoration,				1	15	0

Price per Tod in prefent Money.

" bear hard on the poor, by depriving them
" of a part of their fubfiftance, and *only*
" go

			l.	s.	d.
1660, Wool,	—	—	1	19	8
1670,	—	—	1	8	0
1677,	—	—	0	14	0
1694,	—	—	1	8	0
1698,	—	—	1	1	0
Average, from the Reftoration to the end of the Century,			1	6	1
1706, Wool,	—	—	0	17	6
1707,	—	—	0	16	6
1712,	—	—	0	15	0
1713,	—	—	0	18	0
1717,	—	—	1	5	0
1737,	—	—	0	11	0
1739,	—	—	0	13	0
1742,	—	—	0	14	0
1743,	—	—	1	0	2
Average,	—	—	0	16	8

Smith's *Memoirs of Wool*, Vol. ii. p. 507. The
writer juftly obferves, that when wheat was 8 *d.* a
bufhel, the goofe 4 *d.* and the hen 1 *d.* wool was a
mark a tod, and that the fall in price was a great
burthen upon the landed intereft. And manufacturers
clamoured fo much about the year 1737, upon account
of the decay of our woollen trade, that much was
written on it, and parliament bufied with their complaints; they brought the low price of wool as a
proof of this; but all was falfe, for at that very time
the export of woollen goods amounted to 4,158,643 *l.*
17 *s.* 0 *d.* which was twice what it was in 1698.
Thus the author of the *Britifh Woollen Manufacturers*
to

" go towards increasing farms already too
" large, the advantages attending them
" may

---

to the *Members of Parliament*, 1737 : " Your honours
are fully apprized, even by your tenants, that the
effects of a declining trade are now generally felt :
and no general cause can be ascribed but the great
decay of our woollen exportation trade." The author
of the *Observations on British Wool*, 1738, says,
" Our trade is considerably decreased ; and even the
landholder finds the inconvenience thereof by the
present low price of wool." And the author of the
Essay on the Causes of the Decline of foreign Trade,
1739, (from whose fallacious accounts the *French*
writers have borrowed so much) says, " That the foreign
trade of *Britain* declines, will appear by the following
symptoms, viz. *the low price of wool*. I appeal, says
he, to the experience of every honest man conversant
in trade, whether it does not decline, year after year,
especially *our woollen trade*." And Mr. *Webber* :—
" The present low price of wool shews the great
decay of our trade. Hence it is evident, that we
have not one THIRD PART of the quantity of goods
carried to *foreign markets* which we formerly had."
And Mr. *Lowndes* intitles his Scheme, printed 1745,
by order of the house of commons, " *A Scheme—*
in order to RE-ESTABLISH the woollen manufacture
of *England*."

I have inserted these long accounts to shew the
disposition that is so common of seeing imaginary
evils, and magnifying them as much as possible :—these
writers, and some others, alarmed the nation at the
decline of what was then FLOURISHING ; and it is the
same with our present complainants of luxury and
depopulation.—From the above table, Dr. *Price* may
collect how much reason there is for thinking the
quantity of our fine wool lessened ; for after 1743, the
price

" may not much exceed the difadvan-
" tages *." Hence therefore we find all
thefe improvements very equivocal—Before
it is allowed that converting ling to corn is
beneficial, it muft previoufly be afked if the

im-

---

price continued for many years low; for fome years
laft paft it is rifen to about 20 s. or a guinea; but that
price is nothing (the value of money confidered)
to what it was from the Reftoration to 1699, viz.
1 l. 6 s. 1 d. equal now to double that fum,

* *Obfervations on Reverfionary Payments*, p. 390. While
our own writers, in the ufual manner of depreciating
every thing in their own country and their own age,
would fain make out the mifery of this kingdom, foreigners are ftruck with a very different idea. S'il exifte
une nation qui, fans être tres nombreufe; poffede une
grande quantité de terres bien cultivées; fi cette nation
augmente journellement fon agriculture et fon commerce, fans que fa population augmente en pareille
proportion; en fin, fi elle fait naître beaucoup plus
de fubfiftances fans nourrir plus d'habitans, je dis;
Il faut que cette nation confomme fpécifiquement plus
que les autres; il faut que le tarif de la vie humaine
y foit plus haut. Et c'eft là l'INDICE LE PLUS CER-
TAIN DE LA FELICITE DES HOMMES. Tel eft le
cas où fe trouve l'Angleterre. *Felicité Publique*,
tom. ii. p. 141. And again, fpeaking of our great
national debt, the great evil of which he thinks has
been not expending the money in the improvement of
the waftes of *Scotland* and *Ireland*; he fays, " J'avoue
que je trouverois difficilement d'autres objets que la
guerre ait fait négliger; car *cette heureufe contrée offre
par tout* L'IMAGE DE LA PROSPERITE. Population,
agriculture, manufactures, grands chemins, établiffe-
mens magnifiques, rien ne paroît y manquer, et c'eft
un argument terrible entre les mains des fceptiques en
politique." *Ib.* tom. ii. p. 190.

improvement is wrought by that ghoftly object of dread and terror—a great farmer: before it is acknowledged right to make that fand which would not feed rabbits, produce beef and mutton, we muft know whether the poor were deprived of a part of their fubfiftence :—before you will fubmit to change the heaths of *Lincoln* to fertile fields of fainfoine, you muft demand, *Were the allotments fmall?* I muft own, it is with aftonifhment that I thus fee fuperior minds ftooping to prejudices fo unworthy of their abilities.

How, in the name of common fenfe, were fuch improvements to be wrought by little or even moderate farmers! Can fuch inclofe waftes at a vaft expence—cover them with an hundred loads an acre of marle—or fix or eight hundred bufhels of lime—keep fufficient flocks of fheep for folding—and conduct thofe (for the lower claffes) mighty operations effential to new improvements? No, It is to GREAT FARMERS you owe thefe. Without GREAT FARMS you never would have feen thefe improvements—much I fuppofe to the fatif-faction of thofe who declare themfelves fo indifcriminately their enemies *.

---

* I muft beg leave to tranfcribe from Mr. *Hume*, whofe political ideas have an acumen that diftinguifhes him in an uncommon manner, a paffage or two which highly

SECT. IX.

CONSUMPTION OF MEAT.

THESE points are the great foundation of *Britain*'s agriculture; but there is another circumſtance which though not of equal

highly deſerve attention, and are indeed the beſt reply to moſt of the advice given by Dr. *Price* on great farms, incloſures, luxury and depopulation.

Encouragement by Exportation.

" It was prohibited to export horſes; as if that exportation did not encourage the breed, and render them more plentiful in the kingdom." *Hiſt. of Eng.* Vol. iii. p. 401.

Freedom of Prices.

" Prices were affixed to woollen cloth *, to caps, and hats † : and the wages of labourers were regulated by law ‡. It is evident, that theſe matters ought always to be left free, and be entruſted to the common courſe of buſineſs and commerce." *Ib.* p. 402.

Riſe of Prices.

" Labour and commodities have certainly riſen ſince the diſcovery of the *Weſt-Indies*; but not ſo much in every particular as is generally imagined. The greater induſtry of the preſent times, has en-creaſed the number of tradeſmen and labourers, ſo as to keep wages nearer a par than could be expected from the great increaſe of gold and ſilver. And the additional art employed in the finer manufactures, has even made ſome of theſe commodities fall below their former value. Not to mention that merchants and dealers being contented with leſs profit than formerly, affords

* 4 H. 7. c. 8. † *Ib.* c. 9. ‡ 11 H. 7. c. 22.

equal confequence, fhould not be forgotten — It is the cuftom of eating fuch
quantities

---

afford the goods cheaper to their cuftomers." *Ib.*
p. 402.—And again—" There feems to have been
two periods in which prices rofe remarkably in *England*, namely, that in Queen *Elizabeth's* reign, when
they are computed to have doubled, and that in the
prefent age. Between the two, there feems to have
been a ftagnation. It would appear, that induftry
during that intermediate period encreafed as faft as
gold and filver, and kept commodities nearly on a par
with money." *Ib.* Vol. v. p. 484.—This is an excellent idea, and accounts in one word for the effect
which other writers attribute to engroffing farms, enclofures, and all the nonfenfe we meet with in fo many
volumes.

Enclofures, Farms, and Population.
" The abfurd limitations of manufactures proceeded
from a defire of promoting hufbandry, which however
is never more effectually encouraged than by the
encreafe of manufactures. For a like reafon, the law
enacted againft inclofures, and for the keeping up of
farm-houfes, fcarcely deferves the high praifes beftowed
on it by Lord *Bacon.* If hufbandmen underftand
agriculture, and have a ready vent for their commodities, *we need not dread a diminution of the people*
employed in the country. All methods of fupporting
populoufnefs, except by the interefts of the proprietors,
are violent and ineffectual. During a century and
half after this period, there was a frequent renewal of
laws and edicts againft depopulation ; whence we may
infer, that none of them were ever executed. The
natural courfe of improvement at laft provided a
remedy." *Ib.* Vol. iii. p. 404.

quantities of meat in this country, and,
on comparison with others, so little bread.
—It is true, a very able writer draws from
this a direct contrary conclusion from what
I shall; and as his authority is too good in
general not to demand a proper deference,
I shall offer what I have to observe on this
subject only as doubts that I have conceived.

Whatever a people principally consumes
for their subsistence, must be the great object of the husbandman in his culture:
thus in *France*, where bread, I apprehend,
forms 19 parts in 20 of their food, corn,
and especially wheat, is the only great
object of cultivation; vines answering to
our barley. In *England*, on the contrary,
the quantity of meat, butter and cheese,
consumed by all ranks of the people, is
immense—to a much greater value, I should
suppose, than that of wheat; hence cattle
to our farmers is an object as important as corn: Thus the husbandmen in
France keep scarcely any cattle, addict-
ing themselves almost entirely to corn
—in *England* vast quantities of cattle are
kept. This circumstance I should apprehend would, if every thing else was equal,
give a prodigious general superiority to the
English agriculture. Let us consider on
what principles the farmers of the two
countries

countries muſt neceſſarily manage their
lands. In *England,* they keep ſuch part
of their farms in meadow and paſture as
are by the nature of the ſoil ſo adapted;
they throw their arable land into ſuch
courſes of crops, that ſeveral are introduced which are either ſummer or winter
food for cattle : thus the beſt cultivated
parts of the kingdom adopt the following
courſe :

     1. Turneps.
     2. Barley or oats.
     3. Clover.
     4. Wheat.

In which courſe, there is as much food for
cattle raiſed, as corn ; and as a large part
of the ſecond year's produce, which is
barley and oats, alſo goes to the cattle,
above half the period is applied to their
ſupport, and wheat occupies only a fourth.
After the wheat many farmers add,

     5. Peaſe or beans.

Which is another year given for cattle.
This courſe is that of very good huſbandry ;
but where the culture is not ſo good, more
crops are taken, but the addition generally
oats. Now upon this ſyſtem, a conſiderable part of the whole farm or meadow,
and a large portion of the arable are employed for cattle—the quantity of dung
raiſed is very great, which being ſpread,

              as

as it ufually is on the arable fields, infures good crops—fo much better than if fuch ftocks of cattle were not kept, that I queſtion if three acres are not quite as productive as five would be. Nay, I have in this point no doubt but the barley and wheat in a farm thrown into the courfe abovementioned, with a due proportion befides of meadow, yield a greater value than the corn in general would if one year was fallow, and the three following ones were wheat and barley—of fuch great confequence is this fyſtem of manuring.

Now let us turn to the *Frenchmen* ; their two moſt general courfes are,

        1. Fallow,
        2. Wheat.

And,

        1. Fallow,
        2. Wheat,
        3. Barley or oats.

Much the greateſt part of the farm arable —the meadow and paſture being very trivial, except in fpots that cannot be otherwife applied, and near great towns. Thus very little cattle can be kept, except for tillage; in very many farms no other. Here we find manuring in any degree is cut off at once, confequently the crops muſt be poor; befides this, one half or one third of the land is fallow, at a mere barren expence :

expence : A fyftem which we know from the experience of our open fields is miferable, and not to be compared for profit to thofe in which crops for cattle are made the preparation for corn.

Wheat being in *France* the great objeft, all the expence is applied to that : A year's fallow is given, and what. little dung they raife is all fpread on it; this produces a middling, perhaps a good crop; an effeft we experience in our own open fields, and when the farmer reaps his wheat he often finds himfelf out of pocket, and has to depend for his profit on a poor crop of fpring corn. Thus the little demand for meat, butter and cheefe, neceffitates him to apply all his land to corn—the confequences of which are, he purfues a bad courfe of crops—he has no dung—his produfts are fmall—his profit comparatively nothing.

It muft furely be evident to every one, that there is a great advantage to the *Englifh* farmer from corn and cattle being in equal demand ; fince he is thereby enabled to apply all his lands to thofe produftions only to which they are beft adapted—and at the fame time the one is conftantly a means of increafing the produft of the other.

Nor is this advantage by any means confined to the hufbandman :—the ftate is

intimately

intimately concerned.   A much greater
value is drawn from the earth; of this we
have proof in the open lands in *England*.
A crop of wheat in the courfe, 1. turnips,
2. barley, 3. clover, 4. wheat, on an inclofed farm, with a part meadow, yields
acre for acre, from one quarter to two more
than in the courfe, 1. fallow, 2. wheat,
3. barley, on an open field farm: And
barley in the former fucceeding turnips,
yields on an average, nearly, if not quite
double what it does in the latter fucceeding
wheat: But fuppofing the one 2½ quarters, and the other 4, it is giving as little
fuperiority as can be admitted.   A flight
calculation will fhew this point clearly.

Open field.

	£.	s.	d.
Wheat after fallow, 2½ quarters an acre, at 50s. -	6	5	0
Barley after wheat, 2½ quarters, at 30s. - - -	3	15	0
In three years, - - -	10	0	0
Per acre *per ann.* - - -	3	6	8

Inclosure.

	£.	s.	d.
Turnips, – – – –	1	15	0
Barley, 4 quarters, at 30 s. –	6	0	0
Clover, – – – –	4	0	0
Wheat, 3 quarters, at 50 s. –	7	10	0
In four years, – –	19	5	0
Per acre *per ann.* – –	4	16	3
	3	6	8
Superiority *per* acre *per ann.*	1	9	7

This every practical farmer will allow
me is as little superiority as can be admitted;—yet are the national confequences
prodigious; for there is a much greater
deduction from the open field produce
for expences, than from the product
of the inclofure, where a proper part of
the farm is grafs. Thus more in proportion
is the farmer's profit, confequently he is
wealthier, and more able to work improvements—and at the fame time to pay his
landlord a greater rent: points of vaft importance to the national intereft. But if
the fuperiority of one courfe to the other
was only 1 *l.* 9 *s. per* acre on all the arable
land,

land, it would prove of a magnitude extremely deferving attention.

The author abovementioned therefore
thinking we fhould be more populous if we
lived as much on bread as the *French*, is an
idea that feems doubtful : It is a ftrange pofition at beft, that bad hufbandry fhould add
to our population—that lofing 1 *l.* 9 *s.* 7 *d.*
an acre on our arable lands fhould increafe
the people.   This is fairly ftating the cafe,
for if the demand for meat is changed to an
increafed one for wheat, the farmers muft
either change their good courfe to the bad
one of the *French*, or the wheat muft be
imported ; as the latter can in no country
be depended on, the former muft inevitably be the cafe : and the moment the fale
of meat ftops, thofe crops which beft pre-
pare for corn muft difappear, when there
would be no choice left the farmer but the
old hufbandry of fallow and wheat—unlefs
new refinements were introduced, which
we cannot fpeak of here with propriety.

But this comparifon of population depends on another enquiry : Which yields
moft food for man, 1. fallow, 2. wheat,
3. barley, or 1. turnips, 2. barley, 3. clover, 4. wheat ? The abovementioned author
I apprehend, fuppofes the country of bread
eaters the moft populous, becaufe a given
tract of land applied to yielding bread, will
feed

feed more than if applied to bread and meat : If this is *not* his reafon, I cannot conjecture what *is*. But I fhould fuppofe that the latter courfe yields far more food than the former.

The part of a farm when properly arranged, that is under grafs, is the part more applicable to grafs than corn—fo that when all is converted to corn, the produce of the whole muft not be fuppofed upon a par with the part which is beft for corn. And furely an acre of grafs in three years will yield beef and mutton to fupport a man, as long as one acre of wheat ; for the fecond crop in corn countries is oats for the team. But fuch proportions can only be taken in the value of the crops in money : in the comparifon I gave of the two courfes above, the fuperiority of 1 *l.* 9 *s.* 7 *d.* *per* acre, is what fhould decide it, with this additional point relative to food, that it is gained by a courfe which gives three crops in four years as food for man ; *viz.* the wheat, and the turnips and clover fed by cattle, to fay nothing of the barley ; whereas in the other courfe, only one in three is to be reckoned, *viz.* the wheat. This fuperiority will more than anfwer the inferiority (fuppofing it fuch) of a part of the farm being meadow and pafture ; but it is not clear that good pafture does not

yield

yield as much food for man as corn land without the affiftance of grafs.

Unite both objects as they ought to be, fo as to have the farms from one third to half of meadow and pafture; and the other two thirds or half thrown into a proper courfe for the winter fupport of the cattle, and fuch a farm will, I apprehend, be found to feed more men than if it is all ploughed up, and as much wheat raifed as is poffible upon the *French* fyftem.

Perhaps it may be faid, that there is not fuch a connection between the cuftom of the people in their food, and the courfes of the farmers, as I have ftated, fince what is not in demand at home might be fold abroad. But this reafoning I do not think is juft; if a furplus of corn is raifed, it may, generally fpeaking, be exported—though not always: But as to meat, butter and cheefe, there is no dependance of that fort, the foreign demand is too various and uncertain: Nothing can uniformly encourage the farmer to keep fufficient ftocks, but a great home confumption.

S E C T. X.

INFERIOR OBJECTS, AND DEFICIENCES
IN BRITISH HUSBANDRY.

I BEFORE remarked that it is utterly
vain to recommend minute improvements in the practice of agriculture to any
people who feel the want of thofe effential
and capital articles of encouragement, with
which I began this differtation : but at the
fame time it is neceffary to obferve, that
when a country like *England* is happy
enough to enjoy fuch encouragement, then
it is wife and prudent to give much attention to inferior objects, fuch as the culture
of wafte lands, the introduction of new
branches of culture, the improvement of
old ones, alterations in methods, and abundance of other articles to which it is very
neceffary to attend, if we would have our
agriculture generally good. It is therefore upon very wife and liberal principles
that the fociety eftablifhed at *London* for
the encouragement of arts, manufactures,
and commerce, offers premiums for fuch
improvements, and gives bounties to fuch
farmers and mechanics as excel or invent
any thing valuable.

It

It is very furprizing to think of the general advantages enjoyed by this nation, and yet to fee what large tracts (much the greateft part of the kingdom) are under a culture infinitely inferior to that of other parts. After viewing the hufbandry of *Norfolk*, *Suffolk*, *Effex*, and *Kent*, to obferve the miferable management of fo many other counties, muft convince every fpectator of the importance of fpreading the knowledge of what is good :—of letting the unenlightened parts of the kingdom know what is done elfewhere—and of explaining to them the principles and practice which give wealth to one fet of farmers, mediocrity of fortune to others. This idea urged me to undertake the tours I made through a part of the kingdom, the regifters of which are before the public.

The improvements which are much wanting in fo many parts of *England*, are particularly the fpreading the knowledge of good courfes of crops, fo as utterly to banifh fallows; a practice purfued very generally in the counties I have named above; and which is effected by the introduction of turnips, beans, peafe, tares, clover, &c. as preparations for white corn—covered drains—manuring with marle, chalk, and clay—watering meadows—the culture of carrots, cabbages, potatoes, fainfoine, and

lucerne

lucerne—performing works of tillage with
no more cattle than neceſſary—the uſe of
oxen in harneſs—an almoſt general reform
in implements—the introduction of the
drill huſbandry for beans—the culture of
madder, woad, liquorice, hemp and flax,
on ſuch lands as are ſuitable—with ſeveral
other points too tedious to mention.

Every one of theſe articles, excepting
cabbages and lucerne, are already *commonly*
practiſed by tenants in ſome part or other
of the kingdom; and all of them in the
lands of gentlemen, with great ſucceſs : the
ſpreading the knowledge of ſuch uſeful
practices, is therefore of the higheſt conſequence to the general welfare of Britiſh
agriculture.

But above theſe and all other circumſtances is to be named, the bringing into
culture our waſte lands; which form ſo
large a proportion of the territory, that I
much queſtion if we have not eight or ten
millions of acres waſte in *England,* and a
great deal more in *Scotland.* The want of
public ſpirit in the generality of their proprietors is truly amazing—and no leſs is it ſurprizing that they ſhould be equally inattentive to the advantages of themſelves and
families. Where would be the mighty
exertion in one of our great owners of
moors to ſay to a ſpirited practical man,

You

*You have the knowledge neceſſary for making
a trial of my moors, but not the money: I
have the money, but not the knowledge: fix
upon what ſpot you pleaſe in my eſtate, and I
will ſupply you with a thouſand pounds a year
for ten years to come at common intereſt, and
all the ſecurity I aſk is being convinced that
the money is ſpent upon the land?* Where
would be the hazard in ſuch a caſe? for
ſuch a perſon would have the beſt ſecurity
for his money of all others, his own eſtate;
and he would certainly have double intereſt;
the common, and the advantage of all the
improvements at the end of the term of
years agreed for.

That there are many active practical perſons, no viſionary theoriſts, who would
ſettle the moors upon ſuch conditions, I
have no doubt; and that the great moor-
poſſeſſors in general, proceeding on ſuch
principles, would in no long term cover
them with cultivation, I have as little doubt:
how much this would add to the nation's
wealth I need not ſay. Such undertakings
increaſe the claſſes of the people, that form
real POPULATION.

Nor is it only to private landlords that
theſe obſervations are applicable; it appears to me ſurprizing, that the legiſlature
ſhould never have thought it worth their
pains to attempt ſomething in favour of
cultivation

cultivation on thofe immenfe waftes: A private expenditure of between twenty and thirty thoufand pounds would not make any great figure in the national expences, yet might it be fo managed as to have confiderable effects. I enlarged pretty much on this idea in a pamphlet I publifhed about a year ago *; I explained the practicability and the advantages of fuch an undertaking: but among the infinite fums expended by our government, fuch works poffefs a moft contemptible fhare †.

I have endeavoured to fhew, that as this kingdom enjoys moft of the great fupports of a flourifhing agriculture, that therefore it is right to attend to thefe fmaller circumftances, and the *London* Society judicious in fo doing; but at the fame time I muft remark that they carry their attention too far to the minutiæ of management, and too little to the more important objects: they offer more premiums about drilling and horfe-hoeing, than for the improvement of wafte lands: and as their gold medal is the higheft premium that can be gained, there being but two, the gold and filver one; this *higheft* declaration of merit is often given

---

* *Obfervations on the prefent State of the Wafte Lands of Great-Britain,* 8vo. 1772.

† See Appendix, **No. IV.**

given to very inferior objects, for want of
a better scale of reward. Hence comes
their practice, which totally destroys the
great ideal value of the medal, of offering
*twenty pounds, or the gold medal.—Thirty
pounds, or the gold medal.* Thus the importance of the premium is explained by
the sum given if the medal should be rejected, or if the claimant should be a member *. Hence arises a necessity of classing
objects in the same light, which are of infinitely different merit; and as gentlemen
are more desirous of honorary premiums
than pecuniary ones, there ought to be
some higher reward devised than the gold
medal, which having been given to inferior
objects, is no longer a reward for capital
ones.

Suppose a gentleman has improved five
hundred, or even one hundred acres of moor;
and did it in various methods, in order to
discover the most effectual—he has built a
house, barns, stables, and all the buildings
requisite for a farm; inclosed, planted,
manured, and reduced a desart tract to be
a fertile farm; such a gentleman, that his
experience may be useful to others, sends
an account of his operations to the society:
What do they decree?—They give him
their

* Members can receive only the honorary premium.

their gold medal : that is, they rank his merit in the fame clafs as a man who fats hogs, plants colefeed, drills turnips, and horfe-hoes wheat. Can this be right ? If a fociety inftituted for rewarding merit, confounds all ideas of merit, furely the end of their inftitution is wretchedly anfwered.

They fhould offer an ornamental model of a plough in gold or filver, fo curioufly wrought, as to be an object of beauty and *fhew* ; and on the mould-board the infcription. A man would place fuch a thing in a glafs cafe, and fet it where it might be feen : but a medal, unlefs a hole is drilled through it, and you wear it pendant from a button hole, is feen by no one—a man muft be put to the blufh to bring out his medal and fhew it. A filver or gold cup with the infcription, which paffing round the table, would promote converfation on hufbandry, and raife emulation in every one prefent to gain the like, would alfo be a good expedient. In a word, vanity is very prevalent in this age, and I fee no reafon why we fhould not render the paffions of mankind fubfervient to the good of agriculture.

Perhaps the fpirited endeavours of this excellent fociety in the encouragement of hufbandry, may have been partly the reason why his present Majesty, who has so munificently protected the fine arts and literature, should not have given more attention to the means of advancing the agriculture of his kingdoms, as I am informed that he has founded several establishments with this view in his electoral dominions. The small progress however, which has been made by that society in the great article, the culture of waste lands, shews that a more effective encouragement is wanting. But as I have ventured to make this observation, I shall not refuse myself the pleasure of remarking with how much judgment even the amusements of the young princes are made conducive to just ideas of the importance of husbandry. Nor will the lover of that art fail to congratulate himself on the hands in which the future hope of *Britain* is placed, when I relate an anecdote, which to some may perhaps seem trifling, but appears to me pregnant with excellent consequences.

A spot of ground in the garden at *Kew* was dug by their royal highnesses the prince of *Wales* and bishop of *Osnabrug*; they sowed it with wheat; they attended the growth of their little crop, weeded, reaped, and harvested it. They threshed out the corn, and separated it from the chaff. And at this period of their labour, were taught to reflect

reflect from their own experience, on the various labour and attention of the farmer. Nor did this admirable leſſon ſtop here. The princes not only raiſed the crop; they alſo ground it; and having parted the bran from the meal, attended to the whole pro-ceſs of making it into bread. This bread it may be imagined was eaten with no ſlight reliſh: the King and Queen partook of the philoſophical repaſt, and beheld with pleaſure the very amuſements of their chil-dren rendered the ſource of uſeful know-ledge.—An inſtance, and no trifling one, that a great nobleman from having attended to agriculture, is ſo much the better quali-fied to ſuperintend the education of a prince —and that lord *Holderneſſe* has attended to agriculture both as a philoſopher and a man of practice, I have on another occaſion given the world ſufficient proof *.

This

---

* The inſtance I have now inſerted juſtifies me as a farmer, for ſaying that this country has reaſon to be happy at the princes' education being committed to this nobleman; ſince it is by ſuch a conduct that they will beſt become acquainted with the importance of huſbandry. Not that I would have it ſuppoſed I confine the merit of the governor to points of this ſort: thoſe who know him beſt, would beſt be able to refute ſuch an idea. Nor let his lordſhip's re-commendation of Mr. *Smelt* for an aſſiſtant in his im-portant office, be forgotten—a man whoſe general knowledge

This pleafing idea, I hope, will be a prelude to a farm, in fome of the royal gardens, parks, or chafes, where our amiable young princes may have a farther opportunity of learning the theory and practice of agriculture :—where they might fee a courfe of rational experiments, and gain not a mere mechanical idea of what that ufeful clafs of the people the farmers perform, but a political acquaintance with the connection between the expenditure and the products of hufbandry :—they would learn the neceffity of the farmer being fecure in the poffeffion of that harveft his induftry prepared ;—the dependance of all the orders of the ftate on the foil—the population that flows from a good culture—in a word, they would fee that well tilled fields were the fource of armies, of navies, of conquefts, of fplendid courts, and magnificent expences. They might fet their hands to the plough, and remember that its good progrefs was the teft of a nation's happinefs and a monarch's glory ; and from hence, never forget the maxim of the wife fovereign, THE KING'S FAVOUR in matters of

knowledge and amiable manners, rendered him the delight of an extenfive neighbourhood ; a character formed rather to give luftre than to receive it from a court.—And let me alfo add with pleafure, an excellent farmer.

of agriculture, IS AS DEW UPON THE GRASS.

An experiment from whence such instruction might flow, is surely worth the trial.

*   *   *   *

Thus far I have proceeded in endeavouring to point out the mistakes that may easily be made by adopting in one country the policy of another. Before I conclude, I shall suppose that things will continue much in the same train in most countries ; and in case it should be so, I shall recommend an experiment that might very easily be tried by the legislature of any country ; —I mean the

SYSTEM OF ENGLAND

in matters of husbandry and taxation. Suppose in *France, Spain,* or parts of *Germany,* individuals were backward to engage in it; it might easily be executed in the sovereign's demesne. What I mean is, to ease, in a certain number of parishes, the farmers from all sorts of taxes which are laid any ways in proportion to their wealth, industry or products ; in lieu of them, raise the same sum of money partly by a permanent land-tax, exactly in the manner of that of *England,* not subject

ject to variations, to the amount of about
2 *s*. 6 *d*. in the pound rent; and this,
as in *England*, fhould be charged by the
tenants to the account of the landlords.
Thus the farmers would be exempted from
all taxes except tythe, and thofe general
ones on confumption, which equally affect
every clafs. Let all the diftrict be inclofed
in fields proportioned to the fize of the
farms. Let leafes of 21 years be given to
every farmer at a rent per acre equal, (all
national circumftances, rates and prices
confidered) to what fimilar land lets for in
the beft cultivated parts of *England*. Exempt them abfolutely from all perfonal
fervice; and as to the price of their corn,
in order to anfwer the effect of the corn-
laws of *England*, eftablifh near this diftrict
a magazine where their corn may always
be carried when they chufe to fell at or
under a given price, but from thence to be
carried immediately to the neareft port,
and fent where the confumption of it cannot poffibly affect the price of the diftrict
in queftion. After thefe regulations, let
the farmers purfue their hufbandry in quiet,
in whatever manner they think proper.

In the next place, form out of this ex-
perimental diftrict a farm of 1000 acres, to
be cultivated entirely in the *Englifh* manner,
under the direction of a perfon perfectly
ac-

acquainted with the beft hufbandry of *Britain*. Let the arable part of it, which fhould not be lefs than 800 acres, be divided into four parts, of each 200 acres : one-fourth to be conftantly under turnips, cabbages, carrots, and potatoes; another under fpring corn; another under clover; and the laft under wheat : by means of thefe articles being thus arranged, and perfectly well cultivated, the fuperiority of this fyftem to that of a fallow would foon appear. The ftock of cattle on this farm fhould be fufficient for the confumption of 200 acres of grafs, fainfoine or lucerne (according to the foil) and 200 of winter food; 200 of clover; and 400 of ftraw.

Befides thefe circumftances, the teams of horfes and oxen (the latter the moft numerous) fhould be large and able beafts, a pair of either fufficient to plough an *Englifh* acre in a day. All the harnefs and implements of every kind to be *Englifh*, and of the beft fort. The buildings compofing the farm-yard to be complete, and in every refpect fufficient for conducting the farm in winter on the *Englifh* fyftem, with a view to raifing manure. If fuch a plan was executed completely, the expence of ftocking and fupporting fuch a farm would be 7*l.* an acre, or 7000*l.* for 1000 acres.

Now

Now I conceive that the regulations here propofed, would yield two very important pieces of intelligence: firft, they would fhew the fuperiority of the *Englifh* mode of taxation over that of *France*; and this in refpect, not only to the welfare of the farmer, but alfo to the wealth of the landlord, who fhould calculate the difference of his neat receipts at two different periods, one under the old management, and the other under the new. Secondly, it would fhew what improvements practifed in *England*, are wanting in the country where the experiment was tried; this would evidently appear by comparing the management of the farmers after being eafed in taxes, &c. with that of the *Englifh* farm on the fame foil, and under the fame circumftances: and I fhould add, that the eftablifhment and regular conduct of fuch a farm would be a conftant fource of information to every perfon in the country who was defirous of improving the practice of hufbandry. Among other very fpirited plans carrying into execution for the benefit of agriculture in his majefty's *German* dominions, I fhould prefume fomething of this fort might prove equally beneficial with any other fcheme hitherto devifed.

C H A P. II.

REMOVAL OF OBSTACLES.

HAVING explained the principal causes of the agriculture of this nation being so flourishing, I shall pursue my design by remarking, that other countries that would enjoy the same advantages, should follow the same maxims : it is a little surprizing in this case, that other nations should shew the greatest eagerness to advance their husbandry, manifesting clear ideas of its importance, and yet in most of their plans beginning at the wrong end : if the principles are well understood which prove favourable to agriculture in one country, what should prevent others from adopting those principles as far as climate, government and manners will allow ; instead of which we see volumes written on modes of culture, where political principles should alone be attended to.

We must not, however, suppose that in every country where plans are laid for the improvement of agriculture, that such an admirable constitution as that of *Britain* must first be established, since in disquisitions of this nature, little utility can result

fult if we are not practical. Thus, under the article government, if its nature is unfavourable to induftry, the bufinefs of the ftatefman is to molify its feverity; and as the principles of it are mifchievous, to foften them by a gentle and equitable adminiftration.

In the articles above examined, on which principally depends the profperity of *Engliſh* agriculture, other countries that would wifh to imitate the example, fhould firft remove fuch circumftances as militate moft againft them. That this is the right way of proceeding, can hardly be doubted; to think of making improvements in the modes of culture—in manuring, fencing, tillage, horfe-hoeing, or introducing new vegetables, while the farmers are oppreffed by taxes, flavery, perfonal fervice, or a want of leafes; or where bad corn-laws, defeat every purpofe for which they were intended; or where a want of general wealth leaves him a poor market, is to labour againft the ftream: fuch a conduct, inftead of giving any radical cure, can only make a fhew of little temporary local palliatives; of no confequence in themfelves, and difgraceful to the ftatefman who ufes them. But let us proceed to inftances of great obftacles, which ought firft to be eradicated.

SECT. I.

TAILLE.

IN the article taxation, I shall mention the *French* land-tax, the *taille*, which is laid on the renters and occupiers of all lands, who are not called noble, that is, what we call the gentry are exempted: there is nothing hurtful in such an idea, as the exemption is very fair, the tax being laid on in lieu of the personal military services which were peculiar to the lower classes: the great evil lies in the method of laying it.

The ministry having determined the sum to be raised by the taille, decides the proportion to be paid by every district. This is sent to the intendant, who makes the distribution upon all the parishes in his division, and the sum is raised by collectors in each parish, who impose it on individuals by rules sent them by the intendant. The expression of a well-informed writer is, that these rules of taxing are on—" every species of income, every emolument of industry, even every animal in the possession of those who are subject to this tax. This proportion is calculated to carry the most scrupulous attention to every man's

gain

gain upon all effects belonging to him, and upon every poſſibility of making profit by induſtry *." If the firſt aſſeſſment does not bring in the total demanded, ſecond and even third aſſeſſments are made upon the rules of the firſt, till the total ſum comes in. Here, therefore, we find the taille is in fact a tythe only the full value of the proportion taken inſtead of the product itſelf, and conſequently has all the miſchievous effects of that moſt pernicious tax. A farmer is taxed in proportion to his induſtry and improvements, let the tax be ever ſo juſtly laid on: but the aggravating circumſtance is, that a ſhew of improvement is taken as a ſign of wealth, and a burthen laid in proportion not perhaps to the fact, but the idea of the collector— herein it is worſe than a tythe. Now how is it poſſible that a man can carry on any ſpirited huſbandry if his tax is augmented proportionably for every improvement—for every good crop he gains— for every increaſe of his cattle—for a good dunghill—better implements of huſbandry than common—in a word, to be burthened in every inſtance in proportion to his merit. Would it not be very ridiculous to tell one of theſe farmers that he ſhould ſow beans

in

* *Stewart's Political Oeconomy*, Vol. ii, p. 566.

in drills, that he fhould hoe turneps, cut
drains, and manure fo and fo—would he
not in reply fay, *for whom am I to do this?*
Not for myself.

At the fame time that the principles of
this tax are fo contrary to the intereft of
agriculture, the height to which it is carried exceeds any thing we know in *England:*
We learn from *Duprè de St. Maur* * that
in *Sologne*, the occupier of a little farm, let
for 20*l.* 11*s.* 3*d.* pays 9*l.* 10*s.* 9*d.* taille,
befides 2*l.* 4*s.* 7*d.* capitation. In another
farm, let for 11*l.* 7*s.* 6*d.* the farmer pays
5*l.* 5*s.* 0*d.* and 1*l.* 12*s.* 6*d.* capitation.

It is amazing that a people fo clear-
fighted in various inftances fhould remain
fo blind in this!—Surely it would be eafy
to change fomewhat the nature of this tax
by levying it as a proportion of the rent of a
farm: in the firft place to direct, that all
farms fhould be held by leafe, though only
for a year; fecondly, that all leafes fhould
be regiftered; thirdly, to affefs the tax at
fo much in the pound on the rent; and if
it fell fhort, to have frefh affeffments to
make up the deficiencies, as the intendants
now make frefh diftributions on that account; and as in *England* the parifh-officers
make

* *Effai des Monnoies,* p. 26.

make frefh rates to levy the deficiencies of
former ones. Let all exempted from the
taille be exempted from this tax : the only
objeȼt is to make the affeffment depend
on a certain criterion, which is rent ; and
not to be increafed becaufe of improvements. If a man hires a farm at the rent
of 1000 livres, let this taille be levied in
proportion to that rent without the intendant's having any thing to do with his
crops, ftock, or circumftances ; the farmer
then would not fear working improvements ; and their hufbandry would foon
wear a new face. I fee fome objeȼtions
which I fhould fuppofe a *French* minifter
might ftart ; but none that have any fo-
lidity.

There is no neceffity of extending inftances of improper taxes relative to the
hufbandry of a country ; they may, in any
cafe, be underftood by confidering the principles upon which they are framed ; it is
impoffible agriculture fhould flourifh, if
they are made proportional to the wealth,
ftocks, improvements or induftry of the
cultivators.

S E C T. II.

WANT OF LEASES.

IN the next place, concerning the tenures on which the tenants hold their farms. If the legiſlature of a country would have agriculture flouriſh, encouragement of every kind muſt be given to letting land on long leaſes. If a landlord would have his eſtate well cultivated, he muſt adopt the ſame principles : The endeavours uſed by many of the conſiderable nobility and gentry in *Scotland* to improve their agriculture, will meet with ſucceſs only where this eſſential principle is purſued : How can any man be ſo blind as to ſuppoſe that farmers will enter into a correct and ſpirited huſbandry, which is but another name for great expences, if they have not abſolute ſecurity of a term ſufficient to repay them with a competent profit.

Conſider the common wants of the *Scotch* agriculture ; waſtes to be incloſed and converted to corn and graſs ; bogs and marſhes to be drained ; turneps, and clover to be introduced ; good fences to be promoted ; and expenſive manuring to be wrought ; experienced labourers in ſeveral articles of management, procured

from

from *England.* Where is the farmer from
whom any of thefe articles are to be expected while a tenant at will, or under a
leafe of no more than feven or nine years?
When I hear the gentlemen of *Scotland*
talking of their improved hufbandry, and
underftand that they grant no leafes, or
fhort ones, I guefs what the improvements
are, and how durable they will prove: At
the fame time, however, it is right to obferve,
that there are fome among them who have
juft ideas of this point; and for the fake
of giving this folid encouragement to the
hufbandry of their country, give up the
vanity of having their tenants in a ftate of
dependance, and readily grant leafes of 21
and even 32 years where they are well
deferved.

In *Ireland* the cuftom of granting leafes
of a proper length is coming faft into
practice, yet is it introduced in a manner
well calculated for deftroying much of the
good which naturally attends the meafure.
Lands are let in very great tracts by auction,
with a liberty of re-letting to others; thus
the overgrown tenant, who is probably no
farmer, has that fecurity which the cultivator of the land fhould have, who, on
the contrary, is often only tenant at will:
in this pernicious fyftem, long leafes are

prac-

practifed without one good effect flowing from them.

We have lately heard much in the public papers of great emigrations from *Scotland* and *Ireland* to *America*, not only of poor inhabitants of towns, and country labourers, but even of farmers; if this is true, it muft be owing very much to the mifchievous obftinacy of their landlords in not giving them fufficient fecurity in their tenures; for under fair and proper leafes, it is impoffible that farmers fhould dream of leaving their country. It is greatly to be wifhed that the landlords of thofe kingdoms in their ideas of improving agriculture would attend to this policy of firft removing the great obftacles to their fuccefs; this will prove more beneficial than introducing horfe-hoes, or planting cabbages.

Leafes are granted in *France*, and often of confiderable length, but there it is not a matter of great confequence; for the taille fo effectually crufhes all fpirited hufbandry, that it leaves little mifchief for a want of this fort to perform.

In *Spain* and *Italy* the fale of an eftate vacates the leafe. This is not an evil that operates in common, therefore is not of a general bad confequence; but it deferves attention, and fhould be put an end to.

SECT. III.

TYTHE GATHERED.

AS to the obftacles that arife from tythes, they are great in proportion to their frequency of being taken in kind. Every government defirous of carrying agriculture to perfection, ought to take every poffible meafure for fubftituting fome other method of paying the clergy.

SECT. IV.

PERSONAL SERVICE.

BUT in the article of perfonal fervice, the cafe is different: in this there are no difficulties that might not be overcome almoft without trouble. In *England* the farmers were moft miferably oppreffed by purveyance, while the crown had that prerogative; in which the fervice of themfelves and teams were demanded, and little or nothing returned; befides provifions being taken of them, at one-tenth of their value —and fometimes for no value at all. But in *France* there are great remains of the antient perfonal fervice, which was very important before money was plentiful:

their

their *corvees* have been much complained
of by the modern *French* writers on political œconomy : they are perfonal fervices
performed by all the labouring claffes in
carrying on all forts of works, fuch as
roads, caufeways, navigations, &c. The
value of them reduced to money by compofition is not calculated to exceed 60,000*l.*
through all *France*, and yet the diftrefs
brought on hufbandry by means of the
oppreffion, is probably more than a million
fterling : Nothing can exceed the miferable
policy of fuffering a people to be fleeced
for fo inconfiderable an advantage : The
farmers teams are driven to a great diftance
—their cattle jaded, and often deftroyed—
their carts broken—themfelves ill-ufed—
and this very often, and at all feafons of
the year. Where the labour and carriage of
all public works are thus performed, the
evil muft be of a moft extenfive and dangerous nature,—and one that is very well
adapted to deprefs the agriculture of any
country. But there is in *Germany*, *Denmark*, and in fome parts of *France* (where
the peafants are free) another fort of perfonal fervice, which is that of performing
all the labour and carriage of the landlord's
houfehold and farm ; which is often a confiderable part of his eftate : all his ploughing, carting, dunging, harveft, hay, and,

in

in a word, all the work of a farm : Whatever fuch little tyrants may fuppofe, we
may depend on it that thefe feeming advantages are in reality heavy taxes on
themfelves—their farmers cannot, under
fuch burthens, pay them near the rent that
is paid in other countries—if they would
abfolutely releafe them from fuch fervices,
the increafe of rent would far more than
enable them to do the whole by their fervants. We may guefs what would be the
countenance of an *Englifh* farmer, if his
landlord demanded all his teams in the
middle of feed time.

The fmall real value of perfonal fervice
we experience in the laft remnant of it in
England: The fix days duty in the high-
ways. It is done fo miferably, and fo much
time is neceffarily loft by going to a diftance,
that nobody can doubt but any new road
or confiderable work might be made by
a private man, or an appointed furveyor,
with teams on purpofe, for one-tenth of the
fum which it would coft if performed by
parifh work. Not having fubftituted a
tax univerfally inftead of thefe fervices in a
country fo enlightened as this, is a very
great reflection on our police.

CORN

S E C T. V.

C O R N L A W S.

THE obftacles to good hufbandry, which are found in bad corn laws, have been very much difcuffed of late years—yet there are readers remaining who will not acknowledge the juftice of the innovations recommended. The countries in which very bad regulations have moftly prevailed are, *France*, *Spain* and *Naples*; in thofe and others no tranfportation of corn from one province to another was for a long time allowed, which is yet the law in fome parts of *Spain :* It is but very lately that any exportation was allowed in *France*, even when corn was the cheapeft ; and all exportation has been regularly forbid to this day in *Spain, Portugal*, and feveral other parts of *Italy*. I do not apprehend it is poffible, under fuch a fyftem, to have a flourifhing corn hufbandry—prices will be too fluctuating— fome years will be fo cheap, that the farmers will be ruined—and others fo dear, that the people will be ftarved. Long experience muft convince us, that this is not only reafoning, but fact. Famines never appear in countries that admit a free exportation ;

but

but in all above named, where a contrary policy has been purfued, they have appeared frequently and feverely.

The variations in the earth's products owing to feafons, though not fo great as fome have imagined where the hufbandry is good, yet where it is indifferent muft neceffarily be confiderable : Let us lay down one maxim, which can hardly be contradicted, *the good of hufbandry requires that the price of corn fhould be proportioned to the product.* Let us then fuppofe the common confumption of a nation to be 5,000,000 of quarters of bread corn : the proportion between the common product and the common confumption muft vibrate according to various circumftances :—Suppofe a crop of 6,000,000 of quarters, and no exportation, what muft be the confequence ? There is the furplus of a 6th in the markets, confequently the price is brought down much lower than that proportion : Here lies the misfortune. If corn in fuch a year yielded a price proportioned only to the plenty, the misfortune would not be great—but the addition in the markets of a fixth finks the price probably a third, and perhaps more.—Mr. *King,* the political arithmetician, calculated the proportion; but as it is impoffible to attain any accuracy in fuch a calculation, it is fufficient to fuppofe the

the difference very confiderable. To continue the cafe, we may fuppofe another
good crop with a new furplus of a fixth or
feventh; this coming upon graneries full of a
part of the former furplus, finks the price yet
lower ; and then the farmers are not only
difcouraged, as feveral writers have obferved,
from fowing another crop, but what is as
bad, they are impoverifhed fo much, that
they cannot plough, harrow, dung, drain,
ditch, fence, or do any thing with proper
fpirit. Thefe two circumftances, inability in
future to act well, and difcouragement
from fowing again, can hardly fail of
occafioning in future years a fcarcity, or
probably a famine. Then the farmers
reap of courfe a thin crop from their
former inability, and that too over only
a part of the land ufually fown; in fuch
a cafe, corn muft be very high to recompence the farmer—probably fo high, that
the government of the country is alarmed,
and imports corn from wherever they can
get it, then the price falls, when he again
fuffers. Thus a great crop or a bad one
operates equally againft him, and nothing
can fupport him at all but fuch a product
as pretty exactly anfwers the annual confumption. There is no balance preferved
in the meafures, exportation is prohibited,
yet importation is allowed; fo that it is
im-

impoffible the price fhould with any regularity be fuch as can encourage good hufbandry.

On the contrary, if the policy of the
ftate admits exportation, the furplus of a
large crop being fent away, keeps the price
at home from falling too low: this is an
encouragement to the farmer acting two
ways; firft, by enriching him, he is able
the better to improve all his culture;
fecondly, he is induced to fow as much
corn as poffible, for every man, whatever
be his trade, is defirous of increafing that
commodity which fells beft at market. The
bounty on exportation given in *England*
was a refinement on the policy I am now
recommending—it was given in order that
corn might rife in price, as an encouragement to the country gentlemen; yet, contrary to the expectation of thofe times, it
has made corn much cheaper, by being fo
great an inducement to fow it.

In fuch countries as will adhere to fo
deftructive a fyftem as that of reftraining
the export of corn, it is not of much confequence what other advantages are given to
hufbandry, fince all others united, that can
be named or thought of, will not make
amends to the farmer for the want of a
market: it is of no confequence to enable
him to raife noble crops, if, when he has
got

got them, he cannot fell at a proper price ;
his plentiful harvests tend only to his ruin.
It would be endless to answer the objections
of thofe who have written against the beneficial meafures adopted in the laft century
by *England*; they infift on mifchief having
arifen to manufactures and the poor from
exportation making corn dearer : they affert
a fact which is contrary to record, and on
that they build the falfeft hypothefis that
ever was difplayed; the great end of which
is to prove, that in order to advance the
intereft of a people, their agriculture muft
be depreffed;—and, to make corn cheap,
the culture of it is to be difcouraged !

SECT. VI.

NATIONAL POVERTY.

IN the next place, in relation to the inconveniences arifing to agriculture from
the want of general wealth, we are not to
fpeak with fuch certainty as in other cafes ;
for although laws and regulations are within
the power of a legiflature, yet is not this
the cafe in the great point of rendering a
nation wealthy. It is true, that a uniform
encouragement of manufactures, commerce,
and every branch of national induftry, will
as long as it is carried on tend powerfully
to

to that end; but as the bufinefs requires unremitting attention, and is a long time effecting, we cannot fay to a ftatefman, *Make your people rich*, as lightly as we can advife him to repeal an ill-judged law.

However, this cafe is not without a remedy: if the evil lies in the want of general wealth, the farmer will find himfelf moft oppreffed by a want of a good market: the ftatefman fhould in that cafe, befides taking the ufual methods of encouraging agriculture, endeavour by every means to make the prices of all commodities rife; and refpecting the farmers products, he ought to give a bounty on the exportation, as this remedy bears immediately at the evil, by providing the hufbandman with that market abroad which he cannot get at home:—this I think is in fuch a cafe the moft political conduct he can purfue.

S E C T. VII.

OPEN FIELDS.

AS to the article *inclofures*, he has much more in his power. In this inftance, he fhould lay it down as a maxim, that without inclofures there can be no good hufbandry: while a country is laid out in

open

open field lands, every good farmer tied down to the hufbandry of his flovenly neighbour, it is fimply impoffible that agriculture fhould flourifh. Of what confequence is it that in all the preceding articles the farmer is favoured, if he lies under the weight of this evil? Let taxes be fair, equal and unoppreffive; leafes long; tythe not gathered;—no perfonal fervice; good corn laws, and general wealth in the nation to provide a market. Let all thefe points be eftablifhed, yet of what confequence if the hufbandman cannot purfue the plans which he knows to be right: if he is tied down to a fyftem, which, with all poffible advantages, cannot be made to equal inferior modes in inclofed countries? It is alfo a happy circumftance that this capital obftacle to good hufbandry requires nothing but refolution to be deftroyed. The tendernefs to liberty, which is fo commendable in the *Britifh* legiflature, prevents their interfering in thefe cafes, except when requefted by the parties concerned: this makes the bufinefs much flower here than it need be in other countries; where a lefs proportion of owners applying for the meafure might be made to bind the whole. When the proprietors have the abfolute and free choice of the commiffioners who are to order the divifion, there cannot be any ob-

objections of importance to facilitating the meafure.

Inclofures, like the export of corn, have engaged the attention of many writers, who declare againft them. But if no meafures favourable to agriculture are to be embraced until fuch are difcovered as fhall meet with univerfal approbation, we may fafely venture to pronounce that nothing great or good can ever be performed. I do not at prefent recollect any cafes which ought to be pleaded as exceptions : Doubtlefs there are many *Spaniards* that would be vehement againft them on the principle of their deftroying the immenfe walks affumed by their fhepherds from one part of the kingdom to another : and granting that the inclofure of open dry country, is prejudicial to the finenefs of wool ; yet is nothing to be confidered but wool ? Is not five hundred pounds in corn as good as one hundred pounds in wool ? Befides, the boafted finenefs of the *Spanifh* wool is like their *American* mines, of much greater benefit to foreigners than to themfelves. In all difputes of this fort, the ftatefman fhould enquire what application of the lands brings in the greateft product valued in money, and then univerfally adhere to that party who fatisfies him of the fuperiority, without paying any regard to the contrary pre-

judices

judices—always providing that he lays no prohibitions, no reſtrictions on their antago-niſts. If one party adheres to ſheep, let them ſtick to ſheep, without controul; and whenever he would favour any branch of culture, let it be by ſuch encouragements as ſhall not depreſs another. What! ſays one, would you, for inſtance, encourage corn in *England* to the extirpation of wool for manufacturers? I reply, the caſe is impoſ-ſible: Suppoſe any meaſures were adopted to encreaſe the corn culture to the moſt immenſe extent—ſuppoſing farther, that ſheep ſuffered—yet the very progreſs of ſuch an effect remedies itſelf; for the in-creaſing price of wool would counteract your encouragements of the corn culture, and make the one as profitable as the other. Such fears, therefore, are groundleſs: while prohibitions and reſtrictions keep their diſtance, and every man is left to do what he pleaſes with his land, a general level will be obſerved among all common products *.

---

* It is remarkable, that ſome of the *French* writers, in deſcribing our agriculture, overlook this great point, incloſing.

As an inſtance, among many others, we may turn to M. BUTRE's *Obſervations diverſes ſur la grand et la petite Culture.* In which he entitles one of his ſections, *Grande culture opulente d'Angleterre.* Which great and opulent culture we call a miſerable exploded ſyſtem:

S E C T. VIII.

S L A V E R Y.

BESIDES thefe grand obftacles to the improvement of agriculture, there are others which are not to be properly claffed under the heads with which I fet out: among thefe let me name, firft, the abfolute flavery of the peafants in fome parts of *Germany*, in *Denmark*, in *Poland*, and in *Ruffia*, in all which countries, they were lately confidered as cattle, and transferred from mafter to mafter with the eftate on which they live. In this fyftem the land-lord farms all his eftate by means of thefe flaves,

---

fyftem: But he fays, it is faite avec fplendeur, one plough cultivating 150 arpents, having fix horfes (two for ploughing and four for carting) and the farm is in three divifions, one of fallow, another wheat, and the third fpring corn ! Surely Mr. *Butré* might among our hufbandry writings have found out that this is the courfe of crops peculiar to our old open fields, where the far-mers can practife no other, but that the moment they are inclofed, they reject fo vile a fyftem for many others. They then lay afide fallows, and fow turnips and clover inftead of fallows ; or fome other ameliorating or hoeing crops—this is our fplendid and opulent hufban-dry : that quoted by Mr. *Butré* is a miferable and beggarly culture †.

† Ephemerides du Citoyen, 1767. Vol. xii. p. 75.

flaves, except the fmall portions left for
their own fubfiftence.   It would be rafh to
affert that this fyftem is inconfiftent with
good hufbandry ; for if the landlords enjoy
the advantages which I have ftated before,
they may certainly carry on any culture,
and in whatfoever manner they pleafe ; but
this can only be on a certain extent of land,
no greater than can be well overfeen by the
landlord himfelf ; the appointment of ftewards and overfeers for diftinct eftates will
not do, fince when once the extent is too
great for one perfon to overlook, he muft
neceffarily truft entirely to others, which is
always the common hufbandry of the country, how bad foever it may be : improvements are then introduced with great difficulty.   Yet this is the fyftem in thefe countries ; of whatever fize the eftate, all is in the
hands of the owner, and the peafants affigned in diftricts to the ftewards and overfeers, by whom a very miferable agriculture is ufually carried on, and with all the
oppreffion and cruelty arifing from the fpirit
of flavery.

It will not admit of a moment's doubt,
but that fuch landlords would increafe their
income prodigioufly if they would overturn
this fyftem, by declaring their peafants
free, and let them farms according to their
abilities of ftocking and cultivating them :
many

many advantages would flow from fuch a conduct; the landlord would receive his rents with very little trouble, one fteward would do the bufinefs of twenty overfeers and bailiffs; frauds and impofitions would in a great meafure vanifh; the population of the eftate would much increafe, and as this increafe of people would arife from an increafe of wealth and induftry, it would bring a new market without any difadvantages attending it. As the farmers grew richer, they would keep greater ftocks of cattle, and cultivate their lands better; and of that the landlord might take his advantage without any op-preffion, by raifing his rents with judg-ment on the renewal of the leafes. I am fenfible there are many who will laugh at my talking of freeing peafants, and giving leafes in *Poland:* but fo far from there being any thing idle or extravagant in this idea, that I aver the thing has been done, and with great fuccefs, on a part of the eftate of the Prince de *Maffalfki,* as I was affured by himfelf.

S E C T. IX.

H U N T I N G.

BEFORE I quit thefe remarks on great
obftacles to the improvement of hufbandry, I muft mention the excefs to which
hunting is carried in fome countries by the
fovereign.   I recollect a remarkable inftance
given by Mr. *Hanway* in his travels, that
of *Saxony* under King *Auguftus*, who not
allowing his deer, &c. to be any where
deftroyed, they multiplied all over the elec-
torate to fuch a degree, that the miferable
Saxons offered readily an addition to the
army of 6000 men, only for liberty to reduce the deer to half their number; but
were refufed with contempt.   If fuch a
thing was not well authenticated, it would
be difficult to give credit to fo exceffive
folly.   Wherever hunting and other rural
fports are carried to any fuch excefs, it muft
be almoft to the ruin of agriculture : I have
feen hares in *England* in fo great abundance, as very much to injure the hufbandmen : If the crops when gained, are to be
devoured by game, we may eafily conceive
that all the encouragement in the world,
and the removing of every other obftacle
would

would all be in vain.—Let it ever be laid
down as a maxim, that if the farmer is
not to reap, he will not fow.

SECT. X.

RECAPITULATION.

THERE are abundance of other circumſtances which are real obſtacles
to huſbandry, but which I think do not
demand a particular attention here ; becauſe
I conceive that ſuch are not radical evils ;
if a right ſyſtem of encouragement is
adopted, they would diſappear, without any
particular attack.

The articles I have dwelt upon, are
obſtacles ſo miſchievous, that enterpri-
zing ſpirits among the nobility and gentry who are deſirous of promoting the good
cauſe, ſhould direct their utmoſt endeavours
to remove them. Princes, ſtateſmen, and
the legiſlature of every country deſirous of
a flouriſhing agriculture, ſhould attend to
theſe objects ; and let me further remark,
that it is a vain work for individuals to
attempt the introduction of new improvements in farming : to talk of turnips, cabbages, carrots, lucerne, clover, and other
articles of huſbandry cultivated with ſuch
ſucceſs in *England*, to tenants that have

no

no leafes, to men who pay a taille, to farmers who pay every tenth cabbage, and
every tenth lamb and pig to the parfon;
to people expofed to all the oppreffions of
perfonal fervice; to the hufbandmen of a
country where the exportation of their products is forbidden, yet importation allowed,
or of a territory fo poor that they cannot
find a market for the crops when raifed:
—what can fuch recommendations be .ef-
teemed, but a frivolous infult upon common
fenfe? Gentlemen who act in this manner
may mean well, and they have as much
merit as people can have who begin at the
wrong end—but no general or lafting good
can ever flow from their moft ftrenuous
endeavours.

C H A P. III.

EXAMINATION OF FALSE PROPOSITIONS.

HAVING explained the principles upon which the happy ſtate of agriculture in *England* principally depends, and endeavoured to point out the capital obſtacles which in various countries, oppoſe themſelves to the buſineſs of adopting thoſe principles, I ſhall in the next place touch upon certain new ſyſtems that have been recommended to the world, which it is probable may attract the attention of a ſtateſman in the great work of improving the agriculture of his country. If many ſchemes of public conduct are recommended by different writers of reputation, it may without uncommon attention be difficult to pronounce which plan is beſt. In the caſe before us there have been ſome propoſitions laid before the world with a view to encouraging agriculture, which appear to me to have a very bad tendency; and of courſe it is neceſſary to explain the reaſons for my differing in opinion from gentlemen for whoſe abilities I have not leſs reſpect than others.

SECT. I.

UNION OF TAXES ON LAND.

WITHIN thefe twenty years there
have been an amazing number of
publications in *France, Holland,* and *Germany,* on the means of promoting agriculture; and, as might well be expected, moft
of the writers became ideal financiers: The
evils of the taille could not but ftrike
every eye, and new modes of taxation
were called for with all poffible vehemence.
Syftem upon fyftem was framed, and their
authors looked upon themfelves as the
founders of a new fcience; the *oeconomical
fcience,* or, as they termed it, *Phyfiocratie.*
At the head of thefe writers appear *Quefnay,* the *Marquis de Mirabeau,* and *du
Pont* *, who agree in the great outlines of
their

---

* The number of writers who have publifhed on
this fubject in *France* is very great; among the many
works on the branches of this pretended new fcience,
the following may be confulted:
Encyclopedie, Art. *Fermier Grain,* &c.
Les Eléments de la Philofophie Rurale, par Mirabeau,
12mo. 1767.
L'Ordre naturel et effentiel des Sociétés politiques, 4to.
& 12mo. 1767.

La

their plan, which is to abolifh all the long lift of *French* taxes, and fubftitute a fingle one upon land; no idea of their own, but which is borrowed from *Englifh* writers, from *Locke*, *Decker*, &c. They agree to it for the fame reafons as are advanced by our writers, particularly the capital principle, that all taxes fall ultimately on the land; and as they build fo much on this, it will be neceffary to fay a few words on it.

That the maxim is falfe and founded on nothing but abfurdity, has been very clearly, though

---

La Phyfiocratie, ou Conftitution naturelle du Gouvernement le plus avantageux au genre humain, par Quefnay, 2 tom. 8vo. 1767.

De L'Origine et des Progrés d'une fcience nouvelle, 8vo. 1767, par Dupont.

Lettres d'un Citoyen à un Magiftrat, fur les vingtiémes & les autres impôts, par M. l'Abbé Baudeau, 12mo. 1768.

Doutes adreffés aux Philofophes économiftes fur l'ordre naturel & effentiel des Sociétés politiques, 12mo. par M. l'Abbé Mably, 1768.

Precis de L'Ordre Legal, 12mo. par Marquis de Mirabeau, 1768.

Memoire fur les effets de l'impôt indirect, par Saint Peravy, 1768.

L'Ami des Hommes, par le M. de Mirabeau, 7 tom. 1757.

Tableau Oecconomique, avec fon explication, 4to. par Quefnay, 1758.

Theorie de l'impôt, par le M. de Mirabeau, 12mo. 1760.

Journal d'Agriculture.

Ephemerides du Citoyen.

though elaborately proved by Sir *James Steuart*; but as it is too important a link in the prefent argument to be paffed over merely with a reference to another book, I fhall add a few obfervations to make it plain to every one.

The argument of Mr. *Locke, Decker,* and the *French* writers is, that excifes and other taxes on confumption are blended by every artizan, &c. with the price of his work, which accumulating as they advance, render every thing dearer except to people in trade who draw back the accumulation, fo that the landed intereft not being in trade, receives the weight at laft with the progreffive profits of the whole train.   This ftate of the matter has many fallacies in it : the tradefman who advances the taxes, can draw back only a part of them; the other part he *pays* as much as the landlord does his land tax.   The excifes he pays on the goods he manufactures, he draws back completely; but thofe upon the luxuries he confumes, he cannot draw back.   The brewer is repaid the taxes on malt, beer, and hops, by the confumer, but he is not repaid for the chintzes with which he hangs his rooms, the ftamps on papers and plate, the duty on his coach wheels, the cuftoms on his wines, brandies, and fruit; and in a word, every article out of the line of his trade,

trade. The fhoemaker is refunded his tax on leather ; but let him go to the alehoufe and drink porter ; let his wife be extravagant as fhe pleafes in tea, fugar, and fpices, he pays the taxes on all thofe commodities, but moft affuredly he will never be able to charge them on his cuftomers.

But, fays Sir *Matthew Decker*, taxes make all articles of houfekeeping fo dear, that tradefmen are obliged to charge the higher prices in order to enable them to fupport the expence, and others doing the fame, it comes at laft to the landlord. Nothing is farther from the truth ; they cannot raife their price on any account that does not equally fall on all their brethren : the taxes on leather fall equally on all fhoemakers, and confequently all may raife their prices proportioned to the taxes ; but as to *dearnefs of living*, it affects them merely in proportion as they chufe to be expenfive : if fome are for *living well*, confuming much wine, punch, porter, tea, fugar, and other fuperfluities, and in proportion to THIS *dearnefs of living*, raife the price of their fhoes ; their trade will fpeedily be gone to others who are content with pork, cabbage and ale. What can be more idle than to fuppofe I am to pay in my fhoes an increafed price, becaufe my fhoemaker drinks wine inftead of porter ?

ter? In the name of common fenfe, will he not be underfold by his neighbour, who flicks to porter; and if the porter drinker has raifed his price becaufe malt is taxed, will he not be underfold by the poorer man who is contented with fmall beer?

It is in this manner that the people in trade are able to draw back nothing more than the amount of the tax they pay, with fuch a profit on it, as all their brethren unite in; but as to a brewer's felling his beer dearer on account of the high price of candles, and the tallow-chandler on account of the high price of fhoes, and the fhoemaker on account of the high price of tea and fugar, as *Decker* would perfuade us, it is felf-evidently an error.

The fact is, that all taxes on confumption, fuch as excifes of every denomination—cuftoms and other duties, are all paid by the confumers of the commodity taxed; which fo far from being the poffeffors of land alone, includes every rank of the people; the tradefman when he is extravagant as much as the duke; and in proportion to the wealth acquired by tradefmen, who often are enriched by taxes, is the landed and other idle interefts eafed, becaufe that very wealth is fpent in taxed commodities, and confequently contributes in proportion to itfelf to the wants of the ftate.

Thus

Thus are taxes on confumption the faireft and moft equal, and the leaft burthenfome of all others ; every clafs of the people, every individual in the nation bears his fhare, and that a *voluntary* fhare, becaufe if he forbears confuming he pays no tax, never advancing a penny unlefs he buys a taxed commodity, and his very purchafe implies an ability to pay ; whereas taxes on property, like land taxes, and on houfes, which was Sir *M. Decker's* favourite fcheme, force a man to pay not becaufe he *confumes* but becaufe he *poffeffes* ; the one is a proof he is able to pay, the other no proof at all of it.

As this is the cafe, let any impartial perfon judge of the confequences of throwing the whole weight of taxes upon land, under the prepofterous idea of favouring it. A pretty figure our landed intereft would make if the ideas of thefe gentlemen were realized in this kingdom ; let us ftate the fuppofition.

	£.	s.	d.
The land tax to raife 2,000,000*l.* is in the pound, -	0	4	0
The cuftoms bring in 2,000,000*l.* this is - -	0	4	0
The excife 4,600,000*l.* this requires in the pound, -	0	9	2
Carry over, - -	0	17	2

	£.	s.	d.
Brought over, -	0	17	2
The inland duties, 1,000,000, or	0	2	0
The malt tax 600,000 *l.* or in the pound, - -	0	1	2
	£.	1	0	4

So that for our land tax to abforb all our other taxes, it muft be laid at 20 *s.* 4 *d.* in the pound *; and then we are perfuaded by thefe gentlemen that the landlords would grow

---

* La Hollande eft la preuve la démonftration que les principes de M. *de Mirabeau* ne font pas fondés. Si les impôts ne devoient fe prélever qu'immédiatement à la fource de revenus comme le prétend M. *de Mirabeau*, et qu'on ne pût jamais exiger qu'une partie du produit territorial, il y a longtems que la Hollande n'exifteroit plus.

Elle a peu de productions alimentaires ; elle eft prefque entiérement privée de terres labourables, de vignes, de bois ; quelques près font toute fa reffource de ce côtè-la. Cependant cette république paie des troupes, a une marine, et a figuré fouvent en Europe à côtè des grandes puiffances. Les taxes et les impóts qu'on y prèleve font bien plus forts, en tous genres, qu'en France et en Angleterre ; et cependant cela n'a pas caufé la ruïne de l'etat : il eft meme encore dans une grande opulence. Si la jaloufie de fon commerce ne lui avoit pas attiré tant de concurrens, l'etat ne fe reffentiroit feulement pas des taxes exorbitantes qu'on y paie. Le pain, qui eft un objet de premiere néceffité, paie un impôt qui en double prefque le prix ; tous les objets de confommation y font plus chargés qu'en France. Les biens fonds, comme maifons,

actions,

grow very rich, becaufe they would buy
their fhoes and ftockings much cheaper!

Here is the infallible and immediate
effect of laying all taxes on land; how is
it to be paid? What is to enable the landlords to live after their income is gone in
taxes? Explain this. Anfwer the objection.
Your tax on the net product, lay it how
you will, and realized to the fair proportion *, will amount to about 15s. in
the pound abfolute payment. What is to
be the landlord's return? Will his products rife proportionably in price, fo as to
enable him to bear it? Impoffible. The
very terms of the propofed innovation are,
that all confumption fhould at once be fo
much the cheaper. Will he, in confequence of this change, find that his remaining rental of 5s. will go as far as his former
one of 20? It does not follow; nay it is
by no means clear, that even thofe commodities which were taxed before would be
cheap in proportion to the deduction of fuch
tax, from there not being the fame encouragement to produce them—elfe why do the
real

---

actions, contracts, terres, le font d'avantage; et
malgrè cela la Hollande fleurit, et la machine de la
finance va fon train, par la magie de la circulation et
du credit qui opère ces effets falutaires. *Traité de la
Circulation*, p. 134.

* The *Englifh* land-tax at 4s. in the pound nomi-
nally, is not fo really. The true proportion is nearly
that mentioned above.

real *confumption* of many articles encreafe in *England* upon being taxed? Render any thing by taxes fomething more of a diftinction than formerly, and you will find that the tax, inftead of checking, will increafe the confumption.—It has been propofed to tax horfes and livery fervants: I have no doubt but both would increafe under a moderate tax *. But a confiderable part of the landlord's expenditure is in articles which never were taxed, the prices of which certainly would not fall; confequently he would have no advantage, though his whole income would fuffer merely with a view to a general fall. Nothing can be clearer than the immenfe balance that would be againft him on that account.

There are no taxes on the moft neceffary parts of provifions, except malt; confequently, you cannot pretend to increafe the confumption by lowering the price (fuppofing the one to follow the other, which is not always the cafe) and if beer was cheaper, yet would it be enormoufly rivalled by all forts of foreign wines and fpirits; men who now are curious in ales, would then have *French* wines.—But not to wafte one's time in proving that there is fome diftinction between black and white, there

---

* The fame obfervation I find in *Remarks on the Size of Farms and the Price of Provifions.*

there is one general argument which with me is unanfwerable. The propofition is defigned to eafe the landed intereft in confequence of a general fall in the prices of their confumption ; it is faid they now pay not only the nominal amount of the taxes, but as much more in profits on them ; if all thefe were ftruck off, the œconomical writers exprefly fay the income of land would go as far again ; thus their plan of eafing the land and improving agriculture, is to be by a general *fall of prices* * ! What a monftrous contradiction ! What a contradiction of themfelves ! As if any thing could poffibly be more favourable to agriculture than that general dearnefs which wherever found is the ftrong fign of vigour and profperity.

But let us take a clofer view of the argument of Meffrs. *Mirabeau* and *Du Pont*.

The former fays,—" Ce que j'en ai dit eft feulement pour rapeler en un coup d'œil que de quelque maniére que fe retourne l'impôt, il eft impoffible qu'il provienne
d'autre

---

* There is one article, which is of all others the greateft expence upon hufbandry—*labour*—And this would not fall one penny from the abolition of taxes. They have in fcarce any refpect raifed it, and moft certainly their fall would not fink it. There are alfo many other articles of the confumption of the landed intereft, which would not be affected : thus their *whole* income would be heavily taxed in order for a defpicable advantage in the inferior articles of their expence !

d'autre part que du produit, et que s'il n'eft pris directement fur le produit net qui conftitue le revenu, il n'a plus ni bafe, ni bouffole.—Auffi eft ce directement fur le revenu et fur le produit net que l'auteur affied l'impôt, ainfi que la dîme *." This is M. *de Mirabeau*'s grand idea; firft, that all taxes fall upon land, which I think I have refuted; and fecondly, that they fhould all be raifed on the neat produce, which he ftates thus: the total produce he divides into, 1. the farmer's expences; 2. his profit; 3. the remainder fold at market; out of which third part are to come tythes, the whole revenue of *France*, and the landlord's rent: this fcale is not drawn with much accuracy, but one word is fufficient: His third divifion would not pay one half of what he fuppofes; and as taxes and tythe would firft be paid, the landlord would remain without a penny of rent. He goes on :—" Si l'on veut confidérer quel eft le poids des impofitions arbitraires, foit perfonelles, foit cenfées territoriales : des taxes fur toutes les manieres d'agir de contracter, de fe faire rendre juftice, &c. des *droits fur les confommations,* fur toutes les tranfi des denres des douanes, &c.—on en conclura que les proprietaires feroient fort

---

* *L'Ami des Hommes,* tom. vii. p. 45.

fort heureux d'obtenir par le payement d'une portion égale à la moitié de leur revenu, l'exemption, de tant et tant de genres de fpoliation réunis *.———On voit en général que l'impot doit être pris im-médiatement fur le produit net des biens-fonds, puifque de quelque maniére qu'il foit impofé dans un Royaume qui tire fes richeffes de fon territoire, il eft toujours payé par les biens-fonds †."—This writer thinks the great benefit of his fcheme is the laying the tax on the *net* not the *grofs* produce of the lands ; becaufe he firft fecures the farmer's returns and his profit, before any tax is paid, confequently he efcapes all taxation. But this idea appears to be falfe and im-practicable; for the landlord we muft fuppofe in the firft place lets his lands at a certain fixed rent, let taxes be paid how and by whom they will ; if then the tax is laid on any part of the product, or proportioned in any refpect to the crop, it will evidently fall on the farmers, lay it on how you will; for though the Marquis may proportion the tax to what he calls *neat* produce, yet a proportion will always hold to the grofs produce. The farmer will pay in pro-portion to his crop : if he gets a good crop

he

---

* *L'Ami des Hommes*, tom. vii. p. 47.
† Ib. p. 171.

he will pay more than if he gets a bad one, and confequently fuch a tax would in fact be a new tythe, and a moft mifchievous burthen to agriculture. It is by the direct contrary principle that the land-tax in *England* is harmlefs, where being laid not on any part of the produce, but rent alone, the farmers and landlord pay juft the fame, whatever their crops are—whatever improvements are wrought, the profit is all their own, no part going in taxes. It is a ftrange miftake to fuppofe that becaufe the tax is laid in proportion to the farmer's furplus, that therefore it fhould not be burthenfome, when the furplus being proportioned to the produce, the farmer muft certainly pay in proportion to his crop— which is the very mifchief of tythes, nay, and of the taille too: whereas the glory of the *Englifh* fyftem is, that NO MORE IS PAID FOR GOOD CROPS THAN FOR BAD ONES.

But M. *de Mirabeau*'s idea further appears to be impracticable; how is a tax to be raifed on the farmer's furplus, which he calls *net produce?* how are the tax-gatherers and the farmers to agree in deciding what this furplus is? The latter firft takes his expences—then his profit—and the remainder he leaves to the church, king, and landlord: a ftrange way of ftating it, becaufe the landlord fhould be paid firft, and his rent reckoned among the farmer's expences.

expences. Does the writer mean, that a land
tax fhould be laid proportioned to rent?
This has nothing to do with net produce.
Does he only in general mean, that the tax
fhould never be fo high as to touch more
than the farmer's furplus? This he certainly means in general, but then none of
his particulars have any further meaning,
and he points at no mode of levying it.

Suppofe a farm let for one hundred
loüis d'ors, and to contain two hundred
arpents, how would M. *de Mirabeau* lay
his tax—by the rent—or by the acre? I
fhould fuppofe neither : nor in proportion
to the grofs produce. What is his net produce? he muft divide every crop into three
parts in the field, and taking two himfelf,
the parfon, the tax-gatherer and the landlord
take the third? How can this be practicable! If the farmer carries the whole to
his barns, and a compofition takes place
by valuing it—then would frauds multiply,
and the whole kingdom be in confufion.

Let us in the next place examine if
M. *Du Pont* will caft further light on this
affair, as he has lately entered into a deline-
ation of his ideas on this fubject in his
*Lettre à Meffieurs de la Societé d'Emulation
de Londres* *. Which is a performance that
ftruck

---

* It is an unaccountable affectation in the *French*
writers that they will never call *Englifh* things by
Englifh

ftruck me a good deal, fince it is a leſſon to
Britain to convince us, that our ſyſtem of
taxation is abſurd, and that the profeſſors
of the œconomical ſcience in *France* could,
if we would let them, pull down the fabric
of our finances, and build a far better one
in its ſtead.

He begins with giving *Mirabeau*'s idea
of the *produit net* out of which all taxes
ought to be paid, and goes on—"dans ce cas
c'eſt une très bonne loi que celle qui etablit
l'impôt non pas à une ſomme déterminée,
mais dans une proportion connue et ſtable
avec le prix du fermage ; de ſorte que l'im-
poſition, ſuivant toujours pour régle le prix
du loyer des terres, hauſſe et baiſſe avec ce
loyer.   Par cette loi de nature le gouvernement ne ſaurait accroitre ſes revenus que par
l'accroiſſement de ceux du peuple.—"

Here

Englijh names : why is a ſociety for the encouragement
of arts to be called a ſociety of emulation ? An *Englijh*
writer to talk of the academy of knowledge inſtead of
the academy of ſciences at *Paris,* would but talk like
a fool : and what excuſe ſhould we have for writing
Burdux for *Bordeaux,* or *Kain* for *Caen?* yet *Cambridge*
in their authors is *Catonbrige*; and M. *de Mirabeau*
in *L'Ami des Hommes,* talks of *Goodman's cheſter.* The
French writers that have done me the honour of
mentioning the books I have publiſhed, have ſpelt my
name ſo that I did not always know myſelf. Even
Baron *Haller,* who compoſes in *Englijh,* calls me M.
Arthard Joung. Memoires par la Societé de Berne,
1770, p. 50.

Here M. *du Pont* partly explains M. *du Mirabeau*, that the idea is to rate every farmer with a fum proportioned to the amount of his neat produce; but, fays he, it is then right to tax him in proportion to his rent, by which means the ftate will come in for a fhare of all the improvements that are made.—The very thing—and I will venture to fay the thing alone that renders tythes and the taille mifchievous to hufbandry. " La loi, fays he, qui laiffe l'impôt invariable d'après un cadaftre une fois fait, comme celle de votre taxe fur les terres, *eft moins bonne* *.——Si la nation profpére, au bout d'un certain tems elle fe trouve n'avoir pas une force publique proportionée à fa puiffance réelle—elle fe trouve prefque inevitablement entrainée à des refources ruinenfes, telles que les emprunts, les *taxes fur* les confommations, les droits de douane, &c. &c. C'eft ce qui eft arrivé à votre nation, Meffieurs."—It is amazing that men of fagacity and penetration can fee things in fuch a light. There is no

man

---

* One would think that thefe writers *would* not fee the excellence of our fyftem, for they blame it for the very reafon which makes its merit—fondées fur un cadaftre ou fur de pareilles évaluations fixes, une pepiniere d'abus généraux et particuliers. Certaines terres ne payent pas quinze deniers par livre, et d'autres fon furchargées, vû leur etat actuel. *Ephemerides du Citoyen*, 1767, vol. iv. The fuppofition of the tax ever being *furchargées* is a very great error.

man who has been attentive to the progrefs of hufbandry in this kingdom but what muft be fenfible, that if our prefent land tax of a nominal 4*s.* in the pound was a variable one as here recommended, our agriculture would fuffer confiderably. The grand encouragement it meets with now is the ftability of the land tax. If a landlord takes or buys a farm worth only fifty pounds a year, and by improvement makes it worth five hundred pounds a year, he has no increafe of tax : will any body of common fenfe affirm that a contrary fyftem, a fyftem which divides his profits with him the moment he makes them, which bears on him in direct proportion to his fpirit and his merit—will they affert that fuch a fyftem is beneficial to hufbandry ? But to fo prepofterous a length is this fyftem carried, that thefe writers want to have it include ALL THE TAXES OF A STATE ; fo that in *England* the improver would have his improvements immediately taxed at 15*s.* in the pound ! And on comparifon with fuch a land tax, excifes on the confumption of the luxurious are called *refources ruineufes !* There is a madnefs in this hypothetical rage fufficient to confound perfpicuity itfelf.

But M. *du Pont* does not content himfelf with general reafoning; he gives as an
instance

inftance of the mifchief of cuftoms, thofe
upon *French* wines, (this ftroke of patrio-
tifm I readily forgive him, yet it is amufing)
by affuring us that the forcing our people
to pay fo exorbitantly for liberty to drink
them, is impoverifhing them, and by confequence the exchequer itfelf—*cet impôt eſt
donc payé par les revenus de l'Angleterre.*
Who can doubt but that a man is impoverifhed by drinking claret with a duty of
three fhillings a bottle on it?—But is he
more impoverifhed by it than M. *du Pont*'s
landlord with a land tax of fifteen fhillings
in the pound? But fuppofing it only fifteen-
pence, which is moft politick, to make a
man pay fifteen-pence becaufe he *poſſeſſes*
an acre of land, or to make another pay
3 *s.* for *confuming* a bottle of claret? A
man's having an acre is no proof that he
can fpare 1 5 *d.* for the ftate, but his drinking
a bottle of claret is a certain proof that he
can pay the 3 *s.* becaufe it is blended with
the firft coft, and he pays it before he confumes—and on the other hand, if people
will be extravagant and drink what they
cannot afford, nothing is wifer than to
make the ftate profit by their folly.

Thefe gentlemen complain much of taxes
on confumption raifing the prices of every
thing, and M. *de Mirabeau* calculates how
much farther the *French* landlord's rents
would

would go if they were abolifhed : But this
is an effect which found politicks ought
never to wifh for : the general dearnefs of
every thing is in all ftates the greateft fign
of profperity—no inftance is to be named
of a profperous and flourifhing country
being a cheap one : thofe in which every
thing is to be had cheap, are poor and
miferable, and exhibit in every refpect the
reverfe of what a ftatefman would wifh to
fee. I will go farther, and venture to affert, that there is not a clafs in *France* that
would not fuffer by a general fall of prices ;
it is a circumftance that never happens but
in confequence of a general decay. And it
is furprizing that M. *de Mirabeau* fhould
argue in this manner, who in other parts
of his works fhews a very proper idea of
the importance of a general dearnefs of
commodities, and repeats with approbation
from the *Encyclopedie,* ABONDANCE ET
CHERTE EST OPULENCE.

At page 21, M. *du Pont* declares generally againft all excifes and duties, mentions their being falfly fuppofed to fall
equally on the people ; and obferves, " En
vain les faits fe font éléves contre ces pré-
jugés ; en vain votre dette national perpé-
tuellement croiffante a du vous prouver l'in-
fuffifance & l'illufion d'un impôt ainfi
perçu qui porte fur les depenfes même de
l'ctat

l'etat & qui tarit la source des richesses renaissantes de la nation." This reasoning is extremely fallacious : Does M. *du Pont* suppose that our debt is owing to the publick money being raised by one mode rather than another ? Does he imagine that we should have been free from debts, had all our excises been consolidated into one tax on land ? Should we then have been able to have raised from 15 to 19 millions within the year ? Our debt has been owing to the taxes not producing half what is necessary, by no means to the mode of collecting them. At page 27, he asserts, that taxes on consumption, admit not of equality in their distribution; which is directly contrary to all experience. He says that some lands yield a great net produce, some a middling one, and some little more than the expence of culture; taxes on consumption, which are established equally on all three, he says, must reduce the last to waste. But what can this mean ? What have excises to do with any land ? the excise on malt, hops, &c. is not laid *per* acre, but *per* quarter and *per* cwt.; this supposed inequality therefore is merely ideal.

If he means the taxes on the consumption *of the products of such lands*, then his observation cannot be just because the tax will be

pro-

proportionable to the quantity of product, and confequently cannot be *equally eftab-lifhed on all three.*

Nor will M. *du Pont* take the inftance of this kingdom, which alone is fufficient to refute him. After ftating from *Decker* the mifchiefs of our excifes, &c. he fays, " Et les proprietaires font obligés en outre de fupporter la dégradation de leur patrimoine, laquelle réfulte de la *deftruction progreffive* des richeffes d'exploitation operée par la partie des taxes dont les fermiers des terres ont reffenti le premier coup." This whole kingdom exhibits a fact fo decifively con-trary to this affertion, that M. *du Pont* muft be little acquainted with the effects of our taxes to have let fuch a paffage flip his pen. Inftead of a progreffive deftruction of the wealth of our farmers, owing to excifes, we fee nothing among them but a progreffion of wealth and felicity—we have not a farmer who has any conception of an excife—nay, nor of a tax, except on windows, and poor's-rates ; thefe are all the taxes he feels —and if M. *du Pont* was to queftion them on our duties on confumption, nine out of ten would ftare, and not know what he meant—fo little do they feel the very taxes they pay, from their being blended with the original price of the commodities they con-fume. This writer proceeding with his argu-

argument, tells us, that our exchequer receives but one half of what is raised on the
people by our taxes on confumption. I
quote this only to fet the author right in a
fact he much miftakes; even our excifes
coft only 5 ½ *per cent.* collecting, every
expence included: The following account
of the charges of all our taxes, I believe is
not far from the truth.

	£.
Land-tax, ½ *per cent.* - - -	10,000
Malt, 5 ½, - - -	41,250
Excifes, 5 ½, - - -	308,000
Cuftoms, 15, - -	300,000
	659,250

For which expence the exchequer receives neat above ten millions; but if the
charges of collection run up to one million,
and higher than that no author of credit
ever calculated, whence can M. *du Pont* de-
rive his authority for making it ten times as
much?

From the terms which this gentleman
ufes, there is not the leaft reafon to fuppofe
that he means by 10 millions to include the
profit made by manufacturers and merchants
upon the advance of cuftoms and excifes; but
as he in other paffages complains very much
of fuch taxes raifing prices, let us for curiofity
fuppofe

suppose he had meant to include this, and calculate how near to 10 million such an idea will carry him. We must calculate this by allowing the person in trade 5 *per cent.* interest on his advance; but to obviate objections I shall suppose 7 *per cent.* which gives him 2 *per cent.* profit on the tax.

	£.		£.
Customs,	2,000,000		
Collecting,	300,000		
	2,300,000	on which 7 *per cent.* is -	161,000
Excise,	5,600,000		
Collecting,	308,000		
	5,908,000	on which 7 *par cent.* is -	343,560

But this includes all inland duties, stamps, coaches, &c. on which no advance can be made; however I have reckoned the whole.

Malt,	613,000		
Collecting,	41,250		
	654,250	on which 7 *per cent.* is -	45,797
			550,357

Here therefore we find that manufacturers and merchants charging 7 *per cent.* on the taxes on consumption, amounts to but little more than half a million. I do not think we ought to reckon it at more than 7 *per cent.* and for this reason, the real expence

to

to them is 5 *per cent.*; and as they can
afford to take that, others who charge more
might be underfold.   However, as we are
at prefent endeavouring to elucidate this
matter, I fhall calculate it in another manner; and fuppofe that the merchant and
manufacturer blends the duty with the
prime coft and all other expences, and then
upon the total, charges whatever the neat
profit of his trade is : Suppofe the average
profit on trade and manufactures to be 12
per cent. then we muft calculate the advance
on the taxes at 12 *per cent.*

	£.	£.
Cuftoms and collecting,	2,300,000	
Excifes, &c. - - -	5,908,000	
Malt, - - - - -	654,250	
		8,862,250
On which 12 *per cent.* is, - -		1,063,470

The whole account of *Britifh* taxes therefore will, upon this footing, ftand as follows :

Total of all our taxes neat into the exchequer, - - - - - - - }	10,213,000
Expences of collecting, - - - -	659,250
12 *per cent.* to merchants and manu- facturers on their advance of thofe on confumption, - - - - - - - }	1,063,470
Total, - - - - - -	£. 11,935,720

I do not apprehend that any probable
account can carry the calculation farther;
upon what authority therefore, or on what
prin-

principles, can M. *du Pont* make the total above 20 millions?

But it well deferves the attention of the œconomical writers, that if their ideas and thofe of *Locke* and *Decker* be true, M. *du Pont* is much too low in faying, that for 10 millions the exchequer receives, the nation pays 20; for if every man makes fuch advances on the taxes as they defcribe —if the farmer fells his ox dearer on account of taxes—if the leatherfeller raifes his price on account of taxes on candles and foap—if the fhoemaker adds to his on account of cuftoms on wine—if the hatter raifes his on account of the high price of fhoes—if the mercer raifes his filks becaufe hats rife—if the merchant importer raifes his prices becaufe filks are dearer—and, in a word, if every man in trade adds *all the taxes* he pays to the prices of the commodities he deals in, it is plain, as *Locke* obferved, that the whole muft fall (not on land) but on the idle confumer; but inftead of taxes being thus doubled, they will be multiplied an hundred fold—inftead of our paying 20 millions, we fhould be paying 100 millions, nay, perhaps 1000 millions; the extravagance of which idea fhews plainly that the real bearers of the taxes are much more numerous than they fuppofe —and that in fact people in trade can draw
back

back no other taxes on their confumption than fuch as fall equally and by neceffity on every one engaged in the fame trade. All the other taxes they really pay, and fupport the final weight as much as any landlord in the kingdom.

M. *du Pont* is determined to give our fociety of *Emulation* the meaneft opinion poffible of the whole fyftem of *Britifh* politicks. Not content with overturning our finances, he attacks the navigation act—" cet acte n'a pas peu contribué à retarder les progrés de votre commerce"—I believe the *Dutch* in the laft age would have given a different account; nor can there be any doubt but it was a meafure calculated with the utmoft wifdom, and the experience of above a century has confirmed the reafoning of the politicians who made it; M. *du Pont* feems not to know that our wifeft writers, and thofe whofe works are here in much the higheft eftimation, concur in this idea, which is fo perfectly confonant with the nature of things *.

In

---

* At page 43, M. *du Pont* falls into a very great error in afferting that the *London* Society expends 40 *mille livres fterling* annually. This is an error of a cypher—let him ftrike that out, and he will be much nearer the truth.

In another place he fays, " il a renverfé la conftitution *Britannique*.—Il a appauvri les maîtres de la maifon pour enrichir leurs valets de leurs dépouilles. Il a principale-ment contribué à former ces fortunes pécu-niaires qui ont jetté la *Grande Brétagne* dans le delire funefte des emprunts pub-lics †." What is this to the purpofe? he might as well have faid in general that TRADE had done all this; which has no-thing to do with the enquiry. Has it been an encouragement to trade? This he ac-knowledges in thefe words. And as to its being a monopoly, which is *Decker*'s ob-jection, experience tells us the contrary, and that from the competition between our own ports and our own merchants, freights are as cheap, and commodities as readily tranfported as if all *Europe* had been our carriers. As to navigation, fhipping, and feamen, all thefe *phyfiocratical* writers laugh at fuch matters, but they forget that an extenfive navigation, much fhipping, and many feamen, are the farmers beft markets —they are themfelves markets—they by wealth create markets—not to fpeak of that maritime power which M. *du Pont* mif-takenly fays in the fame piece, is to be bought.

---

† *Ephemerides du Citoyen*, 1769, vol. vi.

bought.—Ships and cannon may be bought, but money will not buy feamen.

He would do well to inftance any export of our commodities in which the navigation act ever proved a monopoly : Let him enquire the freight of the immenfe quantities of corn *Britifh* fhipping landed in *France* in 1748, 49, and 50; and yet the export of our corn is a monopoly to fhips navigated by *Britifh* feamen.

The author in various parts of his letter fpeaks of our taxes on confumption as impoverifhing the people to the leffening of confumption : but herein he is again utterly mifinformed, fince the confumption of every article that has been excifed, has increafed under the accumulated weight. No article has been heavier taxed than malt and beer—and none confumed by people lefs able to bear it; yet has the quantity almoft regularly advanced under all the growing weight of fuch heavy duties.

Upon the whole, this gentleman and the Marquis *de Mirabeau,* with many other *French* writers, feem to have recommended the abolition of all taxes on confumption in favour of a fimple land-tax, rather for the fake of getting rid of farmers of the revenue, and other great abufes, than from any pofitive conviction of the excellence of the plan : and in the purfuit of the notion
they

they have run into the two common errors,
a difpofition to condemn every thing they
find at home; and on the contrary, in their
recommendation to launch into an hypothefis, to which every circumftance, every
fact, and every thought muft be fquared.
I know nothing more likely to lead to erroneous conclufions. It was a ftrange blunder
to carry the fame idea to *Britain*.

Thefe gentlemen do not feem in any of
their works to make a proper diftinction
between different countries. For inftance,
between thofe where the income arifes only
from the foil—thofe where the foil yields
much the greateft income—and others where
trade and manufactures are the moft confiderable. Had they made this diftinction,
they could not have allowed themfelves
the licence of fuch *general* expreffions, as if
their noftrum was equally adapted to every
poffible conftitution. What do they fay to
Holland?—Would they abforb all the *Dutch*
excifes into a tax upon land, which one
might almoft fay hardly exifts? Would
they, like our Sir *Matthew Decker*, lay it
upon houfes, and thereby let the trader,
who fpends five thoufand a year, be taxed
no higher than the fifherman who fpends
only fifty pounds? neither of whom poffefs
one acre of land—And will they venture to
assert

affert the inconfiderable body of *Dutch*
landlords would be eafed by paying all the
enormous amount of *Dutch* excifes directly
in a tax on the produce of their lands,
rather than have, as at prefent, the accu-
mulations of thofe who advance the taxes?
Would thefe gentlemen accept a *Dutch*
eftate in fo bleffed a predicament? This
is an inftance, perhaps the ftrongeft, of a
country, for which their fyftem appears at
firft fight to be ridicule itfelf.

On the other hand, let us fuppofe a
country where there is neither trade nor
manufactures, and confequently where the
national income arifes only from land rents.
If the publick revenue in fuch an one is
raifed by excifes, the landlords, who from
the fuppofition are the only confumers,
pay not only the tax, but the profit made
on advancing it. Here therefore their fyftem is fo far rational ; but even in this cafe
there follows the quere, Whether they would
not lofe more than to the amount of this
advantage, by the new tax on their *produit
net*, which would be a tax on their improvements, in direct proportion to the
amount of fuch improvements. Hence,
therefore, I fhould even in this cafe be
againft their fcheme, and had rather that
the general body of indolent landlords
fhould

fhould pay accumulated excife, than have induftrious improving ones taxed in proportion to their induftry.

Thefe are two inftances, the one in which their fyftem would be prepofterous; the other, in which it would be attended with the feweft inconveniences. The example of *England* lies between both.

The income of our foil is very confiderable, but does not make much above half the total income of the ftate. The profits and labour in commerce, manufactures and arts, are of a vaft amount; confequently to exempt them all from taxation, and throw the whole burthen on land, would be unequal and oppreffive in the higheft degree.

In *France* the income of the foil bears a much greater proportion to the total income than in *England*, and confequently their fyftem would do lefs mifchief there than here. But it is by a ftrange mode of reafoning that they fhould recommend a plan to us, becaufe in *France* it is to a certain point more expedient than in fome other countries.

In anfwer to all this, I know they would advance as before, that their propofition is by no means to burthen the land more, becaufe the land already pays all taxes, and

in

in no fyftem can it pay more than all : but on their plan it would pay the *all* with moft eafe.

By what other logical ledgerdemain than what *Locke* and *Decker* ufed, they make out this pofition, I know not ; that it is falfe, will admit of no doubt—that every thing *Locke* and *Decker* advanced on this point, has been refuted by expe- rience, as well as writings, there is as little doubt.

Suppofe a merchant of *Marfeilles* trades to the *Levant*, and that his commerce con- fifts of exporting *French* cloths in return for cotton, filk, fruit, drugs, coffee, and filver ; and upon this trade makes a profit of forty thoufand livres a year. Now the queftion is, who pays the excifes that in any way affect the manufacture of the cloth ex- ported, or the cotton and filk imported ; the cuftoms on the drugs, coffee, &c. ; and laftly, the manufacturers and merchants profits not only on the direct line of trade, but on the advance of the excifes and cuf- toms ?—*Anfwer*, The confumers of thofe commodities. *No*; fay thefe gentlemen, *it is les propriétaires des biens-fonds*, the land- lords alone.

Suppofe the coffee, for inftance, landed at *Marfeilles*, and a cuftom paid on it ; fup- pofe

pofe it next to pay (as not coming from their own iflands) an excife; and further, fuppofe it to pay at the gates of a city the entrée: it is confumed, part by the merchant who imports it, part by the manufacturer of the filk and cotton, and part by a *French* landlord. Thefe three purchafers of the coffee certainly pay all the duties, and all the profits made by advancing them —what I would urge is, that the merchant who drinks his part, pays in the laft refort, his fhare of the taxes as much as the landlord. And I defire to know in what manner the tax on that drank by the merchant and the manufacturer can poffibly come to the landlord? *Locke* and *Decker* in anfwer will fay, that thefe men will charge the expence on the confumers of the other commodities they deal in : they might as well fay they would do the fame by the money they loft at the gaming tables; and becaufe they loft a thoufand livres at hazard fell their filk and cotton fo much the dearer.

Let us attend to the manner in which a merchant fits down to calculate the prime coft to him of the commodity he deals in. Suppofe it wine; and let us ftate ideal fums, their exactnefs is not of confequence, fuppofe 36 pipes.

	£.	s.	d.	£.	s.	d.
Invoice of 36 pipes, - -				409	10	0
Duty with fees, -	347	15	4			
Port entry with ditto,	79	3	4			
				426	18	8
Freight, &c. - -	63	18	0			
Prifage, - - -	9	0	0			
				72	18	0
Infurance with convoy on 400 *l.* at 5 *per cent.* - - - -				20	0	0
Landing, at 3 *s.* 4 *d.* *per* ton,				3	0	0
Porterage, - - - - - -				3	12	0
Cooperage, at 1 *s.* 4 *d.* *per* ton,				1	4	0
Leakage, 5 *s.* a pipe, - - -				9	0	0
				946	2	8
Which is *per* pipe, - -				26	3	4
Suppofe the merchant's profit 23 *per cent.* - - - -				5	16	8
Coft to the confumer, exclufive of expences in moving from the merchant's vaults,				32	0	0

Now if the *French* writers ideas be juft, the merchant, befides the above charges, fhould add fuch as thefe :

	£.	s.	d.
	32	0	0
Expences in coffee, tea, fugar, &c. beyond what the above 23 *per cent*. will allow,	1	10	0
Point lace, and diamonds for my wife, - -	3	0	0

N. B. Merchants wives in *Eng-land* wear thefe commodities.

	£.	s.	d.
Further, as I am perfectly well inclined to drink as well as to fell wine, and my 23 *per cent*. not being fufficient, *inde*, - - -	1	8	0

	£.	s.	d.
Price which I muft charge the confumer, - -	* 37	18	0

The

---

* Sir *M. Decker*'s idea that every man advances the price of the commodities he deals in, proportioned to the increafe in *all* the articles of his expence; of which he gives an inftance in fhoes; is contrary to common fenfe and all experience. Thus he fays, the grazier adds the advance in fhoes to the price of his beaft: Impoffible; the price of it in the market will not be regulated even by the expence of its food, much lefs of its mafter's fhoes. He farther makes the tanner's journeymen raife their wages on account of the advance in fhoes; another inftance which fhews how little he underftood the nature of taxes. In what manufactory of the kingdom did he find 100 or 50 *per cent*. advance in labour fince the excife duties? And

he

The merchant may charge what he pleafes, but where is the confumer who will pay 37 for what he can get at next door for 32 ?

I fuppofe 23 *per cent.* or whatever is named on the above expenditure; but if the merchant charges more than reafonable, he will be as much underfold by his neighbour as if he charged his wife's gilt chariot, or her loffes at quadrille.

Thus there are certain expences, under which a commodity cannot be procured ; there muft alfo be a reafonable profit for the merchant ; and if there were no confumers but landlords, certainly the land would pay the whole ; but as the commodity is confumed by all ranks—all ranks pay their fhare.

It is the cuftom of fome gentlemen in *England* to import their own wine; they then fave a part of the 5 *l*. 16 *s*. 8 *d. per* pipe

---

he makes every man who deals in leather or fhoes, raife his price proportioned to the taxes on foap and candles ; in a word, he fuppofes every man to make an advance in his commodity, proportioned to the general dearnefs of living—and becaufe fuch a proportion appears reafonable, he took it for granted ; whereas nothing is farther from fact. See *Effay on the caufes of the decline of foreign Trade:* which decline never exifted ; fo far from it, that our exports, and particularly of woollen goods, were then greater than ever known before, as is abundantly proved by Mr. *Smith,* in his *Memoirs of Wool.* Yet Sir *M.* complains moft of the decline in the woollen fabricks.

pipe (not the whole of it)—then, fay the *French* writers, furely the gentleman if he buys of the merchant, pays not only the duty, but 23 *per cent.* more—Certainly, I reply, for all he confumes—*On no more,* fays a dealer in dowlas, who ftands by, *for I buy part of the merchant's wines, and of courfe pay my fhare of the taxes.* But who buys your dowlas? *The Dutch and Americans*—and confequently pay the duties. *I alfo,* fays a tobacco merchant, *buy wine of this man :*—Who confumes this tobacco? *Germany and the North*—they therefore pay their fhare.

But there is a farther circumftance which muft not be forgotten, and which may be faid to eafe the landlord even of the fhare which belongs to him, which is his own confumption :—This is the great national wealth which accompanies taxes, or at leaft is always found, where they and trade abound together, as in *Holland, England,* and *France,* raifing the prices of the land-lord's products, fo as to indemnify him for his taxes, which, though not a regular drawing back in the way a trader does, yet has the fame effect: he is enab'ed from this national wealth, to raife his rents, and the price of the farmer's products rifing with all other commodities; this burthen, like all the reft, falls equally on the whole

body

body of confumers. I do not fay that the fuppofition I have now been making is always the cafe—but if the landlord paid an excife which he could regularly draw back, then the effect would be juft fo, and the circle complete: That is, every man advancing his fhare of excifes, but paying no more than in proportion to his confumption.

In the next place, let us take the cafe of a ftockholder, a man with a thoufand a year in the public funds. The excellency of our excifes is, that they bring every article of this man's confumption to contribute to the public revenue: Excifes and cuftoms are alone what he can feel: he cannot drink a bottle of wine, buy a yard of lace, or an article in furniture, &c. without paying a tax: this idle confumer therefore, is made to contribute—Is this no advantage to land?—He fells nothing which the landlords buy, and confequently cannot accumulate duties on them.

Out of the fuppofed 23 *per cent.* I ftated above, there is to be deducted the intereft of the merchant's capital, or 5 *per cent.*; alfo, all his expences of trade, or charges of merchandize, fuch as clerks, writers, vaults, coopers, paper, books, poftage, long credit, bad debts, &c. which perhaps will reduce the 23 to 12 or 15; and there
are

are many trades and manufactures not fo good as a wine merchant: fuppofe we fay 12 *per cent.* as a medium neat profit.—Now can there poffibly be common fenfe in the landed intereft fubmitting to the total of taxation, in order to efcape 12 *per cent.* addition on the part of their confumption?

Suppofe M. *du Pont*'s propofition executed, and all our taxes laid on land: what would be the confequence, granting it poffible for the land to bear them? Would not trade, manufactures and arts efcape taxation, that is, the poffeffors of half the national income? And is this a way to render taxes an equal burthen? But in what manner is the landlord made amends? This immenfe tax on the farmer's neat produce is to be no excife which he can draw back and throw upon the confumers of corn, confequently he can afford to pay no more rent than before to the landlord; but much lefs; nor is there one attendant circumftance that can raife the price of his products, and thereby recompence him: What advantage is to arife to him farther than the 12 *per cent.* the mercantile advance on the landlord's confumption—No probable one; for, as to the benefits of a free port trade when cuftoms are at an end, the probable confequences

are

are much againſt the nation; one circumſtance of which would be a free import of
corn, not very favourable to the farming
race—but which, in ſome years, would be
heavy enough upon them.—It may be ſaid,
the duties on malt would ceaſe, and the
conſumption of barley be greater. I much
queſtion it; at beſt it is but a conjecture;
whereas we certainly know that with an
increaſe of tax there has been an increaſe
of conſumption *.

Thus,

---

* A modern writer, whoſe information is un-
doubted, and whoſe abilities are confeſſed, ſtates the
duties on conſumption at two periods thus :

	£.
—" Average of net excife ſince the new duties, three years, ending 1767,	4,590,734
Ditto before the new duties, three years, ending 1759, - -	3,261,694
Average increaſe, - -	1,329,040

Here is no diminution. Here is, on the contrary, an
immenſe increaſe. This is owing, I ſhall be told, to
the new duties, which may increaſe the total bulk,
but at the ſame time may make ſome diminution of
the produce of the old.—Let us take, as the beſt
inſtance for the purpoſe, the produce of the old here-
ditary and temporary excife, granted in the reign of
Charles II. whoſe object is that of moſt of the new impoſitions from two averages, each of eight years :

Average

Thus, with a view to very doubtful advantages, they are, in order to eafe themfelves of 12 *per cent.* advance on taxes on
con-

	£.
Average firft period, eight years, ending 1754, - - -	525,317
Ditto fecond period, eight years, ending 1767, - - -	538,542
Encreafe, - -	13,225

Such is the ftate of the oldeft branch of the revenue
from confumption. Befides the acquifition of fo much
new, this article, to fpeak of no other, has rather
encreafed under the preffure of all thofe additional
taxes to which the author † is pleafed to attribute its
deftruction. But as the author has made his grand
effort againft thofe moderate, judicious and neceffary
levies, which fupport all the dignity, the credit and
the power of his country, the reader will excufe a
little farther detail on this fubject : That we may fee
how little oppreffive thofe taxes are on the fhoulders
of the publick, with which he labours fo earneftly to
load its imagination, For this purpofe we take the
ftate of that fpecific article upon which the two capital
burthens of the war leaned the moft immediately, by
the additional duties upon malt and upon beer :

	Barrels.
Average of ftrong beer brewed in eight years before the additional malt and beer duties, - -	3,895,059
Average of the eight years fince the duties, - -	4,060,726
Encreafe in laft period, -	165,667

† *State of the Nation.*

Here

confumption, to accept the whole amount,
and inftead of 4*s.* pay 15 *s.* in the pound,
while all the other idle confumers in the
nation are to drink their claret at 1 *s.* 6 *d.* a
bottle, and wear foreign manufactures duty
free—in a word, their whole confumption

to

Here is the effect of two fuch daring taxes as 3 *d.*
by the bufhel additional on malt, and 3 *s.* by the
barrel additional on beer. Two impofitions laid without remiffion one upon the neck of the other; and
laid upon an object which before had been immenfely
loaded. They did not in the leaft impair the confumption : it has grown under them. It appears,
that upon the whole the people did not feel fo much
inconvenience from the new duties, as to oblige them
to take refuge in the private brewery. Quite the contrary happened in both thefe refpects in the reign of
King William, and it happened from much flighter
impofitions. No people can long confume a commodity for which they are not well able to pay. An
enlightened reader laughs at the inconfiftent chimera
of our author, of a people univerfally luxurious, and
at the fame time oppreffed with taxes and declining in
trade. For my part, I cannot look on thefe duties as
the author does. He fees nothing but the burthen.
I can perceive the burthen as well as he ; but I cannot
avoid contemplating alfo the ftrength that fupports it.
From thence I draw the moft comfortable affurances
of the future vigour, and the ample refources, of this
great mifreprefented country ; and can never prevail
on myfelf to make complaints which have no caufe,
in order to raife hopes which have no foundation."
The *French* writers, who often quote *the State of the
Nation*, fhould read this admirable anfwer to it : it
would enlarge their conceptions not a little. *Obfervations on a late State of the Nation*, 3d edit. 1767. p. 44.

to be exempted from all taxation—and all this mighty operation is to be founded folely on the chimera that the land pays all taxes.—That Mr. *A.* the landlord pays the cuftoms on Lord *B.* the ftockholder's claret. That Mr. *C.* another landlord, is burthened with the duties on tobacco fmoaked in *Germany.* And Mr. *D.* a third, has the excifes on tea drank at *New York* to pay. If thefe ideas are juft, there is a contradiction in mine not far fhort of frenzy.

Suppofe all cuftoms and excifes abolifhed, let me afk this fimple queftion; How would the merchant or manufacturer contribute to the publick revenues ? At prefent he pays taxes in the whole expenditure of his *profit.* The moment he is a mere confumer inftead of a trader, he ranks with landlords, and pays at the laft hand duties on all the commodities he buys.—Further; how would the ftockholder, or him whofe income was from mortgages, contribute to the public ? Not a penny would be paid by them ; if they pleafed they might expend their whole income in encouraging the induftry of *Frenchmen* and *Italians,* by confuming their manufactures, without contributing a farthing to the ftate. To what purpofe, confiftent with common fenfe, could fuch an exemption be given them ? Such would live duty free, while land paid 15 *s.* in the pound!

pound! The firſt, greateſt, and moſt eſſential principle of taxation is *equality :* The
wit of man could never deviſe a ſyſtem ſo
compleat in this reſpect as duties on conſumption ; where can the converſe of their
merit be found ſo perfect as in the union of
taxes on the neat produce of the land ?

A *German* prince, the Margrave of *Baden
Dourlach,* pleaſed with the writings on
what our authors pompouſly call *La Nouvelle Science,* the œconomical ſcience, and
I ſuppoſe meaning perfectly well, has
made the experiment, as we are told *, in
the conſiderable village of *Dietlingen,* in
1770. He there aboliſhed every exciſe, and
duty whatſoever except the tythe, and in
return accepted the 4th of the neat produce
of gardens, graſs and arable lands ; and
the 6th of vines ; that is to ſay,

	liv.	s.	den.
From an arpent of arable land, of the firſt quality	6	10	11
Ditto the medium quality	2	10	11
Ditto bad quality -	1	14	11
Ditto good graſs -	8	14	6
Ditto bad graſs - -	6	0	0
Ditto the beſt gardens -	11	12	8
Ditto the next -	8	14	8
Ditto vines - -	8	14	6

And M. *du Pont,* in a note on this obſerves,

---

* *Ephemerides du Citoyen,* 1771, vol. vii. p. 209.

ferves, that it muſt be changed every ten
years, becauſe an acre in the loweſt claſs
may be advanced by improvement to the
firſt. Thus we ſee that in every inſtance
theſe friends of the farmer are for taxing
his improvements: they muſt have a portion
of the produce varying with improvements:
we know what this is in our tythe; a tax
would be univerſal, which the tythe is not.
—What a curſe upon the agriculture of a
country would ſuch a ſyſtem be! Nay; as
if they would not ſee the effects of their
own taille, he obſerves, that the means to
judge of improvements are the cattle the
farmer keeps—" La quantité des beſtiaux
peut donner une idée aſſez juſte de la ſomme
des avances, dont ils forment toujours la
meilleure partie.—Quand le nombre des
beſtiaux eſt *tel* ſur *telle* étendue de terrein,
les *avances de culture* et les *repriſes du cul-
tivateur* doivent être de *tant*.—Quand les
avances de la culture et les repriſes du cul-
tivateur ſont de *tant* le *produit net* ſur une
récolte de *telle* quantité, à *tel prix*, eſt de
tant."—But in this whole paper there is
no ſatisfaction given us how exciſes are
aboliſhed in one part of a prince's territory
and not in all—This is a difficulty to which
I cannot readily imagine a ſolution without
a much greater expence than the experiment was worth.

M.

M. *Quefnay* gives in the *Encyclopedie* a set of maxims upon which his difciples have founded much of their new fcience; there is in thefe maxims a great mixture of penetration and prejudice. Here they are:

I. *Les travaux d'induftrie ne multiplient pas les richeffes.*

This is the idea upon which they partly found the neceffity of making the foil pay all taxes; but what a ftrange affertion! In what manner will M. *Quefnay* get rid of the exception, *Holland?* Does not induftry in that country multiply riches? Is it not attended with the fame effect in *England* and *France?* To affert that the foil is the original of all wealth, would be juft; but to fay that manufactures and commerce add not to national wealth, is beyond conception. Let us ftate a fuppofition. A country produces befides its own confumption, 100,000 quarters of wheat; 500,000 pounds of wool; 50,000 hides; 5000 tons of hemp, and 10,000 tons of iron; which furplus of its product is exported in 300 fail of foreign fhipping, navigated by 5000 failors. We will fuppofe thefe commodities fell for 500,000*l.* which is of courfe annually received part in cafh and part in foreign produce. Suppofe the legiflature of this country, in order to enrich the people, introduces or enlarges manu-

factures

factures fufficiently to work the wool and hemp into cloth; the hides into fabrics of leather, and the iron into hard wares; and inftead of exporting the wheat, feeds thefe new manufacturers with it. Let us, to make the idea ftronger, fuppofe the ftatefman to erect thefe fabrics within an enclofure quite cut off from the common intercourfe with the reft of the people. What is his procefs? In order for his defigned works he wants a portion of the people; a demand that will in all countries be eafily fupplied. As he encreafes the numbers of workmen in his enclofure, the export of thofe raw commodities leffens, till it ends upon his having hands fufficient for working the whole. Here then is a change wrought, but not to the old inhabitants; before, they fold their furplus products to the foreign fhipping; now they fell it at the gates of the ftatefman's enclofure—it is the fame to them; their intereft is neither promoted nor injured. Now let us attend to the progrefs of the new manufactures; the raw materials being worked into the fabrics abovementioned, amount to the value of £2,000,000—thefe the ftatefman puts on board fhips he has built, and having by degrees trained up feamen, he fends thefe fabrics to a foreign market, where he difpofes of them, and taking in exchange
fuch

such commodities as are wanted in his own country, receives the balance in bullion. Here then we may state some effects of the new policy.

The number of subjects is encreased by .all that are employed in the manufacture and transport of those commodities, which formerly were exported raw.   This increase arises from the increase of demand for labour, the consequence I explained on another occasion.   The people in his inclosure are just the same to him as an increase of territory; they have a regular, permanent income *created* by themselves of 1,500,000 *l.* which is the value their labour adds to the rough materials purchased without the walls of the inclosure.   This income supports them, and is open to levies for the public service as much as the products of the lands. How can M. *Quesnay* possibly assert that the labour of this industry does not multiply the wealth of the whole nation? The inclosure is peopled without lessening the population of the country; 1,500,000 *l.* is gained more than before, which is to support the manufacturers; they in the common course of multiplication will yield a surplus of people for soldiers, sailors, &c. and in the expenditure of their income will add to the national revenue so much by taxes on consumption, that it may be possible for the statesman to ease the landlords thereby of a

part

part of thofe on the products of the land.
I affert that the labour of thefe people is to
all intents and purpofes as really and effectually *wealth* as the income of the lands.
Nor has M. *Quefnay* in any of his works
given one reafon to prove the contrary.
Inftead of an enclofure for manufacturers, fuppofe a fmall ifland full of them
near a large one, a territory under the
fame government; will not the income
gained by the inhabitants of the little
ifland be as much the income of the ftatefman's fubjects as that of the great one?
Will he not have taxes and men from
them? will not his people be increafed?
will not their navigation give him feamen?
To what other purpofe, intent or idea can
the income from the lands in one ifland be
called wealth, and that from manufactures
in the other not allowed the fame definition?
I have kept the manufacturers, merchants
and feamen diftinct from the people, to
throw the idea into the ftrongeft light, but
the effect is the fame if they are fcattered
through the whole territory.

II. *Les hommes fe multiplient à proportion
des revenus des biens-fonds.*

Very true in fome cafes, very falfe in
others. In a ftate where the only income
is land it may, under fome circumftances,
be true; but not in others. Suppofe the
multiplication from the land ftopped (as it
always

always is) for want of a greater demand of the furplus of its population; it then ftops becaufe the people, if it bred more, would not be able to get an income; but if manufactures, arts or commerce are introduced or increafed, to demand more hands from the population of the foil, *then* that population will multiply, though the revenue of the land remains the fame. It is therefore a great error to fuppofe that the income of the foil alone regulates the population of it.

III. *Les travaux d'induſtrie qui occupent des hommes* au prejudice de la culture *des biens-fonds, nuifent à la population, et à l'accroiſſement des richeſſes.*

An ideal cafe, which is impoffible to happen. A demand for hands in every thing creates hands; agriculture is always firft eftablifhed in a country; when manufactures come they demand hands of agriculture, which will have plenty to fupply them: if this goes on fo far that agriculture wants hands, fhe will demand them of the towns, and the towns will fupply her. Both thefe cafes are very common, and no inconveniences follow; if labour and prices in general rife, agriculture does not fuffer by it.

IV. *Les richeſſes des cultivateurs font naitre les richeſſes de la culture.*

It is impoffible to ftate a truer maxim.

V. *L'agriculture produit deux fortes de richeſſes: ſavoir le produit annuel des revenus des*

*des propriétaires, & la restitution des frais
de la culture.*

You may make this diſtinction if you
pleaſe, but with equal juſtice you might
ſay, it produced ſeveral other ſpecies of income. In *England* I ſhould ſay, firſt, the
ſoil yields a groſs product, which forms the
following diviſions of income :

1. The landlord in rent,   5
2. The clergy in tythe,   1¾
3. The ſtate in the land-tax,   0½
4. The induſtrious poor in labour, 3¼
5. The non-induſtrious poor in rates, ⅘
6. The artizans in wear and tear, 1⅓
7. The farmer in his profit.   4½*

And for the information of my foreign
readers I have ſet down againſt each article,
the proportion it bears to the reſt. That
is, if 20 is the groſs product of *England,*
the reſt will be as above.

VI. *Les richeſſes employées aux frais de la
culture doivent étres reſervées aux cultivateurs
& être exemptes de toutes impoſitions.*

Moſt certainly ; and this tythe and rates
excepted is clearly and deciſively the caſe
in *England*; yet would theſe writers perſuade
us that our ſyſtem of finance is a bad one.

VII. *Lorſque le commerce des denrés du
cru eſt facile & libre les travaux de main-
d'œuvre ſont toujours aſſurés infailliblement
par le revenu des biens-fonds.*

A very

---
* Theſe make 17¼, the other 2¾ are feed and teams,

A very juſt idea.

VIII. *Une nation qui a peu de commerce de denrée de ſon cru, & qui eſt réduite pour ſubſiſter à un commerce d'induſtrie, eſt dans un état précaire & incertain.*

Holland is an inſtance that this truth (for there certainly is truth in this maxim) muſt have ſtrong exceptions. *Holland* is in a precarious ſtate, not from ſubſiſting by commerce inſtead of agriculture, but from the ſmallneſs of her territory. Greater neighbours, if permitted by others, might ſwallow up *Holland*; ſo they might *Switzerland*; ſo they always have done *Milan*: this cauſe of weakneſs has nothing to do with the employment of the people: but will any perſon pretend to aſſert, that *Holland* would be more powerful if ſhe ſubſiſted by the huſbandry of a ſoil, the rental of which, would not keep out the ſea! Commerce has made the *Dutch* more powerful than many ſtates, far richer in territory. This maxim therefore is only ſaying, that ſmall ſtates (for ſuch only can come within the deſcription) are not ſo powerful as great ones!

IX. *Une nation qui a un grand territoire & qui fait baiſſer le prix des denrées de ſon cru pour favoriſer la fabrication des ouvrages de main-d'œuvre, ſe détruit de toutes parts.*

Uncontrovertible.

X. *La non-valeur avec abondance n'eſt point richeſſe. La cherté avec diſette eſt miſère.*

*mifére. L'abondance avec cherté (perma-
nente) eft opulence.*

An incomparable idea, which deferves to
be written in letters of gold.

XI. *Les avantages du commerce extérieur
ne confiftent pas dans l'accroiffement des richeffes pecuniaires.*

In what then do they confift?

XII. *On ne peut connoître par l'état de la
balance du commerce entre diverfes nations,
l'avantage du commerce, & l'etât des richeffes
de chaque nation.*

This opinion certainly is not juft. Where
there are no mines, the balance of national
payments (which, with a few exceptions, is
the balance of commerce) is the means of
wealth—and it is wealth that encourages
every branch of induftry, agriculture as
well as manufactures. A great domeftic
circulation—a flourifhing hufbandry—and
abundance of national wealth, without a
favourable balance of trade, is a chimerical
idea—of which an inftance cannot be produced in the whole globe.

XIII. *Une nation ne pourroit entreprendre
contre le commerce de fes voifins, fans déranger
fon état & fans fe nuire à elle même, furtout
dans la commerce reciproque qu'elle auroit directement ou indirectement établi eux.*

Nothing can be more miftaken than fuch
ideas; of which truth innumerable inftances may be given. See the commerce
of

of *India*, which has been fucceffively enjoyed by the *Genoefe*, *Portuguefe*, *Dutch*,
French, and *Englifh* ; and by none of them
without the deftruction of their neighbours.
What is the monopoly of fpices ? What
is the monopoly of the commerce of colonies, which all nations upon fuch good
grounds keep to themfelves ? What is the
navigation-act of *England*, that epoch of the
maritime commerce and power of this country ? What are the duties laid by northern
nations on the commodities of their fouthern
neighbours ? When a country is fituated
like *France*, *Spain* and *Italy*, and at the fame
time enjoying colonies in the *Weft Indies*,
what comparifon can there be between the
demand of fuch a country for the commodities of *Poland* or *Denmark*, with the demand in thefe for the commodities of the
fouth ? Would not an equal commerce
without duties impoverifh the north ? And
would not the diminution of its wealth
ruin the induftry and even agriculture
of their own fubjects ? This is a diftinction between nations formed by nature
herfelf ; and if induftry is equal between them, that fuperiority muft be beneficial to one, and injurious to the other.
A general free trade, as there has been no
example of it in hiftory, fo is it contrary to
reafon. But why will not thofe writers
look around them ? Where does commerce
flourifh

flourish moſt? Upon what principles does it flouriſh? It flouriſhes moſt in *England* and *Holland,* upon principles, and owing to a policy diametrically contrary to what theſe writers would inculcate. Let them produce their inſtances. Why will they eternally wrap themſelves up in hypothetical viſionary propoſitions, of which no experience was ever gained, and in which nothing but conjecture can guide them? Yet upon ſuch foundations do they arraign the policy that carried the COMMERCE of *Holland* to the higheſt pitch of grandeur * ; and the principles which have rendered the AGRICULTURE of *England* flouriſhing, and her people happy!

One word more to my countrymen, in general reply to theſe theoriſts. Our agriculture has long flouriſhed—and is now flouriſhing and improving—our landlords and farmers wealthy and happy—our taxes heavy, but ſo equal and well adminiſtered that nobody feels the weight but the idle and extravagant conſumer :—while our landlords raiſe their rents, and the farmers are happy in paying them; while all claſſes of the people expend more than ever they did in former times; while all parts of the iſland are improved by publick works; and ornamented by private

vate

---

* See the India Commerce, &c. &c.

vate ones; in a word, while the great cha-
racteristic of a flourishing state in every
thing appears, ABONDANCE ET CHERTE
EST OPULENCE, while the nation is happy
in such a variety of circumstances flowing
from her present policy, would it not be
madness to adopt or even to commend a
system which tends so powerfully to eradi-
cate every blessing we enjoy?

But impartiality demands of me a due
tribute to the genius of these writers in
other circumstances than such as I have
quoted. Mess. *Quesnay* and *du Pont* in many
of their works, display great sagacity, much
knowledge, and every where a very sincere
desire of being serviceable to the public: In
a word, they shew themselves to be writers
that no man would wish to oppose, nor
should I have been induced to assert opinions
contrary to theirs, had not the same duty to
my country which they owe to theirs,
called on me to differ from ideas, which
I should have trembled to see realized.
M. *de Mirabeau* in his *Tableau Oecono-
mique* has some admirable observations
on the advantages of great farms; on
the export of corn; on the superiority of
national wealth to population †, and on
some

---

† It is very extraordinary that this writer, after
discovering this most useful maxim, should recall his
opinion,

fome other points. In thefe he fhews the clearnefs of his underftanding, and his freedom from popular prejudices—in thefe I readily allow him diftinguifhed merit, and am forry that on any occafion I fhould feel a neceffity of differing in opinion with a man whofe humanity I love, and whofe abilities I revere.

If in return for M. *du Pont*'s letter to the *London* Society, in which he gives fo much advice to this country, I fhould venture to offer advice to the government of his, I fhould do it in few words. Relative to the material object, taxation, I fhould fay— Your agriculture is deftroyed by your land-tax being proportional to the products of the foil—and you are cramped by the exemption of the nobles : Eafe your hufbandry by abolifhing the taille, and throw the burthen into additional taxes on confumption, you will thereby tax the farmers only when they are luxurious confumers, and you remedy the nobles exemption, by making every rank and clafs pay in proportion to their expences. In cafe the amount of the prefent taille could not be added to the prefent taxes on confumption, then let the deficiency be laid on in the form of the

Eng-

---

opinion, and declare that wealth was an inferior object to population ; and that numbers of people were alone the caufe of riches ; yet this is his pofition in the letters annexed to *La Socrate Ruftique,* 12mo.

English land-tax on rents, and like that, be at an invariable rate. But if the representations of your writers are near the truth, there are such enormous expences in the receipt of your taxes, that a better conduct in that respect, would almost make up for the deficiency of the taille. If this is the case, certainly the interests of your country demand a reform.———

Thus have I gone through this long examination of the sentiments of these authors ; I thought it a work necessary to my design, which is to point out how agriculture may best be encouraged. As I explained the system of *England*, and recommended the imitation of it to foreigners, and endeavoured to shew the great obstacles to husbandry in most countries ; it was natural to throw in the caution against adopting, in the career of improvement, propositions, which, though made by able writers, appeared to me to have a very fatal tendency : this it is that induced me to examine with so much attention, the hypothesis which the modern *French* writers have built in what they call the oeconomical science.

S E C T. II.

POPULATION A SECONDARY OBJECT.

IN the confideration of methods for advancing the interefts of agriculture, a
legiflature may be in danger of following
bad advice not only in matters of taxation,
but in feveral other points: Among thefe
the attention that is proper to be given to
population, deferves particular notice. Since
in feveral inftances recommendations may
be offered, which at firft fight may feem
difadvantageous to population, and on that
account rejected; it will therefore be proper to explain in a curfory manner upon
what principles it is that agriculture fhould
never be in any inftance difcouraged, with
a view to render a nation more populous,
fuppofing fuch difcouragement could be
attended with that effect.

What I would here inculcate, is the
idea (in cafe of a fuppofed competition) of
keeping population ever fubordinate to
agriculture. If a meafure is beneficial to
the latter, give no attention to thofe who
talk of injuring population.—If you act
primarily from an idea of encouraging
populoufnefs, you may injure hufbandry;
but if your firft idea is the encouragement
of the latter, you cannot hurt population.

If

If this idea was acknowledged to be juft, there would be no neceffity for a difcuffion of it—but as many are of a very different opinion, it is neceffary to urge a right conduct, though upon motives apparently deceitful.

I have before mentioned that application of the foil to be moft beneficial, which yields the greateft neat profit in the market —*Aye*, fays another, *provided it be food for man, thereby promoting population.* But I admit no fuch provifion; and I am clear that the population of a country will be moft advanced by the farmer's growing rich, whether by hops, madder, or woad, as well as corn: but granting the truth, ftill let the farmer act as he finds beft, becaufe he had better increafe his wealth than the nation's people.

The farmers are defirous in fuch and fuch diftricts to convert their arable lands to grafs—*No*; they are told, *that will injure population.* This reafoning is all on falfe principles. Do not the hufbandmen beft know what their lands are proper for? If they defire a change, is it not plain they do it for their own intereft? Will they not grow more wealthy from hence? Will they not proportionably encourage and confequently increafe all the claffes that depend on, or are connected with them? And how can a conduct in fuch a train, be in the end an injury to population?

M. *de*

M. *de Mirabeau* has obferved in *France*, and I have repeatedly made the fame obfervation in *England*, that great farms are of far more advantage to hufbandry than fmall ones : the fame gentlemen tell us, *no matter*; *fmall farms are the moft beneficial to population.*—I have proved this to be falfe from the regifter of all the farms on more than 70,000 acres of land in various parts of the kingdom; but granting they are right, yet the advantages of agriculture are never to be oppofed on that pretence; for a good, fpirited and accurate cultivation carried on by wealthy farmers, is of more confequence to the nation than population.

This whole matter is reduced fimply to this; National wealth raifed by induftry, is more advantageous to a nation than an increafe of people. Why are you ftrenuous for population? It can only be with views of national defence. But the number of people in a modern ftate, is by no means the meafure of ftrength * : this is wealth alone. Men were never wanting where money, flowing from induftry, was plentiful; but if money is wanting, your population is of no confequence. All modern experience is but a collective proof of this.

My principles are thefe : I mean to befriend population, and I think the only way

to

* See this farther treated in *Propofals to the Legiflature for numbering the People*, 1772.

to do it is to promote every branch of national induſtry, and never throw out any reſtrictions, laws, or rules with a view to population—ever let it be a ſecondary object flowing from wealth, if you would in fact have it the firſt. Farmers, manufacturers, merchants, &c. conducting their buſineſs after their own ideas, and from the increaſe of their private wealth, enabled to be more active in their reſpective provinces, and increaſing the general conſumption of all commodities, muſt in the very nature of things promote population infinitely more than it is poſſible for you to do by your cautions, your reſtrictions, and your regulations.

Thoſe who are ſo eager in favour of population ſhould reflect, that a very numerous people raiſed by any means but the gradual progreſs of wealth and induſtry, would, in moſt caſes, be burthenſome. Suppoſe the farms ſo ſmall as to be juſt able to feed a family, and that the farmers were (as they muſt be in ſuch a caſe) their own landlords—ſuppoſing by ſuch a minute diviſion of the territory the people ſhould increaſe, but to what purpoſe? Merely to ſtarve one another; they can ſell nothing, wanting the whole produce for their own ſupport—land-taxes on them would reduce them to beggary, and they can conſume no exciſable commodities, for how are they to buy them? Thus ſuch a ſyſtem gives you

no

no public revenue—nor yields any products for exportation, scarce any even for sale— Of what good therefore is this part of your territory? Why it breeds people. True; but does it maintain them? No? Here therefore would be a surplus of population; but you want no such surplus— your army is full; your navy is full, and your manufacturers have far more hands. than they can employ—Why then increase your people?—They can be nothing but a public burthen, if they do not leave a country which cannot support them.

This country, and I have reason to believe it is the same in *France,* and most certainly so in *Germany,* has men enough to spare from industry for any wars that we may find it necessary to wage. Whoever will take the trouble to consult the political tracts and the debates in parliament towards the close of the war in the year 1748, will find re-iterated complaints of the want of men, and bold assertions that none could be found to continue the war; yet in ten years we were in the midst of another that employed more than double the men of the former; and when it was ending again, heard the old complaints of a want of men: and the reason was the high premiums given to those that enlisted in the army. But this did not prove that you had fought off the surplus of your population,

every

every man's experience, I might fay in almoft every village, certainly in every town of the kingdom, would tell him the contrary of that; it only proves that, as the furplus decreafed, the price arofe.—It is the fame in the purchafe of all other commodities; no buyer but what knows that he muft pay according to the quantity in the market—and he feels prices rife, without dreaming that he is to go home without his commodity. That the want of foldiers never went beyond this fcarcity, which would appear in the moft populous countries that ever exifted, we have the greateft reafon to believe, from the quick and mighty execution of all publick and private works at the fame time. It was precifely during the laft years of the war that our mafter manufacturers employed more than ever they did in any former period, our merchants employed more feamen; if you examine the ftatutes of that time, you will fee more turnpike, drainage and navigation bills; and in no former period did you ever know fo large fums expended by private people in buildings, lawns, plantations and lakes: all thefe were fo many bidders at the auction of men againft the government: the confequence was, prices arofe; but are we therefore to fay the fcarcity was real? Are we to fay that there were few goods at a fale, becaufe from many bidders they went high?

S E C T. III.

FREEDOM OF CULTURE.

ANOTHER notion of much the fame kind with this falfe one of population, and connected with it, is the government of a country iffuing edicts againft the culture of certain crops—fuch as vines in *France, Spain* and *Portugal.* Thofe countries have fuffered fo much for want of corn, that they think endeavours fhould be ufed to feed themfelves : this is certainly very right; but the means they take is to drive the hufbandmen from one branch into another ; knowing wine can be better fpared than bread, they want to convert the vineyards into wheat fields; this is falfe politicks. It is evident, that the farmers find the vineyard culture the moft profitable, or they would not be defirous of getting into it, which is alone fufficient proof that they do right in purfuing it.—Probably the money they make by their wine will much more than pay for the corn that could have been raifed on the fame ground.—But fuppofing the government defirous of cutting off any fuch importation, yet the evil is one whofe direct

ten-

tendency is to remedy itfelf; for if the vineyards multiply fo as much to leffen the culture of corn, the price of it will rife, and every day bring the profit nearer to that of vines, and confequently the culture would fpeedily increafe. But if the government of a country is defirous of increafing any product of its lands, the direct and proper way is to encourage the culture of it without depreffing that of any other. If your territory does not yield corn enough, give the farmers a better and more fteady price for it, by encouraging exportation; eafe the hufbandman of thofe taxes which difable him from purfuing his bufinefs with fpirit; in a word, make the culture of corn profitable to him, and fear not but he will raife enough of it. I have been furprized to read in the works of the *French* writers, inftances of edicts not only to prevent an increafe of vineyards, but even to grub up fuch as have been planted fince certain periods. This is a fyftem of abfurdity which appears to me aftonifhing. It has alfo very lately been the cafe in *Portugal*. I have reflected on this policy with as much attention as I am able, and I cannot conceive upon what principles it can be embraced.

S E C T. IV.

RISE OF RENTS.

ANOTHER erroneous idea may eafily take place in relation to rents. In my journies through this kingdom I have often taken notice, of how much confequence it is to the welfare of agriculture here, to improve the rental of eftates; as I have remarked that thofe parts of the country which are much under let, are generally cultivated in a very incomplete and flovenly manner.

This remark I know to be juft in *England*; but that it is fo in other countries is by no means clear. Here our farmers enjoy every advantage that can refult from liberty, law, taxation, and other circumftances; if therefore they do not make ufe of fuch advantages, it muft be owing to their being contented with merely living, by means of low rents, inftead of aiming by induftry at wealth: But in other countries where liberty is precarious—law the will of the prince, and confequently of the great—taxes exceffively burthenfome—markets low—and few circumftances very favourable——in fuch the farmers muft neceffarily have fpurs enough to be induftrious, there muft

be

be more danger of activity being extin-
guifhed by oppreffion, than damped by any
favour in rent; confequently it would be
very dangerous to recommend this conduct
to fuch a country, though found fo beneficial in *England*.

S E C T. V.

FREE CORN TRADE.

ANOTHER inftance wherein it may be
imprudent in one country to copy the
fenfible regulations of another, is feen in
the cafe of the abfolutely free corn-trade of
Holland. I have, in various paffages of
this effay, fpoken much in favour of a free
export of corn—but in fome cafes, I think
a free import would be difadvantageous.

That it is a moft wife meafure in *Holland*
cannot be doubted, and for thefe reafons:
In relation to corn, the *Dutch* have but two
interefts, thofe of commerce, and confumption. For the former, corn, like other
commodities, cannot be too cheap, becaufe
the cheaper it is with them, the greater the
trade muft be with all their neighbours; and
as to the confumers, the cheaper the better
for them. If the States think bread too
cheap, they can raife the price by excifes,
which

which accordingly is their practice; and thus the cheapnefs of corn is beneficial to the ftate.

But carrying thefe circumftances in our eye, they offer a ftrong inftance of the caution with which we fhould recommend the practice of one country to another. Several writers, and efpecially one for whofe abilities I have no flight efteem *, have warmly expreffed their opinion in favour of *Britain*'s adopting this fyftem, which is fo advantageous to *Holland:* But herein I think there are reafons againft them, which at leaft deferve attention.

I have juft fhewn that there are only two interefts in *Holland*, that of trade, and that of confumption. But in *Britain* the cafe is extremely different; for befides thefe interefts, we have another which deferves to the full as much attention as either of the former—that of agriculture—an intereft totally out of the queftion in *Holland*. Here, therefore, is a palpable difference between the circumftances of the two countries, entirely overlooked by the authors I have juft mentioned. To the two interefts in *Holland*, corn cannot be too cheap; but to the third intereft in *England*, it

---

* *Inquiry into the Connection between the Size of Farms, and the prefent Price of Provifions.* 1773.

it cannot be too dear—how, therefore, can the fame policy be proper for both countries? The aim of our police is to keep corn at a moderate price for the confumer, without fuffering it to fall too low, on account of the grower.

The argument which I fhould fuppofe would be ufed in anfwer to this, is the denial of a free import of corn having a tendency to fink the price, becaufe where hufbandry is fo good, it can be raifed as cheap as any where elfe. But the truth of this I can by no means admit. Corn is a commodity which varies very much in price, merely from the difference of crops, and they do not fail in all countries alike—it has been no unufual thing to have a good crop in *Poland* and a bad * one in *England*, a good one in *England* and a bad one in *France*, a good one in *America*, and a bad one in *England*; cafes which, as they have happened and have in future nothing impof- fible in them, we may furely reafon from.

The equality of the price of corn ought not to be regulated by the import, but by the produ&: if the crop is extremely plen- tiful,

---

* Whenever I mention bad crops, do not let it be fuppofed I have the common idea of fcarcity; I mean no more than thofe variations which will ever be found, and which affe& prices beyond the proportion of the plenty or deficiency.

tiful, the price ought certainly, and will
be very low : on the contrary, if it is very
deficient, it ought to be high ; but when
there is a fcarce crop, what would the
farmers do if a free impórtation poured in
corn from a country where the crop was
plentiful ? The author of the *Enquiry* gives
a table to fhew at what price the *Englifh*
farmer can afford to fell according to his
products ; and it is from that table extremely evident, that the import in fcarce
years would do him infinite mifchief, if not
abfolutely ruin him ; and the only reafon
why he has not felt this of late years is,
that other countries have had corn as dear
as our own, and confequently a free import,
when there is none to come, muft be perfectly innocent.

We fhould remember that a good crop in
France, Sicily and *Barbary*, at any time
anfwers the demand of *Spain, Portugal,*
and part of *Italy* ; and then the furplus of
America, in cafe of a free import, might all
be poured into the markets of *Britain,*
with how much danger to our hufbandry
may be feen from the table given by the
author of the Enquiry, where he fhews that
a quarter of wheat is landed at *London*
from *America* for the expence of 14*s.*—
and when their export to the Streights fails,
corn with them is 20*s.* a quarter only : but
fuppofe

fuppofe it 35 s. it makes 49 s. in *England*;
whereas by his other table he proves that
when the *Englifh* farmer's crop is 2 ½ quarters, no bad one on an average, he cannot
fell under 56 s. *

Thofe who think there would not be any
danger of an import from *America* at too
low prices, fhould confider the charges of
fhipping flour from thence. The following is an account of the prices at which
flour was actually brought from *Philadelphia* to *London*, before the late high prices
in *America*.

	£.	s.	d.
A barrel of 2 cwt. at from 8 s. to 8 s. 6 d. *per* cwt. -	0	16	6
Barrel - - - -	0	1	0
Fee for branding - -	0	0	1
Freight - - -	0	4	6
Commiffion and infurance -	0	1	1
Port charges in *London* -	0	1	4
	1	4	6

Another

---

* Our knowledge of the agriculture of the colonies
is too imperfect to allow us to reafon in a pofitive
manner ; but from all the information I have been
able to get, and alfo from the prices in *America*, I am
confident they can afford wheat much better at 20 s.
a quarter than we can at 40 s. The advantages enjoyed

Another account makes this as under:

	Penſylv. *Money.*		
One barrel of flour, weight neat 225 lb. at 13 *s. per* hundred, and to which add, caſk, branding, nails, &c.	1	8	0
Inſurance to *England* at 2 ½ *per cent.* and part policy -	0	0	9
£.	1	8	9

Charges.	*Sterl.*		
Freight to *England per* barrel -	0	5	0
Cartage, warehouſe, &c.	0	1	6
	0	6	6
Exchange, at 165 - -	0	10	9
	1	19	6

joyed by agriculture in that country much exceed thoſe of any other under heaven; let but the following circumſtances be conſidered, and this cannot but appear, *viz.* Land to be had in property at a very ſmall price—and what exceeds every other circumſtance, ADDITIONS AT WILL—No tythe—Taxes very light—No poor rates—Materials for building extremely cheap—Great eaſe of ſupporting cattle.—And in oppoſition to theſe powerful circumſtances, there is no counter article; for I do not think the price of labour to be ſuch, as it does not exceed that of *England.*

225 lb. neat flour, cofting 1 *l.* 19 *s.* 6 *d.* gives 19 *s.* 7 ¼ *d.* for 112 lb. which fterling is 11 *s.* 10 ½ *d.*

2 cwt. therefore (equal to 6 bufhels of wheat) come to 1 *l.* 3 *s.* 9 *d.* landed in *England.*

From *New York* the account is:

	£.	s.	d.
2 cwt. flour - - -	0	18	0
Charges as above - -	0	8	0
	* 1	6	0

Thefe 2 cwt. of flour are equal to fix bufhels of wheat; fo that the *Americans* fold that grain in *London* at 4 *s.* a bufhel from *Penfylvania*; and at 4 *s.* 4 *d.* from *New York*, which is *per* quarter 32 *s.* and 34 *s.* 8 *d.* Will any perfon affert that our *Englifh* farmers can rival fuch prices?

Since that period, prices at *New York* and *Philadelphia* have rifen, owing, as I am informed, almoft fingly to the increafed export to *Europe*, a circumftance depending on the fluctuation of the *European* markets: But in the more fouthern colonies, the prices are yet very low. I have lately received the following account from *South Carolina:*

Price

---

* See Appendix, No. VIII. for prices of flour in *America.*

	£.	s.	d.
Price of wheat *per* bushel -	0	2	10¼
3 bushels make a barrel of fine } flour - - -	0	8	7½
Barrel - - - -	0	1	0
Freight to *Charles Town* -	0	2	0
Ditto to *London*, 10 barrels a } ton at 40 *s.* - -	0	4	0
Landing, wharfage, &c. -	0	0	6
	0	16	1¼

The barrel weighs 2½ cwt. confequently the hundred weight comes to 6 *s.* 5 *d.* ½. a degree of cheapnefs never yet rivalled in *England*.

But without entering into any fuch enquiries, we may in general venture to affert that the great object of a free import is to lower the price of corn; to reduce high prices owing to poor crops to the fame ftandard as the rate of good crops in other countries : if it means not this, it can mean nothing; and how well adapted fuch a fyftem is to encourage hufbandry in the importing country, muft furely be obvious without much explanation.

Following the example of the *Dutch*, is to us highly inconfiftent on a fecond account, which is the difference of government. That of the States is one of the

moſt ſtern and ſevere in *Europe*. Any
meaſure adopted by the legiſlature, is carried
punctually and rigorouſly into execution—
the opinion of the lower claſſes is overlooked—obedience is demanded and enforced. The author of the enquiry gives
a ſingular inſtance of this, that while the
people were almoſt ſtarving—much nearer
to it than any thing we have an idea of,
yet would they not. prohibit for a moment
the exportation of corn, although they
would not allow a potatoe to be ſent away:
Now let me aſk theſe ſtrenuous admirers of
Dutch policy, if any thing of this ſort
is to be expected from a miniſtry in
Britain? They want what they are pleaſed
to call a perfect freedom in the corn
trade: let them explain what they mean
by that freedom : I know not what
they mean; but I can tell them what it
would be—We ſhould have a regular freedom of import—whatever our farmers
might ſuffer, this would certainly be ſe-
cured: but whenever the price became diſ-
agreeable to the mob, then our *freedom* of
export would be at an end : this would be
the event of that *perfect* freedom in favour
of which our bounty on export at low
prices is to be ſacrificed, a meaſure which
has brought ſo many millions into this
country.——I cannot forget hearing the
miniſter

minifter in the Houfe of Commons declare, that *a liberty of export muft not
be given, for the difcontents of the people
were great, and fuch a meafure would make
them yet greater:* a declaration following
an examination which proved the average
price to be only 4*s.* 6*d.* a bufhel. Now, I
beg leave to urge, that while the people
(i. e. thofe who certainly wifh to eat as
cheap as poffible) are in matters of export
to be directors—furely a perfect freedom
in the corn trade is a mere chimera, applicable enough to fome governments, but by
no means to ours.

Is it not therefore a conduct that may
be pernicious to the interefts of agriculture,
to recommend in a country governed as ours
is, fuch fchemes, which every one muft
know to be impoffible to be fairly executed
—the above meafure is likely fome time or
other to be adopted; but as to a free export
when corn is very high at home (a cafe fo
poffible, that it would actually have often
happened of late years) thefe gentlemen
muft be certain it would never be allowed:
So we fhould have the mifchief of their free
import, without the good of their export.

Some of thefe writers, who are fo earneft
for a free trade in corn, alfo plead for
a general free port trade, which is very
confiftent with their former propofition,
being

being a ftroke aimed in favour of manufactures and commerce at the direct expence
of agriculture. It is nothing more than
faying to the landed intereft, *Gentlemen, we
will do you and your hufbandry the favour of
laying* 8 *s. in the pound on you, inftead of four;
and in return for this you fhall have the
liberty of eating, drinking and wearing foreign luxuries cheaper than ever*—very much
to be fure to the national benefit *.

---

* The very ingenious and obferving Mr. *Smith*, in
reply to fome wild performances, remarks; " Thefe
gentlemen, it is to be obferved, are great admirers of
the policies of the *Dutch*, whom they efteem the
greateft mafters in the art of trade, and who poffibly
are fo, for their own fituation and circumftances. But
it does not therefore follow that they are a perfect
pattern for all the world befides; though *London* and
Amfterdam refemble each other, yet *Great Britain* and
Holland are very unlike : The chief ftock of the latter,
comparatively is money. It has not natural product
fufficient for its own confumption, nor manufacture
enough for its domeftic ufe and foreign trade. The
former hath *a large eftate in land* producing ftores of
many kinds in great plenty, and abundance of manufactures far beyond what it can ufe or readily vend.
So that *Great Britain* differs from *Holland* much as a
country farmer does from a *London* fhopkeeper."—
Upon thefe confiderations, I am humbly of opinion
that all the fine notions which fome have entertained
for making *England* what is called a FREE PORT, are
quite chimerical, could the great obftacle in their way,
the duties and cuftoms, be transferred elfewhere."
Memoirs of Wool, vol. ii. p. 523.

SECT. VI.

SIZE OF FARMS.

A STATESMAN, in his ideas of improving the agriculture of his country, ought to give a perfect freedom to landlords and tenants, the one in letting their eftates in whatever fized farms they pleafe, and the other in hiring them. But there are writers that will give very different advice, who will affert, that inftead of giving fuch entire liberty, both landlords and tenants ought to be reftrained in the circumftance of rendering farms great—fince it is fuppofed that great farms are pernicious to population, and raife the prices of provifions too high. Now as liftening to fuch ideas would in any legiflature be a moft mifchievous circumftance, it is neceffary to offer a few general reafons to fhew the neceffity of giving perfect liberty in this refpect. This will be done in few words, as I have in another place from facts fhewn the fallacy of the remark *.

A con-

---

* *Six Months Tour through the North of England,* vol. iv. p. 192. 251. 253. 267.

A confiderable farmer, with a greater proportioned wealth than the fmaller occupier, is able to work greater improvements in his bufinefs, and experience tells us, that this is conftantly the cafe; he can build, hedge, ditch, plant, plough, harrow, drain, manure, hoe, weed, and, in a word, execute every operation of his bufinefs, better and more effectually than a little farmer: In the fame manner as a wealthy manufacturer always works greater improvements in a fabric than a poor one. He alfo employs better cattle, and ufes better implements; he purchafes more manures, and adopts more improvements; all very important objects in making the foil yield its utmoft produce. The raifing greater crops of every fort, fo far increafes the folid publick wealth of the kingdom; himfelf, his landlord, and the nation are the richer for the fize of his farm; his wealth is raifed by thofe improvements which are moft of them wrought by an increafe of labour; he employs more hands in proportion than the little tenant, confequently he promotes population more powerfully; for in every branch of induftry *employment is the foul of population.* Thus he employs more people and he creates more wealth, which again fets more hands to work, and
in

in the whole of his courſe does more effectual ſervice to his country *. The gentlemen who maintain a contrary opinion muſt
virtually aſſert that good huſbandry is pernicious, bad huſbandry beneficial; a poſition
which I leave them to meditate on.

Dr. *Price* has the following obſervation:
—" Let a tract of ground be ſuppoſed in
the hands of a multitude of little proprietors and tenants who maintain themſelves
and families by the produce of the ground
they occupy, by ſheep kept on a common,
by poultry, hogs, &c. and who therefore
have little occaſion to purchaſe any of the
means of ſubſiſtence. If this land gets into
the hands of a few great farmers, the conſequence muſt be, that the little farmers
will be converted into a body of men who
earn their ſubſiſtence by working for others,
and who will be under a neceſſity of going
to market for all they want: And ſubſiſtence
in this way being difficult, families of children will become burthens, marriage will
be

---

* The proper and only right encouragement for
agriculture is a moderate and gradual increaſe of
demand for the productions of the earth: this works
a natural and beneficial increaſe of inhabitants; and
this demand muſt come from cities. *An Inquiry into
the Principles of Political Oeconomy.* By Sir *James
Stewart*, vol. i. p. 54.

be avoided, and population will decline *.
—At the fame time perhaps there will be
more labour becaufe there will be more
compulfion to it.   More bread will be confumed, and therefore more corn grown;
becaufe there will be lefs ability of going
to the price of other food.   Parifhes likewife will be more loaded, becaufe the
number of poor will be greater.   And
towns and manufactures will increafe, becaufe more will be driven to them in queft
of places and employments.—This is the
way in which the engroffing of farms
naturally operates : And this is the way in
which for many years it has been actually
operating in this kingdom."

It is a very barren difquifition to enquire
into the different means of promoting
population, without we previoufly fhew that
the increafe of people will be of any ufe
comparable to the evils that will attend it.
The Doctor fets out with the idea that the
minute fub-divifion of landed property is
favourable to population : It may be fo.
                                                   But

* A writer who had very good information concerning *England*, and knew *France* perfectly, fays, fpeaking of the former : Le payfan & le laboureur font
dans l'aifance ; & n'étant point vexes, ils multiplient,
& fourniffent à l'état des cultivateurs, des marins, des
artifans & des manœuvriers. *Traité de la Circulation*,
p. 71.

But what would a nation of cottagers do
for their defence? They would become the
prey of the firft invader: they are to have
neither manufactures nor commerce; for,
fays he, a flourifhing commerce whilft it
flatters may be deftroying *. What does
this mean but profcribing it? For we muft
take mens fentiments in their tendency, and
not admit the ideal meafure and degree of
trade and luxury which they will allow, as
if it was in human power to fay to wealth,
So far fhalt thou go, and no farther. This
nation of cottagers therefore muft pay all
taxes, which we may fuppofe fufficiently
productive to fupport the magnificence of
a fhepherd king—no army—no fleet—no
wars

---

* I cannot pafs this opportunity of remarking,
that the complaints of commerce, luxury, and an
unequal divifion of the lands being prejudicial to
population, have been very often repeated—If the
reader would fee the fubject treated in a much more
mafterly manner than any late writer has handled it,
let him confult Mr. WALACE's *Differtation on the
Numbers of Mankind*, 1753; where every thing is
faid againft them that can be faid; yet is the author
candid enough to allow much to commerce and the
arts, and fpeaks of them as occafions of depopulation,
not fo much in the country where they are practifed as
in the world at large; fee p. 22. Yet do I not think his
fyftem is well founded: The circumftance that *the
countries wherein the neceffaries of life are the cheapeft, are
the worft peopled*, is an anfwer to three-fourths of his
arguments.

wars—What has fuch a fituation to do with
the ftate of the modern world! If the
author fays it is extravagant to carry his
idea fo far, I reply, fuch a fuppofition
fhews the neceffity of limits—fhews that
we muft have fomething elfe in a modern
ftate than the cultivators of feven jugera.
—If this is admitted, how far is the exception to go? Who is to lay down the
line of divifion, and fay, Here propriety
ends—there excefs begins? In a word, the
great fact proved by this argument is, that
you muft give up a degree of population
in favour of more important objects—that
is, you muft admit commerce and wealth
—This muft be admitted—I defire no other
conceffion : your whole fyftem at once
tumbles about your ears.—My politicks
of claffing national wealth before population, needs no exception—it fets population
at defiance—Yours of giving populoufnefs
the firft rank, neceffitates you to call in a
fuperior to your affiftance—and like all
fuperior powers called to the fupport of
the weaker, it deftroys their independance.

But to proceed : the Doctor fays, when
the land is got into few hands, the little
farmers muft become labourers : Certainly ;
and in that ftate are juft as ufeful to the
nation as in their former. But, fays he,
fubfiftence then being difficult, they will

not

not marry: So marriage, in a given ftate, thrives in proportion to the ability of maintaining families. In the back country of *America*, where every child is 50 acres to the father, and the wife 100—where there is no fociety beyond the cottage, and where a woman is neceffary almoft to the exiftence of a man—I admit this.—In a modern *European* ftate, I deny it : I appeal to every man's obfervation for telling him that celibacy is more common among the wealthy than the poor—and that the claffes leaft able to fupport a family, marry more readily than the rich.—At the fame time, fays the Doctor, there will be more labour : then I reply, there is every thing we want, for labour is the valuable effect of population. In a great farm there is but one idle perfon, in a fmall one there is the fame *. Sure, therefore, the fupernumerary farmers are a mere burthen to the ftate ; an idea applicable to every one who ftands in the place of a labourer without performing his office, but confumes thofe products that ought to go to market.

There is one argument I have heard in converfation againft large farms, which appears

---

* One can fcarce ever be accurate in ufing fuch terms as *large* and *fmall*; by fmall I do not mean only farms of 20 or 30 acres, but others upon which mere idle occupiers are found.

appears more fpecious than any to be found
againft them in Dr. *Price*. It is faid, that
large farms are in fact machines in agriculture, which enable the cultivators of the
foil to do that with few hands which before
they did with many; refembling a ftock-
ing-loom, for inftance, which enables the
mafter manufacturer to turn off half his
hands, and yet make more ftockings than
ever. A lively argument, but falfe in
almoft every particular; indeed the refemblance holds no farther than the capacity of
performing in fome operations much more
with ten men in one farm, than with the
fame number divided among five farms; of
which there can be no doubt: But I appeal
to all perfons converfant in hufbandry, if this
holds true through one-tenth of the labour
of a farm; witnefs ploughing, harrowing,
fowing, digging, mowing, reaping, threfhing, hedging, ditching, and an hundred other
articles, in which one man, feparately taken,
performs the full tenth of ten men col-
lected. The faving of labour is but in few
articles, fuch as carting hay or corn; carting dung or marle; keeping fheep, &c.

But take the comparifon in another light.
Who dungs moft? Who brings moft manure
from towns? Who digs moft chalk, clay
or marle? Who cultivates moft turneps?
Which hoes them beft? Which plants moft
peafe,

peafe, beans, potatoes, &c. in rows for hand-
hoeing? Who digs moft drains? Who digs
the largeft and deepeft ditches? Which gives
the foil the moft numerous, deep and effective
ploughings? Which brought into culture
the moft wafte land? Who in all this, and
many things more, expends moft labour in
proportion to their acres, the great or the little
farmers? That any man who pretends to
know wheat from barley fhould affert fo
prepofterous an idea as the *poorer* occupier
to be the *beft* cultivator, is not a little
aftonifhing. Nothing appears to me fo reafonable as the contrary; and when I compared the population of 250 different-fized
farms, the fact turned out as every one
might fuppofe *.

As to the change of the confumption
from meat to bread, it is perfectly harmlefs
—for I know no good in one being confumed more than in another, as long as
meat is dear enough to induce the farmers
to keep proper ftocks of cattle for manure.
But it is a little extraordinary if the confumption of meat declines fo much, that
the price fhould continue fo high.—Farther,
towns and manufactures will increafe—
This

---

* The fingle circumftance of much of the labour
of fmall farms being fervants unmarried, and nine-
tenths of that of great ones labourers married,
makes a greater difference.

This is a great misfortune in the Doctor's political creed—but I would recommend him, if he will hold national wealth in contempt, to confider manufactures in that moſt beautiful idea of Mr. *Hume's—a ſtore-houſe of labour for the public :* thoſe hands which are employed in theſe fabrics yield a ſurplus always at the ſervice of government —but what navies, what armies are re-cruited from farmers? The people em-ployed in raiſing food muſt be tied to the ſoil, and ſo we every where ſee them. The fewer employed (conſiſtently with good huſbandry) the better; for then the leſs product is intercepted before it reaches the markets, and you may have ſo many the more for manufacturers, ſailors and ſoldiers.

This is a mode of reaſoning, which I think is perfectly fair. I do not expect any reaſoning ſhould convince thoſe who will not be convinced by facts; for I may ſay with a *French* author, La dépopulation étoit devenue à la mode*; who alſo obſerves very juſtly : Je ſuis très porté à croire que les *Anglois* ont auſſi LA MANIE de dénigrer leur population.

---

* *De la Felicité Publique,* tom. ii. p. 133.

S E C T. VII.

MANUFACTURES AND COMMERCE.

IN too many of the writings on the œconomical fcience which have within thefe twenty years appeared in *France*; writings which I mention rather than the publications in *England*, becaufe they have been greatly fuperior, the advocates for hufbandry have feemed too much to arrange themfelves rather *againft* commerce and manufactures, than *with* agriculture: M. *de Boulainvilliers* in his well known work * enters into very long details of the mifchiefs arifing from commerce, colonies and manufactures, and he has been followed by feveral other writers. But I think fuch ideas are extremely mifchievous: on the contrary, I efteem them as of infinite confequence to the well-being of agriculture, whenever the latter is not facrificed to the former by prohibitions and reftrictions on the export of corn laid with a view to feed manufacturers cheaper; views never anfwered by fuch a policy. If the conduct of
a ftatef-

---

* *Les Interets de la France mal entendus*, 3 tome. 1755.

a ftatefman fhews ability, I had rather he
would neglect agriculture than manufactures
and commerce ; and for this reafon, agriculture requires only a negative encouragement—let it alone, and it will thrive ; you
cannot hurt it unlefs you are *active* againft
it, in taxation, corn laws, &c. But, on the
contrary, trade and manufactures are children of more fickly and difficult growth ;
if you do not give them active encouragement, they prefently die; witnefs nine-
tenths of our foreign treaties—witnefs our
public companies, *fuppofed* to be neceffary
—witnefs our eternal wars made for the
defence or acquifition of trade—witnefs
half the acts of the legiflature : every thing
in this country fhews the attention that is
neceffary, or at leaft that is given to commercial interefts. If I am afked, of what
good all this is to agriculture, I reply, it
makes us a wealthy people—it makes every
thing dear :—and I have already fhewn,
that great national wealth is one of the
moft effential points in the encouragement
of agriculture. I do not think it is neceffary to add, that fuch a conduct may be
carried to excefs—Views of trade may fo
exhauft a country's revenues as to bring on
a burthen of public debts, more mifchievous than all the evils that can refult
from

from a want of trade*: I am not reafoning
on the abufe of a right maxim; nor do I
affert

---

* As I have in various paffages found myfelf under
a neceffity of differing in opinion concerning provifion, population, &c. from the very ingenious
author of the *Obfervations on Reverfionary Payments*, I
ought not to let flip any opportunity of paying my
tribute to his abilities in other parts of his work. I
think his propofition for paying or leffening the
national debt by the uninterrupted operation of a fum
facred to compound intereft, is fet forth, explained,
and all objections anfwered in the moft clear and
fatisfactory manner; infomuch that the author well
deferves the thanks of the community for that part of
his performance. Perhaps the idea of ruin from our
debts is carried too far; but be that as it may, the
having an opportunity of placing any fums at compound intereft by way of freeing a portion of taxes as
a treafure in referve, and not doing it, is certainly
infatuation: nor can I conceive a reafon againft it,
unlefs it be the propofition whenever made fuppofing a reduction of our taxes. Such a fuppofition
is extremely impolitick; it is fo contrary to the particular intereft of the crown, that there is an abfurdity
in fuppofing it will ever be thought of, confequently
to connect the circumftance of *payment of debt*, with
reduction of taxes, is to raife a prejudice againft the
whole: Indeed the two circumftances are abundantly
different; payment of debt ftrikes one as highly
neceffary, but as to a neceffity of lowering the taxes,
I fee none; nor do I think any good would flow from it,
except in a very few inftances, which might eafily be
changed without any reduction. The object of freeing
a part of the national income from incumbrances, in
order for other applications, is a much more neceffary
and obvious work than the reduction of taxes.—See
Appendix.

affert that this has yet happened in this country.

Certain it is that manufactures and commerce provide an excellent market for the farmer, at the fame time that they give that wealth to the public, without which agriculture cannot thrive: And this beneficial effect, in every country except *England*, is unattended with any great burthen of unprovided poor in cafe of a failure or decline of a manufacture; becaufe, although the community in general has a load upon their charity, yet is not the evil tied to the farmer. In this circumftance, from the abfurdity of the poor laws, which threaten more than any other circumftance the agriculture of the kingdom, and I might in fact fay every branch of induftry in it; operates very differently from what one could wifh, and occafions, wherever manufactures are eftablifhed, a moft heavy burthen of poors rates, partly borne by the tenant in the cuftomary form, and partly by the landlord, who is obliged to let his farms fo much the cheaper.

Yet as this difadvantage belongs more to the falfe policy of our poors laws than to any circumftance neceffarily flowing from manufactures, it would not be right generally to find fault with them on that account: other nations who make them a

great

great object of their endeavours, fhould take warning by our example, and if they find any fupport of their poor further than charity affords neceffary, that they may take care the burthen arifing from manufactures may fall on manufactures, and by no means on agriculture.

Hence therefore we may venture to affert, that the encouragement of manufactures and commerce, and in general of all branches of induftry, is a fure way to encourage agriculture, provided the legiflature attends to a few circumftances which fhould not be forgotten. *Firft*—Not to burthen agriculture with taxes proportioned to its products, in order to leffen thofe on confumption. *Secondly*—Not to prohibit, or in any way reftrain the export of the earth's productions, on fuppofition of feeding manufacturers the cheaper. *Thirdly*— To make manufacturers fupport their own poor. Thefe conditions are fo fimple, and at the fame time fo juft, that a compliance with them can never be reckoned a reftraint on any branch of national induftry.

APPEN-

APPENDIX.

NUMBER I.

Memoir drawn up, and laid before the Lords Commissioners of the Treasury, containing An Historical Review of the statutes that have been made relative to the Corn Trade; and Proposals for ascertaining the prices of Middling British Corn for the purpose of exportation.

Now first published.

BY GOVERNOR POWNALL.

VARIOUS laws from time to time have been made and enacted, directing when corn might be exported and when imported; marking the prices at which such respective grains shall be sold the rule whereby the ports are to be opened and shut to the exportation and importation of corn: And also directing what duties should be paid inwards and outwards, according to such prices. Yet " no provision was made by the said Acts for ascertaining and determining the said prices *."

H. 6. an. 15. c. 2.
20. c. 6.
23. c. 5.
P. & M. 1 & 2.
c. 5.
El. 1. c. 11. § 20:
13. c. 13.
35. c. 7. § 25.
Ja. 1. c. 25. § 26.
21. c. 28. § 3.
Car. 1. c. 4. § 24.
Car. 2. 12. c. 4.
§ 11.
15. c. 7.
22. c. 13.

Therefore for the first time, an act passed in the first year of *James* the Second, entituled, *An additional Act for the Improvement of Tillage*, directs, That the justices of the maritime counties have power by the

1685.
1 Ja. 2. c. 19.
§ 3.

---

* Words of the Statute of 1 *Ja.* 2. c. 19.

the oath of two men, being neither merchants nor factors for the importing of corn, nor anyways concerned or interefted, and having a freehold of 20 *l.* *per ann.* or a leafehold of 50 *l. per ann.* to determine the common market prices of middling *Englijh* corn, &c. and then to certify the fame to the chief officer or collector of the cuftoms.

§ 4. All foreign corn imported is to pay duty according to thofe certified prices.

§ 3. This enquiry, determination and certificate are to be made by the juftices at their quarter feffions at *Michaelmas* and *Eafter* yearly, for the kingdom at large—and for the city of *London* in the § 5. months of *October* and *April.*

N. B. Thofe prices thus determined and certified are to continue fix months.

1688.
1 *W.* & *M.* c. 12. Several bounties were granted on the exportation of corn, when the prices of the refpective grains therein mentioned did not exceed the prices in that ftatute refpectively mentioned.

Remark. The law of *James* II. had it been actually carried into execution (which it was not) refpected only the rates to be paid by *foreign corn imported.*

There was not at the time of paffing this bounty law any rule for afcertaining and determining the prices up to which the feveral bounties on the feveral grains were refpectively payable.

2 *Geo.* II. c. 18.
§ 5. The law itfelf contains no fuch rule or regulation, nor has any been made fince to this day, except in the cafe of bere *alias* bigg, oatmeal, and malt made of wheat, as fhall be hereafter explained.

We will therefore purfue the various alterations and amendments which have been fucceffively made in the mode prefcribed for afcertaining and determining *the prices* which were to regulate *the importation of foreign corn*—and *the duties payable thereon.*

In

In the 2d year of *Geo.* II. a law was made, called
" An Act to afcertain the cuftom pay-   1729.
" able for corn and grain imported, for   2 *Geo.* II. c. 18.
" better afcertaining the *price* and *quan-*   § 1, 2, 3, 4, 5.
" *tity* of corn and grain for which a bounty is pay-
" able on exportation." The firft claufe recites
the whole act of *James* II. and then recites as the
ground of this new law, " That the juftices of the
" peace for fome of the counties of this kingdom
" have, notwithftanding the laft mentioned act,
" omitted or neglected to fettle the price of corn at
" their quarter feffions, and to return certificates
" thereof—whereby great lofs has arifen to the re-
" venue, and detriment to the farmer and fair trader."

Therefore the act directs, that the juftices   § 1.
who have omitted to fettle the prices of corn at the
quarter feffions after *Michaelmas* laft, are to fettle it
at the next quarter feffions by examining and determining *what the prices were* at or about *Michaelmas*
laft—and all perfons concerned are to govern themfelves by the *prices thus fet*, as though according to
the old law they had been actually fet at the quarter
feffions after *Michaelmas* laft.

Corn imported fince the 1ft day of *Michael-*   § 2.
mas quarter feffions, and duty not paid, forfeited.

If juftices in time to come fhall omit or neglect to
examine, determine and certify the prices as by law
directed, the chief officer or collector of the cuftoms,
" *where foreign corn or grain fhall be imported*," em-
powered to receive the feveral duties of *the corn fo
imported*, according to the loweft price of the feveral
forts of corn or grain, as *per* 22 *Car.* II.

Officers to *meafure* corn *exported:* The   § 4.
bounty to be paid according to the *quantity* thereby
computed.

The act uniting the two kingdoms of   § 5.
England and *Scotland* paffed fince the *Englifh* act,
granting a bounty on the exportation of certain grains.

An article of the union gave a bounty on the exportation from *Scotland* of bere or bigg, and of oatmeal.

By

By an act in the 5th year of the reign of *Anne*,
5 *Anne*, c. 29.   this bounty was extended to bere *alias*
§ 10.   bigg, *exported from England*; and by
the fame act it was determined and enacted, that a
bounty on malt made of wheat, exported, fhould be
payable.   This act therefore of the 2d of *Geo.* II.
fuppofing that the regulations for afcertaining the
prices according to which the duties on *foreign corn
imported* fhould be paid, were general rules and regulations that extended to afcertain the prices of *Britifh
corn exported*—which it is feen herein above they did
not—does under this miftake enact, that the like
powers, certificates and regulations, and other matters
and things abovementioned, fhall extend to the afcertaining the *prices* and quantity of bere *alias* bigg, oatmeal, and malt made of wheat *intended for exportation.*

N. B. The cafe then after this law had paffed,
ftood thus:—There was a method (fuch as it was,
an ineffectual one) for afcertaining the prices according
to which the duties on *foreign corn imported* fhould be
paid; and according to which the bounty on bere
alias bigg and oatmeal, and malt made of wheat
fhould be paid.   But yet the rules by which the prices
at which the feveral forts of corn and grain fpecified
in the bounty act might be exported, and to which
price the feveral refpective bounties were payable, ftill
remained undetermined and unauthorized.

Let u's then fee what the next law refpecting the
matter did.

In the 5th year of *Geo.* II. an act paffed " for
" amending and making more effectual
5 *Geo.* II. c. 12.   " an act made in the firft year of
" King *James* II. intituled, *An additional Act for*
" *the Improvement of Tillage.*"

This recites, that in the act of *James, provifion
was made for examining and determining the common
market prices of middling Englifh corn and grain*; which
was however INEFFECTUAL.   Then directs, that for
the better *afcertaining the common market prices of
middling Englifh corn and grain,* and for *preventing
the fraudulent* IMPORTATION of foreign corn and
grain;

grain ; the juſtices of the peace in ſuch counties of *England*, *wherein foreign corn or grain* ſhall or may be hereafter *imported*, at every of their quarter ſeſſions ſhall give in charge to the grand jury to make enquiry and preſentment upon their oaths of the common market prices, of the reſpective ſorts and quantities of corn and grain mentioned in the 22 of *Car*. II.

N. B. Although this law was made ſince the bounty, yet this aſcertaining of the prices is expreſly only to prevent the *fraudulent importation* of foreign corn—Is to be executed in ſuch counties wherein foreign corn *ſhall or may be imported*, and refers, not to ſeveral ſorts of corn and grain, which by the bounty act and the 5th of *Anne* are to receive a bounty *on exportation*, but only to the 22 of *Car*. II. reſpective to the duties payable on *importation*.

This preſentment to be made in open court, to be certified to the cuſtom-houſe where ſuch corn and grain ſhall be imported, to be hung up there—And all duties on importation appointed to be paid by 22 *Car*. II. are to be paid according to theſe prices ſo certified. § 2. § 3.

N. B. Here the mode of aſcertaining the common market prices is altered ; and the prices certified are by this law to continue only *three months*, which before continued *ſix months*.

The mode of proceeding in *London* to continue as before under the act of *James*. § 4.

Bounty on *corn ground* to be regulated by weight. 24 *Geo*. II. c. 56.

By the 31ſt of *Geo*. II. (an act for the due making of Bread, and regulating the aſſize and price thereof, &c.) another mode is directed for the returns of the prices of grain. But this is done only for the purpoſe of ſetting the aſſize of bread ; and the cuſtom-houſe cannot regulate itſelf by it. 31 *Geo*. II. c. 29.

By an act of the 6th year of the reign of his preſent Majeſty, the Mayor and Aldermen of the city of *London* may determine the prices of corn in the months of *January* and *July*, as well as in *April* and *October* yearly. 6 *Geo*. III. c. 17.

By

By an act paſſed in the 10th year of the reign of his preſent Majeſty, weekly returns 10 *Geo.* III. c. 39. of the prices of grain are to be made, and publiſhed in the Gazette.

But this has no reference to importation or exportation, nor can the cuſtom-houſe regulate themſelves thereby.

The caſe then ſtanding thus ; that the law of King *James* II. is ineffectual—that the law of King *George* II. is not always executed, and that neither of theſe laws have any reference to, or can regulate the prices as to exportation ; the cuſtom-houſe, having *no legal rule* to regulate themſelves by, have adopted without law (if not contrary to law) a mode of their own : They oblige the exporter in the body of the *entry outwards* to ſwear that the prices of the corn or grain ſo entered for exportation, did not exceed the bounty price *the laſt market day*.

For the doing this, they have *no authority* by law : And when done, this does not authorize to give a debenture for the bounty, or even to ſuffer the exportation.

Vide *Crouch*'s Compleat Guide to the officers of his Majeſty's Cuſtoms, p. 42. *N. B.* This is what the Cuſtom-Houſe go by.

They are therefore, as a ſuccedaneum, directed and intruſted by their ſuperiors in theſe words : " If the " officers *are ſatisfied* that the reſpec- Vide *idem*, p. 43. " tive prices of corn do not exceed " the limitations for the bounty (which they are care- " fully to inform themſelves of from market day to " market day, remembering that they muſt be ac- " counted as at the time of ſhipping and not of " entry) and the exporter has given the collector a " certificate under his hand, containing the quantities " and qualities of the corn ſo ſhipped, &c."

Now this is not only, as I ſaid above, without the authority of law, but contrary to law—as the oath to be taken reſpecting the prices of corn, by which the cuſtom-houſe is to regulate itſelf as to the duties on importation (even if it could have reference to the bounty

bounty act and to exportation) must be taken by *two* persons—and neither of these merchants or factors for the importing of corn, nor any way concerned or interested, and must have an estate of 20 *l. per ann..* freehold, or 50 *l. per ann.* leasehold.

The conclusion of the matter is :

I. That the laws for ascertaining the prices of corn which are to regulate the importation and duties thereon, are ineffectual and not carried into practice.

II. That except for the article of bere *alias* bigg, oatmeal, and malt made of wheat, there is no law for ascertaining the prices which are to regulate the exportation and bounty paid thereon.

III. That the mode pursued and practised is unfounded—is open to frauds—and has given occasion to many impositions.

The remedy proposed is to repeal these several vague and ineffectual laws, which neither are executed at all, nor can to the purposes intended—To reduce all the *provisions* † contained in them into one bill, to render them practicable, and to point their effect to the real end intended, by

1st, Reciting the present state and inefficiency of them.

2dly, Repealing them.

3dly, Enacting the purview of them by provision, which may reach the end, taking care to insert all and every regulation *so pointed* as the legislature have already enacted, and all such others as may be farther necessary.

The general scope and purview of such bill will be,

I. That the justices ‡ at their general quarter sessions do, by all such methods, and from all ways of information as the laws direct, or as by this proposed law shall be directed, *enquire* what have been the

common

---

† The Register of weekly prices answers (in the publication) so many good purposes, besides the matter of export, I should apprehend that it might very properly be a part of the provisions Mr. *Pownall* mentions retaining. As it ought to be rendered perpetual, it might very properly be done in a general act. Y.

‡ Of the maritime counties only are necessary,

common market prices of corn and grain for three months paſt.

II. That having ſpecial regard to the caſe, whether the markets have been falling, or riſing, they do *determine* what ſhall for the next three months which are to come, be deemed the prices of ſuch reſpective corn or grain : that is to ſay, what ſhall be deemed the port price.—According to which, importation or exportation ſhall take place, and according to which, the duties and bounties ſhall be paid.

III. That they do certify this to the reſpective cuſtom-houſes within the county.—And that this, and this only, be the rule to be obſerved at ſuch ports.

How to oblige juſtices to do it.

IV. This bill to contain a proviſo to guard againſt the only thing which can happen to the hurt of the landed intereſt, viz. That if, upon the ports being opened (according to the prices certified as above) for importation, any ſuch large quantity ſhould be imported ſo as to load the markets in a way that may prove a diſcouragement of tillage—the facts of which will appear by the falling of the market prices,— that is to ſay, that if the *port price* ſhall have been fixed above 48 s. *per* quarter, and by an overflow of importation the actual market price ſhould, within the next three months to come, ſink ſuddenly or rapidly below 44 s. *per* quarter, that then the ſaid juſtices, at any adjourned or ſpecial ſeſſions, may, for the remaining part of the three months, alter the certificate to ſuch price as the *immediate ſtate of the mar-ket* ſhall juſtify.

Theſe certificates and determinations to be hung up openly at the ſeveral cuſtom-houſes.

All the proviſions reſpecting the meaſurement of quantity, the mode of aſcertaining the quality to be re-enacted. If it were not thought better, as it moſt certainly would be, to determine the quantity which was to pay duty, or to receive bounty, *by the* WEIGHT, both as to corn unground, as well as (which the law now directs) to corn ground.

Such

Such a fimple regulation would have an immediate tendency to encourage good hufbandry † in the tillage of, and to avoid a thoufand frauds in the commerce of grain.

It would prevent many frauds as to the bounty,— many in contracts—and would have an effect to give our Britifh corn a preference in the foreign market— and would, at the fame time, lead to the importation of fuch as would never interfere with our own corn, in our own markets, even upon the moft ample importation of foreign corn.

Although there might arife a thoufand perplexities and difficulties, and hence fome danger, in any law directing corn to be *fold by weight*; yet the thus directing the duties and bounties to be fo paid, could have none. I can venture to fay that this matter has been fully confidered.

I take the liberty of laying this ftate and propofal before the Lords Commiffioners of the Treafury. I wifh it to be referred to the Commiffioners of the Cuftoms—and I will be ready to communicate or give explanations in detail upon every point which may arife.

Richmond, Surry, July 15, 1773.

---

† An obfervation which carries conviction with it. Y.

NUMBER II.
Rife of Prices—page 36.

IT has been, by fome writers, fuppofed that the high prices of corn fince the year 1756, have been confined to *England*; an idea which was favourable to the caufes they attributed the evil to, a worfe police refpecting markets, engroffers, foreftallers, &c. To fay, that prices have of late very generally rifen in other parts of *Europe*, will be a reply to much of this nonfenfe; and it will alfo account, in the moft fatisfactory manner, for the rife in our *American* colonies. I tranfcribe the following tables from M. *Engeli's Effai fur la maniere la plus fure d'etablir un fyfteme de police des grains.* Berne, 1772.

I.

The fack of wheat, weighing 212 pounds, was fold in the divers markets of the *Palatinate* from 1751 to 1769 inclufively, at 4 *florins* and a half to 6*fl.* 5*s.* and in 1770, at 13*fl.*

II.
Price of fpelt at *Berne.*

Batz.		*Batz.*		*Batz.*	
1751 —	70	1758 —	92	1765 —	75
1752 —	70	1759 —	75	1766 —	85
1753 —	80	1760 —	60	1767 —	80
1754 —	65	1761 —	60	1768 —	78
1755 —	60	1762 —	60	1769 —	90
1756 —	65	1763 —	56	1770 —	130
1757 —	85	1764 —	64		

The fack of wheat, or fpelt, weighs 190 to 200 pounds.

III.
Price of wheat at *Dijon.*

	fols				*fols*		
1753 —	62	to	70	1757 —	55	to	65
1754 ——	50	—	65	1758 ——	65	—	76
1755 ——	48	—	55	1759 ——	70	—	75
1756 ——	50	—	56	1760 ——	55	—	65

1761 — *fols* 48 to 58   1767 — *fols* 85 to 88
1762 ———— 38 — 45   1768 ———— 84 — 200
1763 ———— 45 — 50   1769 ———— 85 — 92
1764 ———— 60 — 65   1770 ———— 85 — 107
1766 ———— 72 — 80   1771 ———— 140 — 160

The meafure of *Dijon* weighs 46 to 47 pounds.

IV.

Price of corn in the *Canton* of *Bale*.

	Liv.	s.	d.			Liv.	s.	d.
1754	8	2	6		1763	7	16	8
1755	7	12	6		1764	7	6	8
1756	9	5	0		1765	8	15	0
1757	11	7	6		1766	10	10	0
1758	10	17	6		1767	10	6	8
1759	10	12	6		1768	10	15	10
1760	9	2	6		1769	11	19	6
1761	7	15	0		1770	25	0	0
1762	8	15	0					

V.

Price of corn at *Geneva*.

	Florins.		Florins.		Florins.
1700	30	1720	21	1740	33
1701	33	1721	21	1741	26
1702	32	1722	21	1742	28
1703	34	1723	16	1743	25
1704	32	1724	16	1744	25
1705	21	1725	21	1745	28
1706	18	1726	21	1746	31
1707	21	1727	24	1747	40
1708	45	1728	21	1748	50
1709	95	1729	21	1749	50
1710	36	1730	21	1750	25
1711	36	1731	21	1751	30
1712	36	1732	22	1752	30
1713	40	1733	20	1753	30
1714	40	1734	21	1754	23
1715	36	1735	23	1755	22
1716	24	1736	19	1756	24
1717	21	1737	19	1757	36
1718	20	1738	18	1758	35
1719	25	1739	25	1759	34

	Florins.		Florins.		Florins.
1760	— 24	1764	— 22	1768	— 29
1761	— 24	1765	— 36	1769	— 34
1762	— 23	1766	— 36	1770	— 63
1763	— 22	1767	— 32		

The meafure is the *coupe*; weighs from 108 to 112 pounds, of 18 ounces.

NUMBER III.

Decline of Manufactures—Page 87.

IT is very difficult to know what is the real ftate of any manufacture; fo difficult, that I believe it is fcarcely ever attained, except when a committee of the Houfe of Commons is appointed for the purpofe, with power to fend for perfons, papers, and records. The late appointment of fuch a committee to enquire into the ftate of the linen manufacture in *Great Britain* and *Ireland*, has brought to light fome very important facts relative to that manufacture. The point of fuppofed declenfion, mentioned in the text, after the conclufion of the laft war, appears to be no fuch point in reality: this is an extraordinary circumftance, for in the journies I have made through this kingdom, I found accounts very general of the decline that followed the peace; I am therefore furprized to find that this was not the cafe with the linen manufacture, as appears by the following table of export of *Britifh* and *Irifh* linen from *England.*

Years.	Britifh Linens. Yards.		Irifh Linens. Yards.
1743	——	52,779	—— 40,907
1744	——	49,521	—— 28,255
1745	——	56,240	—— 101,928
1746	——	175,328	—— 695,002
1747	——	238,014	—— 595,277
1748	——	330,747	—— 723,663

Years.	*British* Linens. Yards.	*Irish* Linens, Yards.
1749	414,834	965,897
1750	588,874	742,032
1751	527,976	854,490
1752	437,277	968,319
1753	641,510	1,039,967
1754	1,382,796	843,973
1755	41,367	51,040
Average of seven years peace,	576,373	772,245
1756	394,746	719,135
1757	1,016,754	2,005,575
1758	1,942,667	2,117,109
1759	1,693,087	1,956,572
1760	1,413,602	2,352,583
1761	1,272,985	1,819,329
1762	1,762,643	2,930,476
Average of seven years war,	1,355,226	1,985,825
1763	2,308,310	2,588,564
1764	2,134,733	1,858,780
1765	2,095,933	1,663,670
1766	2,236,086	1,770,634
1767	2,444,181	2,227,142
1768	2,687,457	2,270,160
1769	3,056,950	1,855,159
Average of seven years peace,	2,423,664	2,033,444
1770	3,210,506	2,707,482
1771	4,411,040	3,450,224

Since 1771, the manufacturers have complained much, and their complaints were the occasion of this committee. But upon this I must make two observations which appear to me essential: First, the year 1771 is greater than 1770, by

	British.	*Irish.*
Yards	1,200,534	742,742

Which

Which in the *Britiſh* is a greater riſe by a million of yards than that from 1769 to 1770; this great ſuperiority of 1771 was owing to the flow of trade that followed the diſſolution of combinations in *America*; conſequently is an improper year to take ſingly for compariſon. The only fair method of comparing different periods is to average ſeveral: thus, if 1771, 1772, and 1773 equal on an average thoſe of 1770, 1769, and 1768, no perſon can, upon any principles, deduce a decline. The ſtagnation of credit following the bankruptcies in *May* 1772, was a wound to every fabric in the kingdom; but as in its nature it was temporary, there can be little doubt of a revival: and accordingly trade of every ſort is now faſt reviving.

The linen manufacturers, it is true, came to parliament for relief, ſuppoſing the ſtagnation they experienced not owing to that of credit, but an increaſed import of foreign linens. The following table is tranſcribed from the report of the committee.

Years.	Total import. Yards.	Re-exported. Yards.
1752	27,856,122	7,187,110
1753	35,372,907	7,448,672
1754	30,871,973	6,981,528
1755	31,947,447	7,542,694
1756	31,759,234	8,461,726
1757	28,429,072	8,461,031
1758	29,770,104	7,989,160
1759	25,059,533	10,482 730
1760	27,988,972	10,079,851
1761	30,428,424	6,740,960
1762	18,827,853	5,990,706
1763	26,634,851	8,046,355
1764	28,092,215	7,889,265
1765	25,497,795	6,394,147
1766	25,624,107	7,171,891
1767	21,054,411	7,147,784
1768	23,112,349	8,046,980
1769	25,431,162	7,102,527
1770	27,101,343	8,461,546
1771	28,243,121	10,470,129

Now

Now from this table it appears equally clear, that the import is not increafed to 1771, it is on the contrary leffened; nor is the re-export leffened. If when the accounts come to be made up for 1772, and 1773, a great increafed import is feen, than thefe gentlemen may have reafon to complain.

The tables here tranfcribed being quoted for the purpofe of fhewing that this manufacture went on regularly increafing after the peace, it is not a part of my bufinefs to touch upon what has happened fince 1771—they have proved what I produced them for clearly—as to the reft, I was induced to hint what I did, becaufe I am always, from principle, fufpicious of commercial complaints. The lengths to which the woollen manufacturers carried fuch complaints near forty years ago—the affeverations they made—the proofs they brought—the arguments they ufed--the attention given them by parliament—all tending to evince and *prove inconteftibly*, that the woollen manufacture was *going to the dogs*, at the very time when it was flourifhing in an higher degree than was ever before experienced—this is with me a circumftance that gives fufpicion at manufacturing complaints—and will never allow me to believe facts that do not clearly appear in fuch tables of exportation as thofe I have now quoted. If, on the average of feveral years, a decline is *proved*, meafures of encouragement ought certainly to be taken ; but as to temporary ftagnations, arifing from evidently temporary caufes, they do not appear to call for permanent alterations, if any thing is hazarded by fuch alterations : the alarm of ruin that is gone forth among all our other manufacturers at *the idea* of meafures, carries an appearance of impropriety, for fuch alarms are generally groundlefs. The committee appointed to enquire into the whole affair, will fairly and candidly examine all parties—they will difcover, firft, whether there is any great decline ; next, they will enquire if a correfponding decline has appeared in other manufactures—then the caufes of fuch partial or general declenfion will be examined—

and

and if it appears that caufes, which bear particularly againft the linen trade, have produced fuch effects, they will very wifely recommend to the houfe fuch meafures as may remove thofe caufes. On the contrary, if they find that the effect is not fingular but general, and flowing from caufes which will gradually remove themfelves, they will then, doubtlefs, determine that new and reftrictive meafures are unneceffary.

One circumftance has fallen within my own knowledge relative to the prefent ftate of *Ireland,* which gives me reafon to think the evil complained of is not owing to any caufe particularly bearing againft the linen fabric. The number of farms at prefent upon the landlords hands in that kingdom is very great, and tenants every day throwing up others, or breaking upon them. I have been applied to by feveral very confiderable landlords for my advice on this their fituation ; and upon making enquiries into the caufes of this effect ; afking if the products of the land fell at lower prices than they ufed to do—or if the farmers expences have arifen confiderably—I have been anfwered, that products of all forts fell better than ever they did—and that expences have not rifen.— Nor was it till I had repeated my enquiries of different perfons, that I found the whole of their evils owing to the ftagnation of credit—yet was it proved to me inconteftibly. Very many farmers hired their lands on credit—conducted their bufinefs on credit, and fettled their children in other farms on credit, and this whole fyftem receiving a fatal blow in the bankruptcies of *May,* &c. 1772, fuch a diftrefs followed among thefe fons of credit, that infinite numbers were ruined. Now if agriculture could be fo affected by the failure of credit, is it to be wondered at that manufactures fuffered in a greater proportion, being more dependant on commercial credit : and is not this a very ftrong collateral proof that the declenfion of the linen trade is owing principally to this caufe ?

Before

Before I finifh thefe obfervations, I fhall exprefs a
wifh that the committee may publifh, in their farther
report, a table of the annual export of all woollen
fabrics.—It is a common opinion that that manufacture
is declining—I much fufpect the truth of it; but to
prove the real fact, cannot but have its ufes—it will
probably ftop many groundlefs complaints.

EMIGRATIONS.

In the courfe of the examinations which the linen
committee has taken, the emigrations from *Ireland*
were an object much enquired into—they feemed to
many gentlemen an object of alarm.—What I have
obferved in the preceeding papers was defigned by
way of reply to the falfe ideas too current in books,
pamphlets, and news-papers.—I did not imagine that
fo wife an affembly as a *Britifh* houfe of Commons
would ever defcend to opinions fo much below their
level. Why are you uneafy at thefe people leaving
Ireland? To what purpofe would you have them
ftay at home? their going is proof enough that they
ought to go—or in other words, there were more
than you could employ. *Oh, but that is owing to the
decline of the linen trade, and if that rifes again, the
hands will not be found.* Do not indulge fuch idle
fears: raife the manufacture as quick as you pleafe,
it will, in its moft rapid progrefs, create hands by
every motion: the abfence of thofe that are gone
will be a premium to the induftry of thofe that remain,
by filling their hands with conftant work, and prove
fuch an encouragement to population that nothing
will be able to oppofe its progrefs. It would be a moft
beneficial thing to this country, if the unemployed
people at *Norwich, Colchefter, Sudbury, Bocking,* &c.
were feized with the *Irifh* fpirit of emigration; we
fhould, twenty years hence, be the more populous on
that account. In a word, this is a link of that chain
of reafoning which I traced before. Look firft to employment, as the principal object, and trouble not your
head about population; if you cannot keep up your
quan-

quantity of employment, your people will decreafe in
fpite of fate ; and they will decreafe more from the unemployed hands remaining a burthen on the induftrious,
and ftarving them by competition, than if they fhould
emigrate as faft as their employment declined. Would
but gentlemen reflect on the whole train of this
reafoning, they would not think any part of it para-
doxical. It has been with furprize that I have heard
gentlemen of acknowledged abilities, faying, *If fome
meafure is not taken to keep thefe emigrants at home, the
country will be ruined.* Whereas, the fureft method
of doing mifchief would be to ftop them. Increafe
your employment and you will retain hands enough
to anfwer that employment—let the reft take their
way to that happy clime where *hands create employment.* Which is not the cafe in *Europe* †. But if you
would retain them without doing mifchief, offer them
fome of your wafte land in property, and you will
foon find that they will then ftay in *Ireland*; having
found that at home for which they wanted to go
abroad—*employment.*

The emigration of the hufbandmen from the North
and Weft of *Scotland*, has occafioned as much converfation in that kingdom, as the emigrating manufacturers
in *Ireland*. There is a confiderable difference between
them, for farmers and hufbandmen emigrating are
an extreme clear proof, that they are very unpoliti-
cally treated at home in fome point of rent, houfes,
leafes, or perfonal fervice. For I fhall venture to
affert, that if a landlord conducts his eftate on good
principles, even with his own profit the firft object,
that his tenants and labourers will never emigrate.
Raifing rents with judgment is an excellent operation for all parties, but fome contrive to make it the
very engine of lofs and folly. I find, however, from
fome very fenfible obfervations in the *Edinburgh Magazine,*

---

† I have heard fome perfons exprefs themfelves as if they wifhed a
prohibition laid upon the exportation of men. Such an idea I have
alfo found recommended in *France*, in a book which, from beginning
to end, is a continued ftring of vulgar errors. *Des Caufes de la Dépopulation*, 12mo, 1767, page 201.

gazine, that the emigrations from that country are not confiderable: the authors, alfo, obferve, that the war carried off between 50 and 60,000 of the ableft bodied men in the north and weft of *Scotland*, which, for a time, diftreffed every branch of demand, yet in a very few years numbers were greater than ever, and hands for every demand fo plentiful, that many wanted work : an inftance which is a very ftrong illuftration of the reafoning I have offered ; and proves that the abfence of thofe men operated as a premium to the increafe and induftry of thofe who remained.

Now I am upon the fubject of emigrations from *Scotland* and *Ireland*, I muft add a remark or two on the methods followed in raifing rents. People of large fortune will look only to faving trouble, and they fend an agent to raife their eftates, as if it was a work as eafy as raifing a barn. In *Ireland* the buildings on many eftates confift of labourers cabins only, who may fo far be called farmers, as they have each their little field or two. Thefe labourers depend on and are under-tenants to farmers who live in towns at fome diftance; the landlord deals only with thefe farmers, and the cabbins are left at their mercy. The moft pernicious fyftem that ever was invented. Was I entrufted with the management of a great *Irifh* eftate, I fhould fet all thefe labourers free from the farmers, and make them tenants to the principal ; and fo far from raifing their little farms, I fhould fink the rent where it was fcrewed very high, their cabbins I would put into repair, give them as much more land at a reafonable rate as they defired—and affift the moft induftrious, in proportion to their induftry. In a word, my firft operation fhould make all the mob in the country my friends upon principles of juftice ; and then I would go to work with the farmers, and make them pay what their lands were really worth. In this part of the bufinefs however there ought to be many confiderations, particularly under the circumftances of

1. Buildings ; 2. inclofures ; and 3. leafes. The two firft articles muft either be at the direct or the

indirect expence of the landlord—the latter is in all cafes the heavieft upon him. If he throws an expence upon his tenant, which he ought to bear himfelf, he muft grant ample deductions on that account—and he muft not only do this, but muft farther fee his tenant fpending that money on buildings and fences, which ought to be expended in the culture of the land—This is as heavy upon him as the former—he bears both thefe weights—and he precludes improvements upon the *Englifh* fyftem. Let any man who underftands hufbandry and figures, calculate thefe circumftances, and fee what profit the *Irifh* landlord makes by neither building houfes nor digging ditches. As to leafes, they fhould be for 21 years; never for lives.

NUMBER IV.

Reply to Dr. Price.—Page 91.

To the Printer *of the* St. James's Chronicle.

SIR,

THE Rev. Dr. *Price*, in his very ingenious *Obfervations on reverfionary payments*, has drawn fuch a picture of the declining population of this kingdom, as muft alarm and terrify all well-wifhers to their country, and much exhilerate the fpirits of our neighbours. This *opinion*, for I can call it nothing elfe, is publifhed in a work, the principal part of which confifts of a chain of demonftrative proofs; the author being remarkably attentive not to advance any affertions in his calculations of the value of reverfions, &c. without giving the pofitive facts on which he builds; and at the fame time, being a gentleman of confiderable literary reputation, whatever is found in his book muft carry a much greater weight than the fame fentiments would have if found in inferior company. The confequence is, that the idea of our depopulation will become more general;

clamours

clamours about engroffing farms, and the high prices of provifions, will be more riotous; and the old worn-out declamations againft luxury be again common in the mouths of our politicians. It is not only an author's readers that converfe about his fentiments; the difcourfe is retailed among numbers. *The kingdom is depopulated!* Who fays it is depopulated? *Why Dr. Price, who has written fo excellently on reverfions.* Immediately the affertion fpreads, and connected with the idea of being as clearly proved as any other affertion in his book. *Engroffing farms depopulates the kingdom.* This is fuppofed to be proved as fatisfactorily as the *value of joint lives for a given number of years.*

But here, Sir, I beg leave to obferve, by way of confolation to my countrymen, that a very great diftinction is to be made in the doctor's book. The pofitive affertions he has ventured on the number of the people, engroffing farms, &c. are by no means attended with any but conjectural proofs ; no pofitive ones; that is, he offers us fuch and fuch *opinions,* fupported by *arguments*; which, if you approve, you may accept ; and if not, reject. But this is not the cafe with the other parts of his work ; he there commands your affent by facts ; not folicits it by arguments founded on fuppofitions.

The following are the propofitions which Dr. *Price* labours to eftablifh :

I. That the number of the people is fallen a million and a half fince 1685.

II. That the prefent number is four millions and a half.

III. That the depopulation is partly owing to the engroffing of farms.

From an attentive perufal of the work, I can find no other data from whence thefe conclufions can be drawn than the following :

1. The number of houfes calculated from the hearth books by *Davenant,* were,
at the reftoration, - - - 1,230,000

In 1685, ditto - - 1,300,000
In 1690, ditto - - 1,319,215

2. The number in 1759 *(from Confide-*
rations on Trade and Finances) - 986,482
In 1766, ditto - - - 980,692

3. Individuals per houfe at *Norwich,* found
to be in 1752 - - - 5
Ditto in *Oxford* (exclufive of the colleges)
and at *Wolverhampton* - - $4\frac{4}{5}$
Ditto in *Birmingham* and *Coventry* - $5\frac{3}{4}$
Ditto in *Shrewfbury* - - $4\frac{1}{3}$
Ditto in *Holy-Crofs* - - $4\frac{1}{3}$
Ditto in *Northampton, Manchefter* and
Liverpool - - - $4\frac{3}{4}$
Ditto in *Ackworth, Newbury* and *Speen* - 4
Ditto in *Calne* - - $4\frac{1}{2}$
Ditto in *Altringham* - - $4\frac{1}{7}$
Ditto in *St. Michael's, Chefter* - - $4\frac{5}{6}$
Ditto in *Leeds* (partly conjectured) - 5

4. Individuals *per* Family in 14 Market-
Towns *(from Dr. Short.)* Little more
than - - - $4\frac{3}{4}$
Ditto in 65 country parifhes ; not quite - $4\frac{1}{2}$
Ditto in *Leeds* - - - $4\frac{1}{5}$

Upon thefe authorities I fhall obferve, that the
number of houfes given by *Davenant* is not from an
actual enumeration, (for none was ever yet made) but
calculated from the hearth tax. This may be juft ;
but reafons are not wanting to think the contrary.

Here it is to be obferved, that Dr. *Halley* calculated them (fee *Houghton's Hufbandry*) from the fame
authority, in 1691, at 1,175,951, which agrees fo
badly with that of 1690, as to make a prodigious
error in one account, and fhews how extremely fallible
the authority is.

Dr. *Brakenridge* gives the number, in 1710, to be
911,310, which is lefs than at prefent. It is to be
noted, that Dr. *Price* takes no notice of thefe accounts.
It may be faid, that Dr. *Brakenridge* does not mention
the office whence he got the lift ; but his character
is

is too well eftablifhed to fuppofe him utterly miftaken.

If the lifts from which the Doctor calculates be
true, the number of houfes in 1766 were lefs by
249,308 than in 1660.

The lift of 1691 gives 56,826 more houfes in
Yorkfhire, *Middlefex*, *London*, *Kent*, *Effex*, *Surry*, and
Suffex, for that year, than for 1758, which is fimply
impoffible. *(See Three Tracts on Corn Trade.)* From
hence is to be feen what credit is to be given to the
calculations of the laft century.

Let us compare the two periods.

	£.
Cuftoms at the Revolution, produced	*1,015,000
At prefent, above - -	2,000,000
The excife at the Revolution -	† 666,383
At prefent - - -	4,600,000
Total of imports and exports in 1668	‡ 10,000,000
In 1763 - - -	26,651,854
Rental of the kingdom in Sir *William* *Petty*'s time, after the Reftoration - - -	**9,000,000
At prefent - - -	20,000,000
Years purchafe of land then ‡‡	17½
At prefent - - -	33½
Intereft of money from 1660 to 1690,	£. 7 6 6
From 1730 to 1760 - -	3 13 6

Agriculture needs no comparifon.

In the name of common fenfe, if the kingdom
contained in the former period a million and a half of
fouls more than in the latter, about what were they
employed?

Does the Doctor imagine, that the fuperiority of
all thefe circumftances can indicate a *lefs* numerous
people, by a *quarter*, than in the former period? If
Dr. *Price* can conceive thefe circumftances to exift,
and at the fame time mark a population inferior to
that of 1660, I muft fay, by the fame rule, that the
moft

---

* *Davenant's Effay on Ways and Means*, 1695, p. 36.   † Ib. p. 36.
‡ *Davenant's Works*, Vol. II. p. 15.
** *Petty's Political Arithmetic*, p. 151.   ‡‡ Ibid.

moſt populous age of *Britain* muſt have been the reign of the Conqueror.

In the next place, reſpecting the preſent liſt, it is ſuppoſed (and I apprehend juſtly) that theſe are much the moſt accurate ever taken; but I muſt remark, that a gentleman (equally eminent for his abilities, his eloquence, and his accurate inveſtigation of theſe affairs) has informed me, that by taking particular accounts of ſeveral pariſhes, the inhabitants, houſes, births, &c. he finds the number of houſes falſely reported to government in 1759, &c. being in *every inſtance* FEWER than the real number. This is extremely probable to be univerſal; and of which the Doctor might have taken a hint, from the great difference between the number of houſes in *London*, as appears in the pariſh books, and from *Maitland*'s accurate and laborious examination. This circumſtance is *eſſential* : It deſtroys the foundation of all the arguments to prove our depopulation,. at one ſtroke.

Laſtly, as to the number per houſe :—Suppoſe the houſes 980,692, and the average

5	to a Houſe,	as at *Norwich*, the total is	4,903,460
5	———	as at *Leeds*, ———	4,903,460
$4\frac{4}{5}$	———	as at *Oxford*, ———	4,717,320
$4\frac{4}{5}$	———	as at *Wolverhampton*, ———	4,717,320
$5\frac{3}{4}$	———	as at *Birmingham*, ———	5,638,979
$5\frac{3}{4}$	———	as at *Coventry*, ———	5,638,979
$4\frac{1}{3}$	———	as at *Shrewſbury*, ———	4,249,665
$4\frac{1}{3}$	———	as at *Holy Croſs*, ———	4,249,665
$4\frac{3}{4}$	———	as at *Northampton*, ———	4,658,287
$4\frac{3}{4}$	———	as at *Mancheſter*, ———	4,658,287
$4\frac{3}{4}$	———	as at *Liverpool*, ———	4,658,287
4	———	as at *Ackworth*, ———	3,922,768
4	———	as at *Newbury*, ———	3,922,768
4	———	as at *Speen*, ———	3,922,768
$4\frac{1}{2}$	———	as at *Calne*, ———	4,413,114
$4\frac{1}{7}$	———	as at *Altringham*, ———	4,062,867
$4\frac{5}{6}$	———	as at *St. M. Cheſter*, ———	4,740,008

Average, - - 4,587,000

At *Oxford*, the Colleges are rejected—at *Ackworth*, the Hofpital—and at *Calne*, the Poor-houfe: Thefe omiffions are named; nor have we any information that fimilar deductions are not elfewhere ufed. But upon what principles can fuch a calculation be made? As the application of the facts is to know the general average not *per* family, but *per* houfe, the largeft feminaries of people ought to be included, or the refult cannot come near the truth. This is fo apparent, that it muft ftrike every one at firft fight. Yet does Dr. *Price determine* the general number by the average of the particulars, after all fuch buildings are rejected. So that a houfe with a family of ten, two of whom are at college, is called eight, yet the college no where included—And the fame with hofpitals, poor-houfes, &c. This is fuch a method of calculating as I cannot comprehend—for in it 2 and 2 do not make 4.

No parifh at *London* is included, where the numbers *per* houfe muft certainly be more confiderable, though perhaps more than a tenth of the total are there*. No place in which any great nobleman or rich commoner refides.—What allowance is made for all the body of feamen? the army, which in 1759 was above 100,000; alfo the men fought off by the war, but which peace foon recruits? The number taken *per* houfe of only one family, we find 4,587,000: To thefe are to be added the fuperiority of *London* and

its

---

* It deferves notice, that Dr. *Price* procured an account of part of *Pancras* parifh, wherein the numbers are above feven to a houfe; which is explained away by faying many were lodgers.

Within the Bills there were in 1737, 95,968 houfes, *Pancras* and *Marybone* not included; call it only 100,000, and if they are claffed in whatever probable manner you may fix on, the number will turn out greater than the Doctor's idea.

20,000	at	12	240,000
20,000	at	10	200,000
20,000	at	8	160,000
20,000	at	6	120,000
20,000	at	5	100,000
			820,000

its environs to 4½ *per* houfe; the inhabitants of all colleges, fchools, hofpitals, poor-houfes, and prifons; all foldiers and feamen; all perfons without fettled habitations, &c. You are farther to add the deficiences in the lift of houfes, which *cannot* exceed, and which *may* fall fhort, as we know it does, and reckon for thefe the *real* average *per* houfe. And when all thefe circumftances are confidered, the reader, it is apprehended, will not approve of the pofitive expreffion ufed by our author. "Four millions and a half are *probably* too large an allowance; five millions *certainly* fo." (Page 60 of *Supplement.*) To what purpofe fuch an affertion can be ventured, unfupported by facts, unlefs to convince the world that *the nation is ruined*, I know not.

As to the number of individuals *per family*, it is in this enquiry ufelefs, unlefs it was proved that every houfe contains but one; which is impoffible to prove. But I fhould be glad to know, whether an hofpital, a prifon, a college, a fchool, &c. were reckoned as families? The author takes no notice (except in the cafe of *Leeds*) of the difference between *houfe* and *family*; fo that we have no certain fatisfaction on this head.

Laftly, Sir, I come to the caufe of this imaginary depopulation, which the Doctor attributes chiefly to *engroffing farms*. I will offer no *reafons* in fupport of that which I have already *proved*. From a comparifon of the population of 250 farms, containing more than feventy thoufand acres, I have fhewn that farms of above 500 acres are in population fuperior to fmaller ones, as 8¼ to 6½ (*Six Months Tour*, vol. iv. p. 192, 251, 253, 267). I will change my opinion when a longer lift, taken with more care and impartiality, is produced, that proves a contrary fact. And I have there given the reafons why it is impoffible the fact fhould be otherwife.

Attributing the high price of provifions (*Supplement*, p. 19) to any caufes that can be remedied by government, muft have an extreme bad effect on the

minds

minds of the people; it is like all we hear about jobbers, badgers, foreftallers, &c. It is a miftake to
fuppofe, that large farms can have any fuch effects,
unlefs the foil, when well cultivated, yields lefs food
than when full of beggary and weeds.

The Doctor from M. *Muret* fpeaks alfo of laying
arable lands to grafs, as a caufe of depopulation.
This has nothing to do with the fize of farms.
This *Swifs* writer fpeaks alfo of engroffing farms;
but the author fhould recollect an effential difference
between *England* and *Switzerland* in this refpect. In
the latter, the fmall farms M. *Muret* fpeaks of, are
generally fmall eftates, that is, the property of the
farmer. I find this in almoft every page of the *Berne
Memoires*; but this is a direct exception to fmall
farms. It is poffible (but this again is a point
which wants proof) that fmall farms *in property*, may
be favourable to population; for the farmer may
afford a much better culture than that miferable one
univerfally feen on them when rent is paid.

No part of this fubject will admit of general,
random affertions; exceptions muft be made, or a
writer can only miflead.

If the prices of provifions be high, it muft be owing
to the cheapnefs of money, or a natural fcarcity; but
the people never recur to natural caufes; they always
drefs up a phantom among their neighbours, and call
it jobber, badger, butcher, or what not, to whom they
attribute every evil under the fun. But who will be fo
hardy as to affert that provifions are dear? What do
you mean by dearnefs? Would you have wheat at the
fame price when a kingdom has thirty millions of
fpecie as when it had but twenty; or when it has
twenty, the fame as when it had ten? Before you
talk of the comparative dearnefs of two periods, prove
to me, that the quantity of fpecie in both is equal.
For want of attending to this circumftance, the people
are blown up into difcontent, by writings which cannot poffibly have any good effect. If my commodity

is wheat, and I pay for moft of my confumption double the price of 80 years ago (and juftly too ; owing to the different value of money) ought I not to receive double the price for my wheat?

But the truth is, the prices of commodities muft always vary according to the variations of *demand* for them ; and the *quantity* that is brought to market to anfwer that demand. If the people either increafe in numbers, or confume more, or a better fort of food than formerly, in either cafe the demand increafes and prices muft rife : If on the contrary, the demand continues the fame, but the quantity is lefs, the fame effect muft follow. If the people decreafe, or eat lefs, or a worfe fort of food than formerly, and the fame quantity is brought to market, then prices muft certainly fall. In all which cafes, whatever is found to be the price of a commodity, OUGHT TO BE the price of that commodity ; fince it is evidently regulated by the variations in the demand, and the quantity which fupplies it. Nothing, therefore, can be more pernicious, and at the fame time futile, than to attempt to regulate that by laws, rules, ftatutes, and proclamations, which regulates itfelf by the vibrations in the market. And I do not comprehend, how a country can greatly increafe in wealth, through induftry, without the *quantity of wealth* having a confiderable effect in thefe vibrations. (*But for a contrary opinion, fee Sir James Steuart*, vol. i. p. 394).

To return to population—I have lately taken great pains in procuring lifts for fatisfying me on this head. —I fhall continue to collect them, and doubt not being able to convince the publick, as far as any authority, except directly numbering the people, will allow, that the numbers, fo far from declining, advance confiderably ; which may be feen by the great increafe of births in very many places fince the Reftauration. The gentleman I mentioned above has made fimilar refearches, and the event is with him univerfally the fame. Dr. *Price*, though he has been

fo

fo converfant in fuch regifters, takes not the leaft notice of this ; from which I conjecture, that he alfo might find it thus.

But whether the people are increafing or not, it is certainly of high importance to know the real and the whole truth ; this can only be gained by numbering them. I publifhed laft year, *Propofals to the Legif-lature*, for that purpofe ; and fince opinions ftill continue fo contrary, the neceffity of that meafure is greater than ever.

It is my being an enemy to all writings that can increafe the groundlefs difcontents of the people concerning the rates of provifions, &c. or convert into the melancholy profpect of a ruined nation the unparalleled profperity of this great and populous kingdom, that has urged me, Sir, to trouble you with this letter ; and by no means a fondnefs for contradiction : I honour the abilities of the author from whofe opinion in one point I differ ; and my aim, believe me, is nothing but the acquifition of real facts.

I am, Sir, your's, &c.

ARTHUR YOUNG.

North Mims, March 28, 1772.

NUMBER V.

Law of Settlements.—Page 95.

SINCE the above paffage was written, a bill has been brought into parliament, and is now under confideration, to prevent unneceffary and vexatious removals of the poor. I have read this bill, and been prefent at the debates that happened on its progrefs, and I am induced to add a remark or two on the propofition ; becaufe, to find fault with our laws as I have done in the above paffage, and to take no notice of a propofed amendment, might be thought an inattention.

The

The argument fhould, I think, go principally to
this point : To remove the POLITICAL evil, incur-
ring as fmall a PRIVATE inconvenience as poffible.
So great an object cannot be acquired without hazard-
ing fome inconveniences ; but in queftions of this
fort, it ought to be an eternal rule, at the fame time
that you look at the inconvenience, to view alfo the
benefit. Compare them, and then draw your conclufion. That it is an object of vaft importance, no
body can doubt ; the prefent laws are cruel, injudicious, unpolitical, and pernicious. To tie a man
down to a fpot where his legal fettlement may be,
and cut off that natural liberty of mankind of moving where he pleafes, is certainly a cruel law, and in
its nature, a direct effort of tyranny, for the effect is
flavery.—To fuppofe that the expenditure of the poor
rates, is the price at which this right to tyrannize is
purchafed, appears very erroneous, for the evil falls
where the benefit never comes—nor is the latter,
individually taken, the confequence of the former.
Yet if the one was to be fuppofed the price of the
other, both will be acknowledged the effects of mere
power—you chufe to inflict an unnatural reftriction,
you chufe to give a benefit—but both are the efforts
of your power. It is therefore impoffible to fay, with
any propriety, that the maintenance of the poor in
their age fhould be confidered as a fufficient compen-
fation for the flavery of their youth.

But the ftriking light in which the bufinefs fhould
be viewed, is that of a POLITICAL evil. In this
refpect the obfervations I made at the paffage referred
from, are fuch as I fee no reafon to change; the
caufes of population in this country are fo powerful, that we do not feel the effects of contrary caufes ;
but that they exift, no one can doubt, in the laws of
fettlements. And if population was out of the queftion, the effect on the general aggregate of induftry,
ought alone to evince their abfurdity. The preventing a man from living in the place where he thinks
he can beft maintain himfelf and family, and forcing
him

him to ftay where he finds that he cannot, is fuch an abominable fyftem, that to attempt to eftablifh its abfurdity is almoft an affront to common fenfe. In fhort, the firft principles of the propofition are found, and founded upon the moft immutable laws of nature and policy.

The only queftion is, how will you get rid of the evil ? Will you make the poor the judges of the propriety of their own removals—or will you lodge that truft in juftices of the peace, by giving them a power of refufing certificates ? The latter propofition appears to be one of thofe palliatives, which plaifters over an evil, but can never effect a radical cure. Such a truft ought to be lodged in no man—much lefs in a juftice, who living, perhaps, in the neighbourhood of the man who afks a certificate, and who wants, poffibly, to remove into a parifh where the juftice has an eftate, is refufed, left that burthen fhould be the confequence which, at prefent, people have fuch an idea of. Gentlemen of fortune who perhaps fit in parliament, and know the liberal principles which actuate their brother members, may be too apt to fuppofe that juftices in general act upon fuch principles—but he muft be a poor obferver that is not fenfible, very many of the tribe deferve no fuch idea— merit no fuch truft—and ought not to be confided in for acting contrary to what they think their intereft.

A propofition was made, that the perfon wanting to remove fhould bring proof before the juftice, that he cannot get employment—but this would be open to fuch horrid abufes and impofition as would totally defeat the ends of the bill ; fince nothing would be eafier than to prove, that the man might have employment at home ; and by that means kept from moving, though his ftay at home be under the moft oppreffive circumftances.

The great objection made to the bill, was the idea that it would encourage vagrancy and frivolous removals, increafe litigations, and raife poor rates. I fhould not have any great fcruples at recommending

mending the meafure, even if all thefe evils were
proved decifively to flow from it. Becaufe it is much
better to incur fuch inconveniencies, than to continue in a fyftem fubverfive of the firft principles of
policy. But this conception is out of the queftion:
for—*firft*, the bill abfolutely excepts vagrants and
other delinquents. *Secondly*, removals being frivolous, that is, the reafon for them not fufficient, is a
contingency that muft depend on individuals exerting
their natural right in any point of conduct whatever.
The poor muft remove at their peril; if they find
themfelves miftaken in their expectations, and cannot
find the employment they looked for at one place, they
will feek it at another; but to fuppofe they will take
up their refidence where work is not to be had, is
an idle idea, and when they become chargeable, then
the old law comes again into play, and they are removed. It is impoffible to attain the good looked for
from this bill, without the attendant evil of many
removals being injudicious—but it would be a moft
tyrannical fyftem to reject the exertion of this natural and political liberty, becaufe that liberty, like all
good things, *may* be abufed.

Refpecting the increafe of litigation, it is very difficult to gather this confequence from the meafure:
—at prefent every man may be removed that fettles
where he has not a legal fettlement or a certificate,
and removals are common every where, and every day:
how difputes can increafe from cutting away five
fixths of the opportunities of removing, does not
appear to me. Whether a man is chargeable or
not, litigations from removals now are common—
But if this bill paffes, the removals can only take
place after being chargeable; thus the removal orders
are leffened; furely, therefore, the litigations muft
leffen with them.

As to poor rates increafing from this meafure, it
is the ftrangeft affertion that any man could well
make. Enabling the induftrious poor to fettle where
their induftry can be exerted to the beft effect, is
indif-

indisputably a premium upon that industry; and how an encouragement of that fort should impoverish them to such a degree as to raise the poor rates for their support, is a contradiction in terms. Nor can I see how the granting this liberty to the industrious can fail of proving beneficial to their industry; how many are the instances wherein men are tied down to the profit of their own labour, without being able to make any advantage of that of numerous families, from the want of power to move where a more general demand exists! How many others wherein a man is forced by those cruel laws to support his family upon eight or nine shillings a week, when by a removal, he might with equal ease earn near twice the money in a different calling! How many instances of ploughmen being sent, from mere suspicion of becoming chargeable, to places where weavers only are wanted—weavers being packed away to coal-pits, and colliers sent to fishing towns. Is this rational? And will any man give the idleness of his imagination so much play as to indulge such inconsistencies as asserting, that such a conduct is judicious, and a means of enabling the poor so to support themselves, as to prevent rates from increasing!

One word more as to population—Is it a rational system to keep industrious workmen from filling empty houses? To keep industrious men and women from marrying, and becoming the parents of an industrious progeny? Does not such a conduct effectually operate against the population, the wealth and the happiness of the kingdom? But do your work effectually, and repeal that ill judged law which prevents any cottage being built without four acres of land annexed to it.

NUMBER VI.

Obſervations on the Regiſter Act.—Note, page 144.

To the Printer *of the* St. James's Chronicle.

SIR,

HAVING juſt received intelligence that a motion was very ſoon to be made in the Houſe of Commons, for the repeal of the act for regiſtering the price of corn, I think there will be no impropriety in examining the principles upon which ſuch a propoſition can be made; that if thoſe principles are cogent enough to ſatisfy the people of the expediency of the meaſure, we may applaud the idea, and, on the contrary, condemn it in caſe they are found nugatory and inſufficient.

It is near two years ſince the average prices of corn have been laid before the public by authority of parliament. This has been a period ſufficient for the conſideration of all objections to ſuch a publication; and it has alſo been ſufficient for the friends of it to reflect on the advantages which they ſuppoſe may flow from it. I ſhall begin with the former, and enquire into the force and validity of thoſe objections which have come to my knowledge.

It is in the firſt place aſſerted, that publiſhing the price of corn has this ill effect: It diſſatisfies the farmers in the eaſtern counties, upon their finding that corn is ſo much cheaper there than in the weſt of *England*; the conſequence of which is, inducing them to raiſe the price.

Thoſe who found their objections upon this plea, muſt be very ignorant of the nature of the corn trade, and alſo of the common effect of ſuch knowledge. That the farmers in one part of the kingdom would wiſh to have their corn as dear as in any other part, I readily allow; but I utterly deny that they can poſſibly realize their wiſhes, and becauſe they want it
dearer,

dearer, make it fo. Who can be fo weak as to imagine, that the low price in the eaft is owing to the
moderation of the farmers, or the high rate of the weft
to their avarice? Corn is cheap in the eaftern counties
becaufe fo much is raifed; they are, properly fpeaking,
corn counties; the *demand* likewife is lefs, for want
of manufactures, *Norwich* being the only capital manufacturing place in all the eaftern part of the kingdom.
It is dear in the weft, becaufe their lands are more
generally grafs, and becaufe their demand is greater;
owing to the immenfe manufactures there carried on.

Thefe are the reafons for the difference, Sir, and
by no means the wifhes and avarice of farmers, or
their poffeffing a knowledge of the prices in the different parts of the kingdom. If this caufe of high
prices, *(viz.* the proportion between the price and
the quantity raifed) was better confidered, we fhould
not fee the Houfe of Commons bufying themfelves fo
long in counteracting or remedying the decrees of pro-
vidence.

But the idea of keeping the kingdom ignorant of
the truth, is founded on the fame principles as the
old injunction in *France* of tranfporting corn from
one province to another: They would not fuffer it to
be fent from *Normandy* to *Brittany*, left the former
fhould want it and pay too dear at home; and we
have fome politicians who are not for letting the
farmers in *Norfolk* and *Suffolk* know how dear corn is
in *Warwick* and *Staffordfhire*, left they fhould ftop
the fale and make it ftill dearer. This is all abfurdity. On the contrary, take every meafure to let
them know this fact: let the farmers, factors, and
dealers, know how dear it is in certain counties;
they will only be fo much the quicker in fending
corn to fo good a market; the confequence of which
is to fink it, and reduce the price the nearer to that
general level at which it ought to be throughout the
kingdom. Were it poffible to keep one part quite
ignorant of the price in the other, can there be any
doubt but the difproportion would be vaftly greater?

How

How is a demand to be supplied, if the exiſtence of it is not known?

But, Sir, we may grant the truth of this prepoſterous poſition, and yet theſe gentlemen will be never the nearer their mark; for granting that the eaſtern counties knowing corn to be ſo much dearer in the weſtern ones, ſhould enable them to raiſe the price, I reply, that upon the ſame principles this knowledge among the weſtern *conſumers* would be equally powerful in making it cheaper. The ſame regiſter which tells the eaſt that corn is dearer in the weſt, likewiſe tells the weſt that it is *cheaper* in the eaſt; and why ſhould not ſuch knowledge as well enable them to lower their own prices, as to allow the other part of the kingdom to raiſe theirs? A *Norfolk* farmer ſays to a conſumer, *I will not ſell my wheat at* 5 s. *You ſee it is* 7 s. *in* Warwickſhire. *Why are we to ſell cheaper?* This is the argument. Surely the conſumer at *Warwick* may as well ſay to the farmer, *I will not give you* 7 s. *for your wheat; you ſee it is only* 5 s. Norfolk; and he may add, *if you will not take tſee ſame, I will go to the importer.* This, I think, is ſufficient to ſhew the fallacy of ſuch an argument.

In the ſecond place, the enemies of the regiſtry bill aſſert, that it does not give the prices of corn; on the contrary, that it gives falſe prices, and therefore had better give none.

This is an objection I have often heard in converſation, and as often anſwered, by obſerving that *the price of corn at market*, ſpoken in a general way, is not the price of ſome fine ſample which Mr. *this* or Mr. *that* ſells at, but the average of the market; that is to ſay, if all the wheat ſold at market was thrown into one heap, the price of a ſample taken from that heap would be the average price of the market: Nor is the price that of the cuſtomary buſhel, which varies greatly, but of the Wincheſter meaſure.

Whenever theſe circumſtances are duly attended to, the prices publiſhed by Mr. *Cook* will be found the

true

true average prices of the market. I have examined them fince the firft publication, and I find fuch a confiftency throughout them, that it is impoffible there fhould be any material errors in the account.

Thefe are the only objections I have heard which feem to carry any weight; others there are, but too trivial to deferve an anfwer. As fuch objections have been thought fufficiently ftrong to found on them a motion for a repeal, I fhall take the liberty to examine the contrary fide of the queftion, and fee if no good refults from the publication.

It has at one ftroke overturned the lying reports which ufed to be circulated of the high price of corn. When the world was ignorant of the truth, every man quoted that price which was convenient to his argument; and 8, 9, and 10 s. a bufhel were not unfrequently heard of, when no fuch price fairly exifted.

When a man had a mind to harangue on the price of wheat, he told us that fuch a neighbour of his fold at fo and fo ; not adding that his corn was the fineft fample in the market ; and another juft arrived from a diftance, lifting up his hands and eyes at the mifery of the poor, ufed to tell us, that wheat at fuch a place was 9 s. a bufhel ; forgetting at the fame time to inform us, that the meafure was 11 or 12 gallons : and yet, on fuch vague intelligence were the ideas of people on this important point founded ! Before this act paffed, parliament and the miniftry were bufied in remedying evils that never exifted ; and all the information they could gain of prices was from factors and dealers, who could never be uninterefted in their opinion. Now the cafe is changed, and they have every day much better authority before their eyes than that of all the dealers in *Britain :* authority particularly valuable, becaufe it is *difinterefted.*

It is almoft incredible that there fhould be any men fo totally blind as to delight in darknefs ; and becaufe they cannot or will not fee themfelves, urge the propriety

priety of hoodwinking all the reſt of the nation. Till
this act paſſed, we never fairly knew what was the
price of corn, and every meaſure of the corn trade
was tranſacted in the dark. Our knowledge of this
branch of national œconomy would now be wonder-
fully different from what it is, if we had ſimilar
regiſters from *James* the firſt's reign; ſuch would
be abundantly more ſatisfactory than the *Windſor*
prices of the *beſt* wheat, and in only *one* market of
the kingdom. This part of our domeſtic policy
would then have been long ago underſtood, and
inſtead of volumes of conjectures, we ſhould have had
tables of facts.

The regular publication of the price of corn tends
more ſtrongly than any other meaſure to prevent its
being extravagantly dear in certain counties; becauſe
the knowledge of ſuch an evil is the immediate occaſion of a remedy. It enables the nation to judge
rationally of exportation: and the common means of
collecting the prices will, by degrees, familiarize the
officers through whoſe hands the buſineſs goes, to be
accurate and careful in the buſineſs, to a degree of
which we do not at preſent think; a circumſtance
which may in future prove of no ſlight conſequence
to quite different views.

If any perſon proved to me (which, by the way,
is impoſſible) that the prices publiſhed were not abſolutely accurate, I ſhould ſtill be of the ſame opinion:
If the authority is not good, give me better. Who
will aſſert, that a more exact knowledge of the price
of corn may not be gained from the tables than from
the random impertinence of converſation; from the
aſſertions of dealers and factors; from the reports of
travellers; and from the lying tales of boaſting gentlemen farmers; who, to give you an opinion of
their huſbandry, talk of prices which have as much
to do with the national concern, as prices at *Jericho?*
If the regiſter bill gives us not this, I will agree in
its condemnation.

It is for theſe and other reaſons, Sir, that I cannot
but eſteem this act as the moſt valuable in corn affairs
next)

(next to the general prohibitions of the import of foreign corn, and the bounty act) that ever paſſed the legiſlature of this kingdom, and, as ſuch, moſt heartily wiſh, that inſtead of its repeal, I may ſee its perpetuity.

The Houſe of Commons, I ſee, is much employed in endeavouring to lower the price of proviſions. As far as gaining intelligence goes, they will do good; for the knowledge of facts can never have any other tendency. But by facts I do not mean ſuch random aſſertions, calculations, and opinions, as I have ſeen in the papers among the evidences they have received, ſome of which, whether true or falſe, are little to the purpoſe in point; they may receive much more ſuch, and at laſt find that parliament is unable to cope with nature; and that the effect of much money or bad crops is not to be remedied. Opening the ports is a meaſure that pleaſes the people, but *England* will not be fed by imports from countries where wheat is much dearer than with her. Our poor rioted laſt year becauſe they paid ſeven farthings a pound for bread, while their brethren in *Holland* eat it at four-pence and fourpence farthing. In ſome parts of *France* it was five-pence; in *Switzerland* ſix-pence; and in *Germany*, barley, beans, horſe-dung, and the bark of trees, formed the bread eaten by the poor, through a conſiderable part of laſt ſummer. A fact I have from good authority. Had it not been for the encouragement agriculture has received in this kingdom, our poor might have been in the ſame predicament; and if parliament is zealous in lowering prices, it muſt be done by the ſame means. Let them take means to bring into culture ten millions of our waſte acres: a ſingle vote to raiſe fifty thouſand pounds to begin ſuch a work, would at one ſtroke do more than all the nonſenſe that will be talked, or all the acts that will be paſſed, for two months to come.

There never was a ſcarcity of corn in any country that was remedied by meaſures taken after ſuch ſcarcity was felt; an hundred proofs of this will occur at once to thoſe who are in the leaſt converſant in

the

the corn hiftory of *Europe*; even attempts to effect it have proved mifchievous, in alarming the people; for they are apt to thing a fcarcity much greater than it is when they fee government employed in reducing it, and an alarm of this nature never fpreads without prices rifing much beyond the proportion of the real defect in the crop. Nothing can be more pernicious than addreffing parliament to do impoffibilities, unlefs it be parliament's undertaking them; and, for the fake of quieting the minds of the foolifh part of the people, acting as if it thought the evil to be remedied; the confequence of which is, leaving the mifchief much greater than it was found. While the houfe is bufied upon provifions, the poor will be quiet; but when they find nothing done, they will not be perfuaded that nothing could be done; and then they will riot, and pull down graineries, and burn barns full of corn, in order to make wheat cheap.

The meafures to be taken to remedy the fcarcity, are fuch as are applicable to any period: firft, gain a knowledge of ufeful facts, in which the publication of the prices of corn ftands foremoft; and, fecondly, fink the future prices by increafing the quantity raifed, which can only be effected by bringing our immenfe waftes into culture.

Excufe, Sir, the incorrectnefs of this letter, which is written immediately on receiving intelligence of the motion for repealing an act, the good effects of which are every day felt. I am called away to the care of a few fields, in which I endeavour to produce more corn than they produced before; and this, I think, is the way to make wheat cheap.

I am, Sir, your's, &c.

ARTHUR YOUNG.

North-Mims, Dec. 14, 1772.

P. S. Corn Dealers, I can eafily believe, may be againft the act in queftion; for fuch an open and honeft publication can little fuit the purpofes of private intereft, which are peculiarly anfwered by the kingdom in general being ignorant, and the dealers poffeffing the little knowledge to be found.

NUMBER VII.

Smallnefs of Sums voted for National Improvements.—Page 171.

THE following paper of the expences of government from the revolution to the feventh year of his prefent majefty, I drew up fome years ago with a different view; but I infert it at prefent to fhew in comparifon the attention that has been given by our legiflature to the demands of war, and the arts of peace.

		£.
Expences of the revolution, -		1,020,000
Navy, - - -	140,743,623	
Army, - -	166,551,041	
Sundries, - -	23,273,795	
Subfidies, - -	13,404,204	
Eaft *India* company, for } military force,	120,000	
Enemies' depredations	285,075	
Total war and its confequences, -		344,377,738
Foundling hofpital, -	418,527	
Public buildings, -	691,200	
Britifh mufeum, -	36,000	
Streets and roads, -	66,500	
Rye harbour, - -	23,363	
Longitude, - -	5,000	
Land carriage fifh fcheme,	* 2,500	
Prifons, - - -	20,800	
Total public works and } ufeful eftablifhments, - -		1,266,890

Colo-

---

* This article was meant well, and therefore I have inferted it, but certainly it was a moft futile trifling affair. A premium to fupply the tables of people of fortune: had it been defigned for the poor, it would have been confined to fprats and herrings.

Colonies, - -	908,615	
Survey of *America*, -	5,203	
Manufactures, - -	14,000	
Pot-aſh, - - -	3,000	
African ſettlements and trade,	546,715	

Total colonies, trade, and } manufactures, }	- -	1,477,533
Sufferers by the earthquake } at *Liſbon*, - }	100,000	
Ditto, by fire at *Charles Town*,	20,000	
French proteſtants, -	13,000	
Mrs. *Stephens*'s medicines,	5,000	

Total charities and gratuities,	- -	138,000
Capt. *Cornwall*'s monument,	3,000	
To Sir *Wm. Johnſon*, -	5,000	

Total rewards for bravery exerted } in the ſervice of the public, }	-	8,000
Coinage,	887,655	
Burning infeced ſhips,	23,935	
Caſh ſtole, - -	4,191	
Loſt by an agent, -	8,715	
Maſters in Chancery,	11,485	
Mr. *Lowndes*'s mortgage,	1,280	
Jeykil's legatees, -	13,582	
Rebels and forfeited eſtates,	158,753	
Heretable juriſdiction,	152,037	
Union tolls, - -	7,641	
Journals - -	7,278	
Expences of law, -	372,050	

Sundry articles, - -		1,648,602
Expences of the court, - - -		56,936,733
Intereſt of debts, - - -		170,298,551
General total, being the amount of all } the money raiſed on the ſubject for } the public ſervice during 79 years, }		577,172,047
General medium *per annum*, 7,305,988		

In

In the following fpecification the intereft of the debt is divided among the above articles, in the exact proportion between them and the whole amount.

Revolution, - - -	£. 1,438,581

War.

Navy, - -	202,813,683
Army, - -	233,969,431
Sundries, - -	32,500,602
Subfidies, - -	18,604,604
Eaft *India* company, and depredations, }	540,204
	488,428,524
Public works, - - -	1,790,760
Colonies, trade, &c. - - -	2,105,433
Charities and gratuities, - - -	195,200
Rewards of bravery, - - -	11,300
Sundry articles, - - - -	2,336,602
The court, - - - -	80,865,647
	£. 577,172,047

If we fuppofe the total 20, the parts will then be ;

Revolution, - - - -	$0\frac{1}{21}$

War.

Navy, - - - -	$7\frac{13}{58}$
Army, - - - -	8
Sundries, - - -	$1\frac{68}{587}$
Sudfidies, - - -	$0\frac{1}{2}$
Eaft *India* co. &c. - -	$0\frac{1}{52}$
	$17\frac{695}{587\frac{1}{2}\frac{1}{12}}$
Public works, - - - -	$0\frac{1}{17}$
Colonies, &c. - - - -	$0\frac{1}{15}$
Charities, &c. - - - -	$0\frac{1}{160}$
Rewards, - - - -	$0\frac{1}{2700}$
Sundries, - - - -	$0\frac{1}{13}$
The court, - - - -	$2\frac{430}{587}$

This ftate of the expenditure of the public money ought to filence the anfwers which are ufually given to propofitions for fmall fums being voted as an encouragement to that part of agriculture which evidently

dently wants it, from the lands remaining in the same state of waste and desolation that has disgraced the kingdom for a thousand years. While the national wealth is dissipated by millions in military projects, why refuse a few thousands for the solid advantages of cultivation to the wastes—industry to the people—popularity to the minister—and fame to the monarch?

I have classed the Foundling Hospital rather as it was intended, than from its effect. If the principles of population explained in the preceeding pages be well confidered, I apprehend it will be thought that the policy of establishing hospitals for foundlings is contrary to those principles. It is encouraging that vicious population which cannot support itself. You save many lives, it is said; but the very saving these lives must have the effect of starving other people. The thing wanted is not people, but employment; if you increase employment with the foundlings, you do good; but the increase of employment alone would have the same effect in a much better way. You affert, that you bring up many people, who would otherwise have died in the cottages; and encourage the increase of children by rendering them no burthen to their parents. But why are they a burthen? Why do they not increase? Because there is no demand for them. They would increase fast enough if you employed them: and your taking these children, bringing them up, and fixing them elsewhere, is (like naturalizing foreigners) only starving those with whose labour they come into competition, and consequently destroying with one hand as many as you rear with another. This ought to convince us that all measures, taken professedly with a view to encourage population, are nugatory and idle; and that the only possible means of doing it is by increasing regular employment.

But there is another circumstance which has rendered our foundling hospital pernicious. This is the irregularity of its support; the progressive grants of

par-

parliament gave a great encouragement to that fort of increase I mentioned above, and then comes a fudden ftop: What could be the confequence of this, but great diftrefs among thofe people who had entered into procreation of fome fort or other under the idea of their furplus being taken off by the hofpital? the fudden ftagnation of this demand muft have juft fuch effects as the fudden decline of a manufacture—doing more mifchief to population than it could before have done good.

This four hundred thoufand pounds I confider, therefore, as thrown away: but fuppofing it had been laid out progreffively in bringing into cultivation our moors,—this would have anfwered the defign moft effectually, for the increafe of employment would have increafed the people, without taking the bread from any one, or throwing the leaft difficulty on the increafe of other places: at the fame time that this was effected, the whole progrefs of the expenditure would have added to the national income and wealth, and thereby have become a new caufe of farther populoufnefs. WHEN WILL THERE ARISE A MINISTER WITH SPIRIT AND PATRIOTISM SUFFICIENT TO INDUCE HIM TO LET ONE POOR TWENTY THOUSAND POUNDS FOR WASTE LANDS APPEAR, IN THE LONG GRANT OF SO MANY HUNDRED MILLIONS!

NUMBER VIII.

Price of Flour in America.—Page 282.

IT will appear from the following table of the prices of flour in *America*, that the idea of the colonists not being able to rival the farmers of this country in their own markets, is a very false notion.

New-York.		
Flour.	*s.*	*d.*
March, 1760, at 17*s.* 6*d. per* Cwt.	17	6
Cask, contain. 2 Cwt.	1	0
Insurance, weighing and carting, at 4*d. per* cask,	0	2
Currency, -	18	8
Exchange at 165, is sterling, -	11	3¾
Commission, -	0	6¾
	11	10½

1760,	*April*, —	18	0
	May, —	18	0
	June, —	18	0
	July, —	17	9
	Sept. —	18	0
	Oct. —	18	3
	Dec. —	18	0
1761,	*May*, —	18	0
	Aug. —	16	0
	Nov. —	17	0
1762,	*Feb.* —	18	0
	March, —	18	0
	May, —	18	6
	Sept. £. 1	2	0
	Oct. - 1	3	3
1763,	*Jan.* - 1	4	0
	Feb. - 1	2	0
	March, 1	1	0

Philadelphia.		
Flour.	*s.*	*d.*
March, 1760, at 15*s.* 6*d. per* Cwt.	15	6
Cask, containing 2 Cwt. 2*s.* 4*d.*½,	1	2¼
Commission on 16*s.* 8*d.*¼, at 5 *per cent.*	0	10
Currency, -	17	6¼
Exchange at 154, is sterling, -	11	4½

1760,	*April*, —	16	8
	May, —	15	9
	June, —	15	3
	July, —	15	3
	Sept. —	15	0
	Oct. —	15	3
	Nov. —	15	9
1761,	*March*, —	15	0
	April, —	14	6
	June, —	14	10
	Aug. —	15	0
	Sept. —	15	3
	Oct. —	16	6
1762,	*Jan.* —	15	9
	Feb. —	16	0
	March, —	16	0
	April, —	16	0
	Oct. —	17	9

New-York.		s.	d.
April,	—	17	0
May,	—	18	6
June,	—	18	9
July,	—	17	6
Aug.	—	17	9
Sept.	—	17	0
Oct.	—	16	0
Nov.	—	15	3
1764, May,	—	14	6
June,	—	12	6
July,	—	13	0
Aug.	—	13	9
Sept.	—	14	0
1765, Feb.	—	13	3
March,	—	12	6
April,	—	13	3
May,	—	14	0
June,	—	15	0
Aug.	—	16	0
Nov.	—	15	6
Dec.	—	14	6
1766, Jan.	—	15	6
June,	—	16	0
July,	—	16	0
Sept.	—	16	0
1767, Feb.	—	19	0
April,	—	19	0
May,	—	18	0
June,	—	18	0
July,	—	19	6
Aug.	£. 1	0	6
Sept.	1	0	6
Dec.	—	19	6
1768, March,	—	19	6
May,	—	19	0

Philadelphia.		s.	d.
1763, May,	—	16	0
June,	—	15	8
1764, June,	—	12	0
Sept.	—	13	0
Oct.	—	12	10
Nov.	—	15	3
1765, April,	—	12	9
May,	—	12	6
June,	—	13	8
1767, July,	—	19	0
1768, May,	—	17	4

From this table it appears, that fine flour fold there fometimes at from 12 s. to 16 s. per cwt. and generally at 15 s. to 18 s. currency, which is from 7 s. 6 d. to 10 s. and from 9 s. to 11 s. fterling per cwt. Say on a general average 9 s. for that which is equal to three bufhels good wheat.

NUMBER IX.

Effect of Compound Interest in payment of the National Debt.—Page 299.

THE effect of compound interest as given by Dr. *Price* fuggefts, I muft own, to me a different idea from that of eafing the nation of taxes which are no burthen to it. I fhould rather apply it to eftablifhing a fund for increafing the revenues of the nation in future, in order to enable the government to expend confiderable fums in the encouragement of agriculture, manufactures and commerce.

It is evident from the Doctor's tables, that a moderate annual appropriation to finking debts might be made the means in future of commanding the greateft fums of money.

Let us fuppofe the fcheme adopted in 1774, and fix hundred thoufand pounds a year applied inviolably to the extinction of debt, which we will fuppofe to bear 5 *per cent.* intereft, and let us call our prefent debt 130,000,000 *l.* and fuppofe it increafed in future as below.

Years.		Debt.	Debt paid.	Debt reduced to.
1774,	——	£.130,000,000		
1784,	——	130,000,000	7,546,734	122,453,266
1789,	——	130,000,000		
	Suppofe a war to have added }	100,000,000		
		230,000,000	12,947,136	217,052,864
1804,	——	230,000,000	39,863,307	190,135,693
1824,	——	230,000,000	125,608,800	104,391,200
1844, Twenty years encouragement of agriculture, manufactures, commerce and colonies, at 8 mill. a year,		160,000,000		
		390,000,000	353,117,106	36,882,894
1861, Seventeen years ditto, at 10 mill. a year,	}	170,000,000		
A war, &c.		264,855,094		
		824,855,094	824,855,094	

Without attending to the minute accuracy of fuch a calculation (fomething of which fort I wifh the Doctor had given, to fhew what might yet be done with the debt of this country) it appears from it that by means of applying only 600,000 *l.* a year, which is not one-third of the finking fund, we might fafely continue to run in debt for ever; but fuppofe for 87 years longer; during which period we might expend in war above 364 millions; and in cultivating the arts of peace 310 millions, by means of which every uncultivated acre in the three kingdoms might be made equal to the moft fertile foils, great bounties might be given on the export of manufactures, new colonies eftablifhed, and commerce extended, and at the end of the period, the nation might find itfelf without a penny of debt, and in poffeffion of an immenfe clear revenue. By this means, thofe exertions in the arts of peace fo neceffary and important, and which are fo much neglected in this country, might with eafe be executed. To borrow at fimple intereft for thefe objects, while a fund for payment rolls on at compound intereft, is making the higheft advantage poffible of the funding fyftem: inftead of expending the eight and ten millions *per ann.* in peace at the periods minuted, if a fmaller fum was begun with in 1774, and continued regularly through the 87 years (for inftance near four millions) it would be the fame thing in the payment, and every branch of the national induftry fo greatly encouraged, that all taxes would be abundantly more productive than at prefent, and render the intereft of 217 millions, a weight not much heavier than 130,000,000 *l.* at prefent. I have been induced to run into this perhaps wild note, to fhew what may yet be done by a fmall beginning. Dr. *Price* laments the paft much more than he propofes for the future: if fuch a plan was now begun, we fhould have no reafon to lament its not having been executed; and when once it is begun and really deftined to its end, the more you borrow

the

the better ; for, it will difcharge more than you can
know what to do with, and after it has been operating
fome years, you may fafely borrow any fums, as it
will be difficult to run in debt fo faft as your fund
will pay.

NUMBER X.

Corn Laws.—Page 40.

THE corn laws of *Britain* being entirely changed
by the late permanent act, which was brought
in by Governor *Pownall*, it is neceffary, for the information of foreigners, to give an abftract of that act,
by which they will fee what our prefent fyftem is.

I. The act took place the firft day of *January*, 1774.

II. When Wheat is above 48 *s. per* quarter,   48

      Rye — above 32 - - - - 32

      Barley — above 24 - - - - - 24

      Oats — above 16 - - - - 16

all duties on importation to ceafe.

III. Inftead of former duties, new ones laid of

      6 *d. per* quarter on wheat,

      2 *per* cwt. on wheat flour,

      3 *per* quarter on rye,

      2 *per* quarter on barley,

      2 *per* quarter on oats.

Thefe duties defigned to afcertain the quantities
imported.

IV. When prices are fuch, that importation by this
act is not allowed, wheat or wheat flour, rye, barley,
or oats may be imported duty free, if immediately
depofited in warehoufes in the prefence of the proper cuftom-houfe officer, and under the joint locks
of the king and the importer. The corn not to be
taken out for home confumption till the duties are
paid as if commonly imported. But for re-expor-
tation,

tation, it may at any time be taken, a bond being given as security, that it shall not be landed in any part of *Britain.*

The design of this clause is, to enable merchants to carry on a trade in corn at a time when the prices here will not allow importation for home consumption.

V. When wheat is at or above 44 *s. per* quarter,

    Rye ———— 28,
    Barley ———— 22,
    Oats ———— 16,

exportation to cease ; except

   2500 qrs. to *Gibraltar,*
   3500 qrs. to *Minorca,*
   500 qrs. to *St. Helena,*
   5000 qrs. to *Guernsey* and *Jersey,*
   2500 qrs. to *Isle of Man.*

VI. When the price of wheat is under 44 *s. per* qr.

     Rye —— 28,
     Barley —— 22,
     Oats —— 16,

the following bounties shall be paid on exportation ;

  For wheat   -   -   -   5 *s.* 0 *d. per* quarter,
  For malt made of ditto   5   0,
  For rye   -   -   3   0,
  For barley   -   -   2   6,
  For malt made of ditto   2   6,
  For bear or bigg   -   2   6,
  For oats   -   -   2   0,
  For oat-meal   -   -   2   6.

VII. Merchants re-exporting corn, which on importation paid duties, to have such duties repaid them.

NUMBER XI.

Proportion between the price of meat and wheat.
—*Page* 137.

FLEETWOOD quotes from *Stowe* another set of prices for the year 1533. A fat ox, 1*l.* 6*s.* 8*d.* A fat wether, 3*s.* 4*d.* A fat calf, 3*s.* 4*d.* A fat lamb, 1*s.* Wheat is not regiftered, but the price of the year before is 8*s.* 10*d.*

The ox is 24 bufhels.
The wether and calf, 3 bufhels.
The lamb, 1 bufhel.

Thefe at 6*s.* 6*d.* are,

	£.	s.	d.
The ox, - -	7	16	0
The wether and calf,	0	19	6
The lamb, - -	0	6	6

Which prices for fuch cattle as the hufbandry of 240 years ago would fupport, I confider as high as any rates at prefent at *Smithfield.*

* * * *

There is an inexpreffible difficulty in difcovering the proportion between the prices of antient times and thofe of the prefent. Till the 43d of *Elizabeth*, the coin varied perpetually, fo that the number of grains of fine filver in the fhilling vibrated between 20 and 264; the proportions between thofe numbers and 86 mark the proportions between the fhilling of that age and of this. Thus, when the writers of *Hen.* VIII. and *Ed.* VI.'s time complain of the prices of all commodities rifing to *huge, immoderate,* and *exceffive* prices, and attribute it to inclofures, we have the cleareft evidence of their errors, by turning to the value of money; there we find that thofe princes fo debafed their coin as to reduce the fine filver in the fhillings down to 40 and even to 20 grains. The immediate confequence of which was, a prodigious

con-

confufion in prices, which created an alarm that made moft things rife greatly.

For the better underftanding antient prices, I fhall here infert a table of the variations in our fhillings. One fhilling contained of fine filver,

28	Ed. I.	— 1300	——	264 grains.
18	Ed. III.	— 1345	——	236
27	Ed. III.	— 1354	——	213
9	Hen. V.	— 1422	——	176
1	Hen. VI.	— 1422	——	142
4	Hen. VI.	— 1426	——	176
49	Hen. VI.	— 1471	——	142
1	Hen. VIII.	— 1509	——	118
34	Hen. VIII.	— 1543	——	100
36	Hen. VIII.	— 1545	——	60
37	Hen. VIII.	— 1546	——	40
3	Ed. VI.	— 1549	——	40
5	Ed. VI.	— 1551	——	20
6	Ed. VI.	— 1552	——	88
2	Eliz.	— 1560	——	89
43	Eliz.	— 1601	——	86

And fo has remained ever fince *.

But having found the proportion between the fhillings, there then remains a farther difficulty : which is, the difference in the value of money. This is impoffible to be difcovered with accuracy, but conjectures upon it are numerous. Lord *Lyttelton* obferves, that fome reckon the proportion between the value of money, *for fome centuries after the conqueft,* at 20, fome at 15 or 16, and fome at 10 times the prefent rate, but his lordfhip calculates it at only 5 times †. His reafon, however, appears to be very fallacious, for he founds it on making the prices of thofe days correfpond with the prefent, which they very probably did not. Mr. *Hume,* upon better grounds, calculates it at 10 times ‡, a proportion I fhould be inclined

---

* *Lowndes's Extract from the Mint,* p. 69.
† *Hift. of Henry II.* vol. i. p. 403.
‡ *Hift. of England,* vol. i. p. 228.

inclined to follow; he further adds, that confidering we have fix times more induftry, and three times more people, we may multiply the fums mentioned by hiftorians *for fome reigns after the conqueft* by 100. That ten times is not at all extravagant, we may gather from the conclufion of Bifhop *Fleetwood's* elaborate enquiry, who made the proportion between the reign of *Hen.* VI. and that of Queen *Anne, fix times.* Now, whoever confiders the immenfe rife of prices fince the beginning of this century, will allow that ten times, taken for the prefent period, is moderate.

But the difficulty continues after the 43d of *Eliz.* when the prefent ftandard was fixed; for there certainly is an immenfe difference between the value of money, for inftance, in the reign of *James* I. and the prefent time: intereft was then $8\frac{1}{2}$ *per cent.* and land fold at 14 years purchafe. But what the general proportion is, remains, neverthelefs, a great difficulty; in which every man, who has reflected much on thefe fubjects, muft be left to form his own conclufions.

The moft remarkable rife of prices was in the reign of *Elizabeth*, when the produce of the *Spanifh* mines had circulated throughout all parts of *Europe*, that had any induftry. I fhould apprehend the value of money to be now ten times greater than it was before that period, and that for a long time afterwards, perhaps till late in the reign of *Charles* II. *five times* might be the proportion. And that fince that period the fall has been gradual.

If this idea (or indeed any moderate one that may be ftarted, which takes in all circumftances) be confidered, it will be found that thofe modern writers who complain of the *high* prices of the neceffaries of life in the prefent period, compared with thofe of remoter ages, have very much miftaken the cafe. A few inftances will fhew this.

We

We find in *Fleetwood* *, that in 1302, a fat mutton fold at 1 s. ; as there were 264 grains in the shilling, this in prefent money is about 3 s. which multiplied by 10 gives 1 l. 10 s. not a low price at prefent.

At the fame time a cock or hen fold at 1 $d.\frac{1}{2}$, which at prefent would be 3 s. 6 d.—much higher than our prices.

Hogs (I fuppofe fat) came to 3 s. 2 $d.\frac{1}{4}$, which makes at prefent 4 l. 15 s. 7 $d.\frac{1}{2}$, the price of our largeft hogs.

In 1314 the shilling continuing the fame, a fat goofe is 2 $d.\frac{1}{2}$, or 6 s. 3 d. prefent money ; a very high price.—I have taken very moderate articles, fome oxen and sheep run up to fuch prices that we rarely know any thing like them ; for inftance, in 1314 a ftalled ox fold at 1 l. 4 s. equal to 36 l. at prefent, which for fuch oxen as theirs would be moft enormous ; even a grafs fed one at 16 s. which now would be 24 l. An ordinary cow 10 s. or 15 l.

In the fame year, four pigeons fold for a penny ; this is 2 s. 6 d. prefent money, or 7 $d.\frac{1}{2}$ each, which is a high price.

In 1315, and 1316, wheat 1 l, the quarter, which is 30 l. at prefent ; but it was a great dearth. Some records make it double that price. But the changes were fo great, that in the fame year it was 4 l. and alfo 6 s. 8 d.

In 1336, wheat reckoned very plentiful, at 2 s. the quarter, yet that would now be 3 l. A fat ox, 6 s. 8 d. which makes 10 l. In 1344, a cow, 5 s. or 7 l. 10 s. ; a good price now.

In 1348 (the shilling 236 grains) commodities were reckoned to fell very cheap. A good fat ox at 4 s. which now would be 5 l. 10 s. In 1349, a fat ox, 6 s. 8 d. now 9 l. 3 s. 4 d. In 1407, a cow, 7 s. which would now be 8 l. 15 s. Labour in this period was
enormoufly

enormoufly dear, which, from many circumftances, particularly the fmall number of people, and ftill lefs induftry, might eafily be conceived. In this year a threfher had 2 d. a day, equal to 4 s. 2 d. at prefent. In 1425, a fawyer and a ftone-cutter had 4 d. a day, equal to 5 s. 5 d. at prefent. Threfhing a quarter of wheat, 3 d.½, equal now to 4 s. 7 d. At the fame time a bay horfe for a prior came to 1 l. 6 s. 8 d. which now would be 21 l. 10 s.

In 1444, a calf, 2 s. As the fhilling then contained 176 grains, this is equal to 40 s. at prefent; a good price for fat calves. A porker, 3 s. equal now to 3 l. which is a great price. A goofe, 3 d. now 5 s. Pigeons, the dozen, 4 d.⅛; now 6 s. 10 d.½.

In 1445, hay, the load, 3 s. 6 d.½, which is 3 l. 10 s. 10 d. a very high price in any part of the kingdom : fuch a price of hay explains the high price of cattle, yet rents were low. Oats, 2 s. a quarter, equal to 40 s. at prefent. Bullocks and heifers, 5 s. each, equal to 5 l. now.

In 1449, fheep, 2 s. 5 d.½ each, making now 2 l. 9 s. 2 d. Hogs, 1 s. 11 d.½, now 1 l. 19 s. 2d. and not faid to be fat. In 1459, wheat, the quarter, 5 s. equal now to 5 l. Two years before it was 7 s. 8 d. or 7 l. 13 s. 4 d.

The ideas of parliament in thofe days were confonant to thefe prices, fo high on comparifon with ours. In 1463, it was enacted, that no corn fhould be imported if wheat was not above 6 s. 8 d. rye, 4 s. barley, 3 s. the quarter; which now would be for the wheat, 6 l. 13 s. 4 d. the rye, 4 l. the barley, 3 l. It is plain that thefe prices were not at all oppreffive.

In 1475, a load of hay, 6 s. 8 d. equal now to 5 l. 8 s. 4 d. And in 1498, it came to 8 s. 2 d. which now is 6 l. 10s. Nay, Stow makes it half as much again; and fays, the ufual price was 5 s. equal now to 4 l.

In 1510, a load of hay, 9 s. equal now to 6 l. 2s. 6d.

In 1533, the ftatute price of beef was ½ d. per lb. equal now to 6 d. Mutton, ¾ d. equal to 9 d. at
prefent;

prefent; proportions decifive in the prefent argument.

In 1551, a load of ftraw, 5 s. which, as the fhilling contained but 20 grains, is equal to 10 l. at prefent; another fign how unimproved their tillage muft be, and how miferably they muft fupport their cattle in winter. In the fame year wheat, 8 s. a quarter, that is at prefent, 16 l. In 1562, a load of hay, 13 s. 4 d. or 6 l. 13 s. 4 d. A load of ftraw 6 s. now 3 l.

After this period (the beginning of the reign of *Elizabeth*) the method of computing muft be changed: the fhilling contained the fame number of grains as at prefent, and inftead of multiplying by 10, we muft multiply only by 5.

In 1574, beef, at *Lammas*, 1 s. 10 d. a ftone, equal to 9 s. 2 d. at prefent, but it is called very dear: it fhews that their *fcarcities* happened in meat as well as wheat.

In 1595, a hen's egg fold at 1 d. equal now to 5 d. A pound of fweet (I fuppofe *frefh*) butter, 7 d. equal to 2 s. 11 d. at prefent, but it was then a high price.

I think all thefe proportions prove, in the moft fatisfactory manner, that the writers who complain of the prices of meat and cattle being at prefent out of proportion to what they were in former ages, have utterly miftaken the difference in the value of money, and from that miftake have been led into declamation upon our prefent mifery, which has raifed riots among fome of our poor, and infufed difcontent into the minds of the reft.

To fay, in anfwer to this, that their pay is not now equal to what it was then, is no anfwer: for, in the firft place, if the importance of bread be confidered, and we were to fet down *all* the old prices and compare them with the prefent, I am miftaken if the prefent pay will not be found equal to that of old. In
the

the fecond place, we fhould reflect on the want of
people and induftry; the civil wars and confufions
common; the number of labourers kept in fubjection
to the barons, and the want of communications for
the fupply of one place from another: if all thefe
circumftances are confidered, it will be found that
labour muft have been very dear, without any reference to the price of provifions.

I muft alfo defire the reader to keep in his mind
what I advanced at page 135, &c. concerning the
difference between the oxen of thofe days and the
prefent. They had no turnips, and the price of hay
and ftraw was fuch, that very little cattle could
be wintered, and thofe which were muft have been
almoft ftarved; fo that they could fcarcely have any
thing like the oxen now fold at *Smithfield*. In con-
firmation of this, I may quote the practice recorded in
1321, of falting all the oxen and fheep that were
confumed in the winter; a circumftance decifive of
what their hufbandry and their cattle muft have been.

It may poffibly be faid, that the prices of commodities did not rife and fall in fuch exact proportion
to the quantity of filver in the coin—This may be
true, and may not be fo—but the prices in the preceeding pages will, without injury to my argument,
admit deductions on this account—But I am not
inclined to admit this reafoning; for we find in our
hiftories, that the *clamour* and *confufion* arifing from
alterations in the coin, were very great; and if fo,
I fhould fuppofe that the general alarm would raife
prices *beyond* the true proportion.

NUMBER XII.

People gathering into Towns do not depopulate.—
Page 71.

DR. *Campbell*, in his *Political Survey of Great Britain*, juft publifhed, vol. ii. p. 254, a work which fhews how deeply the author has reflected on thefe fubjects, has a remark which I fhall tranfcribe, being much to my purpofe.—" Many think the great increafe of towns, and the reigning inclination of people to refide in them, hath a vifible tendency to depopulate the country, and thereby leffen its produce. But whence does this defire of living in towns proceed? Becaufe induftry enables people in towns to live better. Numbers living better muft create an increafed confumption. But of what? Moft clearly of the produce of the country. If therefore the confumption be enlarged, the cultivation muft be augmented in proportion, and thofe employed therein be confequently benefited thereby? The voice of reafon feems loud, but the language of facts is ftill louder. All the lands in the neighbourhood of thefe towns, from which lands the inhabitants, occafional vifitants, and paffengers, are fupplied with milk, butter, cheefe, lamb, mutton, veal, and beef, are much raifed in their value, and not a little improved by plenty of manure which towns conftantly fupply. It may be faid, this regards only pafturage. It would be faid with truth if thefe people ate no bread. But by the help of their turnpike roads, they may receive corn and flour from even diftant markets."

In another paffage the Doctor reafons very fenfibly in favour of inclofures.—" As to the popular clamours formerly againft inclofures, they might have fome foundation: as tillage was then neglected, we had few manufactures and little commerce, fo that the common

people

people had few refources. But this has little to do with the prefent ftate of things. By the depopulation complained of muft be meant a local, not a national lofs of people ; which however would be difficult to prove, fince the villages and towns in the vicinity of thefe inclofed commons are as well or better inhabited than ever. As to the nation, the confumption and price of provifions *fhew our people in general do not decreafe.* In truth, this fpirit of inclofing proves it. For the intent of inclofing is to encreafe the quantity of provifions, and nothing could excite, or at leaft nothing could fuftain this, but an increafed demand. In refpect to decreafing tillage, it alfo is hardly to be proved. It is certain the produce of arable lands in general is greatly augmented, that the tillage of commons was inconfiderable, and a great part of it beans. In refpect to the poor (to whom the greateft regard is due) they only change the kind of labour ; and this not to their difadvantage, for wages are higher, and employment in inclofed countries more eafily obtained." Vol. ii. p. 278.

NUMBER XIII.

Inclofures.—Page 127.

A S there has not been an age in which complaints
againſt inclofures were not common, ſo no
period has paſſed in which thoſe complaints have not
been ſatisfactorily anſwered. Of this I have given
feveral inſtances—Another has occurred ſince theſe
ſheets were printed; it is taken from a pamphlet, en-
titled, *England's Intereſt conſidered in the Increaſe of
Trade,* by *Samuel Fortrey,* 1663. — " 1. Our care
ſhould be, to increaſe chiefly our ſtock of cattle.
Firſt, by a liberty for every man to enjoy his lands in
feveralty and inclofure, one of the greateſt improvements this nation is capable of; for want whereof we
find by daily experience, that the profit of a great
part of the land and ſtock of this kingdom, as now
employed, is wholly loſt. And this appears, in that
the land of the common fields almoſt in all places of
this nation, with all the advantages that belong unto
them, will not let for above one-third part ſo much as
the ſame land would do inclofed, and always ſeveral.
  " 2. But it may be objected, that inclofures would
cauſe great depopulations and ſcarcity of corn, as hath
been conceived by former parliaments.
  " 3. To this I anſwer, corn would be nothing the
ſcarcer by inclofure, but rather more plentiful, tho'
a great deal leſs land were tilled: for then every ingenious huſband would only plough that land he found
moſt fitting for it, and that no longer than he found
it able to bring him profit. And as to depopulation
by inclofure, granting it increaſeth plenty, as cannot
well be denied; how increaſe and plenty can depopulate,
cannot well be conceived: nor ſurely do any imagine
that the people which lived in thoſe towns they call
depopulated, were all deſtroyed, becauſe they lived no
longer there, when indeed they were only removed to
other

other places, where they might better benefit themselves, and profit the publick. Certainly they might as well think the nation undone, should they observe how *London* is depopulated in a long vacation; when men are only retired into the country, about their private and neceffary employments; and the like might they think of the country in the term time, yet a man is not thereby added or diminished to the nation.

"4. Further; as many, or more families, may be maintained and employed in the manufacture of the wool that may arife out of one hundred acres of pasture, than can be employed in a far greater quantity of arable; who perhaps do not always find it moft convenient for them to live juft on the place where the wool groweth, by which means cities and great towns are peopled, nothing to the prejudice of the kingdom.

"5. Wherefore then, if by inclofure the land itfelf is raifed to a greater value, and a lefs quantity capable of a greater increafe; and if it really caufeth no depopulation, but at moft a removal of people thence, where without benefit to the public, or profit to themfelves, they laboured and toiled, to a more convenient habitation, where they might with lefs pains greatly advantage both: And if the manufactures and other profitable employments of the nation are increafed, by adding thereto fuch numbers of people, who formerly ferved only to wafte, not to increafe, the ftore of the nation, it cannot be denied, but the encouragement of inclofure, where every man's juft right may be preferved, would infinitely conduce to the increafe and plenty of this nation, and is a thing very worthy the countenance and care of a parliament."

Authors much more ancient were of the fame opinion. *Fitzherbert*, in 1534, recommends inclofures greatly as working an high improvement, keeping four times the number of beafts. *Tuffer* in 1590 is equally in favour of them. *Blythe* was of the fame opinion in 1650, and *Hartlib* in his Legacy 1651, like *Fortrey*, anfwers the great objection to them,
that

that of depopulation from laying down to grafs, in the following paffage :

"Pafture employeth more hands than arable, and therefore pafture doth not *depopulate*, as it is commonly faid ; for *Normandy* and *Picardy* in *France*, where there are paftures, in a good meafure are as populous as any part of *France* ; and I am certain that *Holland, Zealand, Friezeland, Flanders*, and *Lombardy*, which relye altogether on paftures, are the moft populous places in *Europe*. But fome will object and fay, that a fhepherd and his dog formerly hath deftroyed divers villages. To this I anfwer, that we well know what a fhepherd and his dog can do, *viz.* look to 2 or 300 fheep at the moft ; and that 2 or 300 acres will maintain them, or the land is extremely barren ; and that thefe 2 or 300 acres being barren will fcarcely maintain a plough (which is but one man and two boys) with the horfes ; and that the mowing, reaping and threfhing of this corn, and other work about, will fcarcely maintain three more with work through the whole year. But how many people may be employed by the wool of 2 or 300 fheep, in picking, carding, forting, fpinning, weaving, dying, knitting, fulling, I leave to others to calculate. And farther, if the paftures be rich meadows, and go on dairying, I fuppofe all know that 100 acres of fuch land employeth more hands than 100 acres of the beft corn land in *England*, and produceth likewife better exportable commodities. And farther; if I fhould grant that formerly the fhepherd and his dog did *depopulate*, that I may not condemn the wifdom of former ages ; yet I will deny that it doth fo now : for formerly we were fo unwife as to fend over our wools to *Antwerp* and other places, where they were manufactured ; by which means one pound oft brought ten unwrought to them ; but we fet now our own poor to work, and fo fave the depopulation. Yet I fay, it is convenient to encourage the plough ; becaufe that we cannot have a certainty of corn, and carriage is dear both by fea and land, efpecially into the inland countries; and our commodities of wool do cloy the merchants *."

Thefe obfervations are ftrictly true at this day, if the comparifon is made with what it ought to be, the tillage of open field lands under the univerfal courfe of 1. Fallow; 2. Wheat; 3. Spring Corn; in which vile hufbandry not one of the modern operofe improvements is to be found. The fact is fo clear, that it is not to be wondered at that fome of thefe writers fhould appear to treat the contrary opinion with contempt; juftly remarking, that it proceeded from people who knew little of hufbandry, and who therefore muft be very ignorant of the employment in either cafe.

---

* Legacy of Hufbandry, p. 44.

F I N I S.